CYNTHIA GLIDEWELL

The *Red Hat Society*®
TRAVEL GUIDE

HITTING THE ROAD *with* CONFIDENCE, CLASS, AND STYLE

THOMAS NELSON
Since 1798

NASHVILLE DALLAS MEXICO CITY RIO DE JANEIRO BEIJING

Published in Nashville, Tennessee, by Thomas Nelson. Thomas Nelson is a registered trademark of Thomas Nelson, Inc.

Thomas Nelson, Inc., titles may be purchased in bulk for educational, business, fundraising, or sales promotional use. For information, please e-mail SpecialMarkets@ThomasNelson.com.

Page Design by Casey Hooper

Library of Congress Cataloging-in-Publication Data

Glidewell, Cynthia, 1956-
  The Red Hat Society travel guide : hitting the road with confidence, class, and style / Cynthia Glidewell.
    p. cm.
  Includes bibliographical references and index.
  ISBN 978-1-4016-0364-9
  1. United States--Guidebooks. 2. Middle-aged women—Travel—United States—Guidebooks.
  3. Older women—Travel—United States——Guidebooks.
I. Red Hat Society. II. Title.
  E158.G625 2008
  917.304009'05--dc22

                                    2008003177

Printed in the United States of America
08 09 10 11 QW 5 4 3 2 1

For my grandmother, Virginia Pence,
who defined sass and style before sass and style were cool

Contents

Part One: Let's Get Started!

Part Two: Sleeping, Traveling, and Tipping

Part Three: Eating Out

Part Four: Profiles of Twenty Cities

Acknowledgments

Writing *The Red Hat Society Travel Guide* has been truly a blessing and an adventure. The opportunity to write this book came about by something I can only describe as "a God thing," and I am ever thankful for His blessings. Writing this book gave me the chance to collaborate with my son, Cole Wakefield. His significant contributions helped pull all of this together.

I would also like to thank and acknowledge the following people:

My dear husband and helpmate, Jerry Glidewell, who makes any place he is *my* favorite place to be. I could not have done this, or so many other things, without his amazing love and support.

My children at home, Emily and Jay Glidewell who, along with Jerry, meet me at the airport, not at the curb but inside, with open arms each and every time I travel; they make it all worth it.

My children with their own homes: Zack, Laura, and Noah; Cory and Chris; Cole and Jason, who motivate me and tolerate me, and have blessed me so incredibly.

My parents, Eldon and Betty Pence, who have encouraged me to always be my best and a little more.

The members of the Royal Red Hat Sisters of the Road, my Red Hat travel partners and an awesome group of sisters, spread out across this great country, who allow me to be "Queen." Their contributions, encouragement, support (some gentle and some not so gentle when I needed that extra push), and prayers helped shape *The Red Hat Society Travel Guide* into what it is today.

Preface

Until six or seven years ago, about 90 percent of my life took place within a fifteen-mile radius. I worked as an RN less than ten miles from my house, my children went to neighborhood schools, and my dry cleaner, grocery store, and church were all within a ten- to fifteen-minute drive of home. And, quite frankly, that suited me just fine. An interesting turn of events led to my joining a consulting firm to write an adverse event reporting manual for RN's. (I'd written another instructional book for nurses several years earlier.) I was warned that some travel would be necessary—about 20 percent—but my husband insisted that would be no problem and at the very least I should try it. (His vision, support, and encouragement have pushed me to grow and achieve more than I ever believed I could.)

My role with the consulting company evolved rapidly. I went from writing an instructional manual in Chicago to managing an international regulatory compliance team. My 20 percent travel escalated to 85 percent travel, and before I knew it, I was working in places like Copenhagen, Amsterdam, New Jersey, and San Francisco. As a matter of survival I soon learned the tricks of the Road Warrior trade. I learned every alternative airport, airline, and flight schedule that had any chance whatsoever of ensuring that I would get home by Thursday night. I was forced to rent my first rental car, ride my first subway, hail my first taxi, and eat in a restaurant alone for the first time. I never would have attempted any of these things (or even had the desire to) had circumstances not necessitated it. I learned there was a whole new world outside my little fifteen-mile radius. And even though some of my travels were international, my most interesting travels were right here in the continental United States. I also learned the importance and value of having friends "in every port." Being part of the Red Hat Society gave me an instant network of dinner companions, chapters to visit, or just a contact for a restaurant or show.

Sure, I have my passport, as do my husband and all my children, but honestly there is so much to do between the shores of the U.S., you will never grow bored. Whether you are shopping in view of the Brooklyn Bridge or the Golden Gate, I hope the tips and tales in *The Red Hat Society Travel Guide* help to make your adventure a pleasant one and one to remember.

—Cyndi Glidewell

Introduction

My husband and I raised our family in southern California. In less than an hour's drive we could be at the beach; a two-hour drive got us to the nearby mountains. In less than a day we could reach Yosemite National Park, Mammoth Mountain Resort or San Diego and the Mexican border. In 1985, we surprised ourselves by taking our family on a once-in-a-lifetime trip to Europe. It was one of those "If this is Tuesday, this must be Belgium" type of trips. Despite the hectic schedule, it was still glorious, and our eyes were opened to new realities in an unforgettable way. I believe that we can trace our love of travel back to that summer.

Travel expands your world. Seeing new sights, meeting new people, sampling local culinary specialties, visiting museums, restaurants, and shopping areas take you out of yourself and your own circumscribed world. You get a chance to examine your life from a new perspective and when you arrive back home, with your memories and your souvenirs, you feel renewed. Everything just looks a little different, and, if you're like me, it won't be long before you are planning your next trip!

In my capacity as Exalted Queen Mother of the Red Hat Society, I have been privileged to travel widely throughout the United States. I've discovered the immense variety—geographically, traditio nally, culinarily, economically—our country has to offer. There is a whole new world out there—or, perhaps I ought to say "in here"—since I'm referring to destinations within our own borders. The rodeos, upscale shopping, and fabulous BBQ of Dallas or Houston offer an experience totally different from the quaint, rocky terrain, whaling museums, and clambakes of Boston. A jaunt to the concrete canyons of New York City bears very little resemblance to a sojourn in the wooded hills of North Carolina. Every destination offers something for everyone, yet every town or city retains its own unique character.

Since one of the primary values of the Red Hat Society is encouraging its members (actually all women) to embrace middle age and beyond with gusto, there is an obvious need for a book like this. Hundreds of thousands of like-minded women have responded to our battle cry, "We're not done yet!" Seeing the world—beginning with the United States—is on our "to do" list. Since travel has changed during the past few years—and so have we—what could be more helpful than a whole book of tips created especially with the mid-life woman (member of the RHS or not) in mind?

Some of us will be traveling with family, but many of us will set out with other female friends "of a certain age." Red Hatters are discovering that other Red Hatters make fabulous traveling companions! (There is no better place to find lively, vibrant friends!) Through our website, our members can contact other Hatters in their destination city and arrange to meet face to face. It's so enjoyable to see an unfamiliar city in the company of new-found "sisters." When traveling to our conventions, we not only see the city, but make plenty of new friends, and have the time of our lives, all at once! Our office will even match single travelers up with roommates!

Some of us are veteran travelers; some are just beginning to find the time (and courage) to actually do some of the traveling we've always promised ourselves we would do. Regardless of which category you fall into, this book will be an invaluable "insurance policy," helping to ensure that your travel experience will be positive and memorable. There is aid in choosing a destination, advice regarding the sights not to be missed, and solid guidance to help you successfully prepare for any unexpected circumstances or "surprises" that could suddenly arise. Armed with the knowledge and encouragement this book offers, you will be ready for anything!

Many lively ladies of the Red Hat Society have generously contributed solid advice and encouraging words to this book. If they can get out and go, the rest of us can certainly get out and go too! Slap on your red hat (or, at the least, your RHS membership pin) and GO! Remember what Dinah Shore used to say: "America is asking you to call!"

In friendship,
Sue Ellen Cooper

PART ONE

Let's Get Started!

Getting Started

*G*etting started can present two of the most difficult challenges of any trip, deciding where to go and when to head in that direction. There are a few things that you can do before you make those difficult decisions that can help get you in the mood for adventure.

JOIN THE CLUB

Before you start planning your trip, even when it is just a twinkle in your eye, do the following:

Join the Red Hat Society. First and foremost, if you are not a member of the Red Hat Society, there is no time like the present to join. Fun after fifty is for women everywhere, no matter where or when your journey begins! Tapping into one of the largest networks of women anywhere who believe that now is the best time to be alive, is an amazing feeling. The Red Hat Society provides endless opportunities to communicate, share information and ideas and even meet new friends around the world. Not only do you get the benefit of being part of a growing phenomenon, but with the Red Hat Society Purple Perks Membership, you have access to incredible travel benefits as well. Go to <u>www.redhatsociety.com</u> and click on membership benefits. Check out the Purple Perks benefits section for Travel Discounts. You will find discounts on rental cars, cruises, and over 40,000 hotels worldwide. Red Hatters get tremendous discounts on Amtrak as well. Even more travel discounts are available when you book your Red Hat Society travel through Carlson Travel.

Join AAA. The benefits of AAA are countless. The Web site holds many treasures, including hotel discounts, travel planning guides, fuel price finder, and maps, maps, maps! Joining AAA, which has a proven track record, costs about $62.00 per year. You probably do not need a premier membership; the basic one provides many advantages. To top it all off, AAA makes all of the information available in hard copy too. If you are not Web savvy, no worries! Call AAA or go by a local office and pick up your TripTik. As a side note, even if you never take that trip, any woman out there driving or riding in a car should have AAA. Go to www.aaa.com or call 866-222-2582.

Check out AARP. AARP membership costs $12.50 per year. I don't know that I would join AARP for the travel benefits alone, but it has some great discounts that are worth a look. If you haven't yet joined AARP for its general discounts and the great magazine, that is something to think about. Go to www.aarp.org or call 888-OURAARP (888-687-2277).

Sign up for hotel rewards and membership programs. By signing up for the hotel loyalty programs, you can earn points toward stays. When I originally started traveling, I did not sign up because I did not think I would ever be on the road enough to make an impact. Boy, was I wrong. I soon figured out that even if I never earned a free night, the benefits of the free membership were well worth the few minutes it took to sign up for it. Some include other travel partners and/or discounts within their memberships, such as the ability to earn airline miles or rental car discounts. Check out the programs and determine which work best for you. Check out which hotels have locations you are likely to visit, which ones have suite hotels or hotels in the price range you are interested in frequenting, and which ones have point programs in which the points do not expire. You will soon learn that earning those points will factor into your deciding where to lay your head at night. (This is exactly why they have them.)

It may take you a few stays at a few different hotels before you decide which program is best for you, but be sure to sign up so you don't lose any nights. At a minimum, I would sign up for the following clubs. (I've listed the hotels and their brand partners so you will know which ones are included with each membership. Note that the phone number listed is *not* the number for reservations. It is the number for signing up for the loyalty club.)

MARRIOTT REWARDS
www.marriottrewards.com or 800-450-4442
Marriott | Renaissance | Courtyard | Residence Inn | Fairfield Inn
TownePlace Suites | SpringHill Suites | Sheraton

STARWOOD PREFERRED GUEST
www.starwoodhotels.com or 888-625-4988
Four Points | Loft | W Hotels | Le Meridien | Westin | St. Regis | The Luxury Collection

HILTON HONORS
www.hilton.com or 800-HHonors (800-446-6677)
Conrad | Double Tree | Embassy Suites Hotels | Hampton Inn | Hampton Inn & Suites
Hilton Garden Inn | Homewood Suites by Hilton | The Waldorf-Astoria Collection

HOLIDAY INN–PRIORITY CLUB REWARDS
www.holidayinn.com or 800-272-9273
Holiday Inn | Intercontinental | Crowne Plaza | Holiday Inn Express
Staybridge Suites | Candlewood Suites | Hotel Indigo

BEST WESTERN–GOLD CROWN CLUB
www.goldcrownclub.com or 800-237-8483

You may be surprised at how quickly you can earn that first free night.

If you are not a member of your local Sam's Club, look into signing up. The clubs have the best gas prices around and nifty travel packages too.

MONEY-SAVING TIPS

I have a friend, Anne, who has the most incredible knack for finding bargains. She seems drawn to them like a moth to a flame. I bet you have an "Anne" in your chapter. She is that gal who walks into your favorite bargain basement store about 4:00 PM after a blood-and-thunder sale and is successful among the chaos. You know the scene. The clothes are piled up in heaps. Sizes and colors are mixed and next to impossible to find. The pants are dangling under the carousel in no certain order whatsoever. Yet within ten minutes she can find a three-piece designer suit, in her size no less, for $29.99. Rebecca, another friend, will spend thirty minutes and a gallon of gas to drive across town to save $0.40 on a twelve-pack of Coke. And then there are those like me. I am all about a bargain or a sale, and I spend a fair bit of time seeking them. But as I have grown into this awesome age of fifty plus, I have discovered that I factor in more than price alone, especially when it comes to travel. Through my travels in the last several years, I have found that some things are not worth discounting. Peace of mind is one of them.

The age of the Internet, which some of us have joined wholeheartedly and others not so much, has launched a plethora of discount travel sites, lures, and enticements that can quickly consume you. You could spend days searching and researching air fares, hotel deals, tour packages, and so on. (I will cover that aspect of deal finding in the booking section.) But what about those of us who just aren't ready to put the time, effort, and learning curve into surfing the Internet? Well, there are still ways to save money and possibly get a few extra perks along the way.

It doesn't matter whether you are an "Anne," a "Rebecca," or just you. Anyone getting ready to travel should do some very basic things. They will cost you little or no money but can add benefits to your travel experience.

Rule #1: Ask!

You have heard the saying, "Ask and you shall receive." At the very least, *ask!* You may be surprised at the number of discounts and special rates out there for you. Always ask for the best rate available and an upgrade.

THE BEST RATE AVAILABLE

Whenever you make reservations—for car rental, air travel, any type of public transportation, restaurants, *anything*—always ask if there is a senior discount. Senior discounts start anywhere from that magic fifty to sixty-five. Ask for your discount *before* you purchase or consume the product or service:

before you order your meal, when you make your hotel reservation (not when you are checking out), or when you make your car reservation. Many places have a senior rate but do not offer it unless you ask for it. *However,* the senior rate may not always be the best rate available. Check the regular rate and the senior rate, and take advantage of the better deal.

AN UPGRADE

An upgrade may not exactly be a discount, but it can certainly turn out to be a nice little sprinkle on top of the whipped cream. Depending on your level in your chosen loyalty club, the current load of an airplane, hotel rooms available, or the type of car sitting on a lot, you can sometimes score an upgrade simply by asking.

Airlines. Some airlines now allow you to buy upgrades at the gate. You could end up with a pretty good deal and a new experience if you have never gone first class before. But if you are going to spend money to upgrade to first class, save it for a trip that is at least two hours long. That way you can enjoy the full benefit of what is left of first-class service.

Hotels. You can pretty well bet that your hotel will not offer room upgrades unless you specifically request them. Granted, in some hotels, they claimed to have upgraded my room, and the only difference was that a shower cap was included in the bathroom amenities. A few other times, I was upgraded to a suite that knocked my socks off! If there are no room upgrades available, at a minimum, ask for access to the concierge lounge. Depending on the hotel, the concierge lounge may serve a continental breakfast and/or evening appetizers! These upgrades are much more likely to happen for you if you are a member of the hotel's loyalty club.

Car rentals. Upgrading from a compact to a midsize is not very likely to happen because the midsize is the most popular rental and there are fewer of them just sitting around. However, if you have rented a midsize and would like to upgrade to a full size, ask. All they can do is say no. Make clear that you want to upgrade at *no additional cost* to you. Lately, due to the increase in gas prices, the larger cars are less popular with customers so they are waiting on the lot for someone to ask for them. Last week my son was renting a car in Houston, and he signed up for a midsize and got an upgrade to an H3 (Hummer). It was fun for a day! Hey, it's vacation. Enjoy the extra leg and trunk room!

CAR TRAVEL

Whether you are driving your own car or a rental car, check the air pressure in the tires. Not only does it impact the life of the tires, but it will make a difference in your fuel usage.

Make sure your engine is tuned up and your oil changes are up to date.

You can calculate your approximate mileage by using <u>AAA.com</u>, <u>mapquest.com</u>, or some other mileage calculator. AAA and MapQuest even have places on their Web sites that will help you find the best gas prices in a specific area.

Rent a car. Although this may sound a bit crazy, sometimes renting a car can actually be less expensive than taking the airport shuttle. This can especially be true when the airport is more than twenty miles from your destination, parking at the destination or hotel is free, or you are traveling in a less urban area with sparse public transportation. It is worth considering.

If you are heading out on a road trip, it could also save wear and tear on your car. If you do rent a car, do it far in advance. Car rental prices fluctuate daily according to the supply and demand at the time. Trying to get a rental car when the Mary Kay convention is in town will cost you a pretty penny.

HOTELS

Eat breakfast free. Many hotels include a continental breakfast and some include a full breakfast in their room price. Figure that into your accommodation cost. Paying for breakfast can add up to $20.00 per day in travel costs.

Eat dinner free. Some hotels, Marriott Residence Inn for instance, offer an evening meal at no extra charge. It doesn't usually rank in Fodor's for a food review, but it is edible. It is typically a casserole or salad and hot dogs, self-serve style, in the hotel's breakfast area. Dessert is usually cookies. These meals are served only during the business week, Monday through Thursday evenings, starting about 5:30 PM or so. By 7:00 PM the pickings tend to get a little slim. If you've joined the hotel rewards programs, you may have access to the concierge lounge, which usually has at least hors d'oeuvres in the early evening. If you have been out sightseeing all day and had a huge lunch, a light snack may be all that you want.

Use hotels that provide kitchens or kitchenettes. Now, I'm not suggesting cooking full-course meals while on vacation, but having a small refrigerator to keep snacks and bottled water handy or being able to microwave popcorn can really give your budget a boost. Hotels such as Residence Inn will even do the grocery shopping for you. You give them a list (for example, a six-pack of water, diet sodas, cookies, and so forth) in the morning, and like magic, when you return in the evening, the food will be waiting in your room. Last time I used this service there was no surcharge— just the price of the groceries and the nice tip I left for the consideration.

Use the complimentary shuttle service. Many hotels have a complimentary shuttle service from the airport to the hotel. They may also provide a shuttle to prime area attractions. As you make your reservations or check in, ask about this service.

Be coupon savvy. All sorts of coupons are available for discounts at almost every travel destination. Research your destination on the Web, and request information, including discount coupons, from the local tourist organization.

Save water bottles and refill them. Can we really complain about the $3.00 per gallon gas prices when in the last five years, we have started paying more than $1.00 for eight ounces of water? There are very few places in the United States where the drinking water is unsafe to drink. If you have questions about it, ask at the front desk, but in most cases you can refill your water bottle from the tap and save considerably.

Research and/or book online. Doing research and booking online can usually save from a few dollars to a significant sum. At the very least do your research online, and read the hotel reviews on sites such as Orbitz.com or Hotels.com. They are usually pretty accurate and will let you know right away whether you are headed for a great stay with fluffy sheets or a kiddy haven with screechers up and down the halls.

When you plan your trip, use the tools on Travelocity.com and Expedia.com that allow you to see which days the air travel is cheapest to your destination. You can sometimes save $100.00 just by shifting your travel dates a day or two.

Decide what is important and use it. If the hotel has a hot tub, pack that swimsuit and indulge yourself!

Travel close to home. I'm always amazed at how much there is to do within an easy day's drive of home. Transportation is often the largest expense of any travel budget. Get tour information on your own state and surrounding states. You may be pleasantly surprised at what is in your own backyard. Grab your girlfriends and take that two-hour drive to the city, have dinner out, stay in a nice hotel, shop till you drop the next day, then drive home. It can be an awesome forty-eight hours!

Plan ahead; buy in advance. If you know where you are going and when you are going, planning early and buying in advance are wise moves.

AIR

At this time I hesitate to even mention that any of the airlines, other than Southwest, may have senior travel rates. Too often I have found that the senior program is a 10 percent discount of the standard full-fare ticket. If you ask, "Is that the best available rate?" they will disclose some other discounted rate that is far better than the senior fare discount you would have gotten if you hadn't asked.

Southwest is one of the few airlines left that offers true senior discounts. They start at age sixty-five.

The best way to get a bargain airfare is to book twenty-one days in advance. (See more on airline discounts in the booking section.)

TRAIN

Amtrak often has senior discounts of 10 percent on certain routes. Discounts start at age sixty. However, if you are a member of the Red Hat Society, Amtrak discounts can be as much at 20 percent! To receive your RHS member discount you must make your reservations at least three days in advance. You will need to show your Purple Perks membership card when you pick up your tickets. Go to www.amtrak.com or call 800-USA-RAIL to find a complete list of destinations, routes, and schedules that qualify for your RHS discount.

RESTAURANTS

Many large chain restaurants offer discounts for people aged fifty-five and over: Applebee's, KFC, IHOP, and Wendy's, just to name a few. Also, often smaller local restaurants offer senior specials. Once again, it never hurts to ask. Some hotel restaurants provide discounts if you are a member of their loyalty club. Many places have implemented an early bird special for meals during nonpeak hours. You can usually find a restaurant with a lunch special, but also check around for the early bird dinner special. It can sometimes be your best bet.

OTHER DISCOUNTS

Ski resorts. Ski resorts often offer senior discounts for the season. Most discounts start at sixty-five, but some start at sixty. Check the resort Web site or call the resort to see whether there is a senior program. People over seventy may sign up for free programs at some ski slopes!

Research, research, research. Do your research and be flexible. You can often save money by changing your travel dates or times of day. When researching fares, use the Web site's best available fare option. The Web may not be the only source for discounts. It never hurts to pick up the phone and ask someone. If you are working with a travel agent, ask the travel agent to check for discounts.

Deal alerts. Sign up for last-minute deal alerts with your preferred air carrier, car rental agency, www.orbitz.com, www.travelzoo.com, or other companies. You may be able to save hundreds.

SeaWorld and Busch Gardens. SeaWorld and Busch Gardens offer discounts through AARP. They are available at the admissions gate, and you will save $5.00. On designated "Terrific Tuesdays" they have special programs on health, horticulture, behind-the-scenes talks with the animal experts, and other things. You may also be able to get other discounts by purchasing tickets in advance on their Web sites (www.seaworld.com or www.buschgardens.com).

National Park Service. The National Park Service (www.nps.gov) issues an interagency senior pass for people over the age of sixty-two. The lifetime pass costs only $10.00! It will gain you and three of your friends access to all of the national parks and various other sites. The pass holder can also receive 50 percent savings on some expanded amenity fees charged at the parks. The passes must be purchased in person and are available at most national parks.

CityPass. If you are going to Atlanta, Boston, Chicago, Hollywood, New York, Philadelphia, San Francisco, Seattle, or Southern California, you should really look into CityPass. CityPass has combined the main attractions in these cities with significant discounts and advantages that make CityPass a tremendous value. In some instances you may be able to skip long ticket lines, and you can enjoy up to 50 percent discounted admission

Red Hat Recommendations
for Saving Money on the Road

- Fix breakfast in your hotel room and eat lunch out (it is cheaper than dinner).
- Take very little cash and only one credit card, and prebook excursions.
- Eat a large breakfast and a late lunch. That way, you can often skip dinner or have a light snack in the evening.
- Carry snacks—peanuts or packaged peanut butter crackers can go a long way.
- Make a budget and keep it.
- Purchase admission tickets for venues in advance.
- Use regional and local public transportation. Purchase public transportation all-access passes.
- Drink water with meals.
- Eat fruit instead of lunch, and keep shopping.
- Stay in hotels that offer free breakfast.
- Travel in an RV and cook rather than eat out a lot.
- Visit free attractions.
- Ask locals about interesting and low-cost places to see.
- Plan in advance.
- Check out local stores for meat, cheese, and bread to make sandwiches.
- Find a package store for a bottle of wine. Have a glass before dinner and after. Skip the high price per glass at the restaurant.
- Research the route, travel with friends, and share expenses.
- Take an inconvenient 6:00 AM flight instead of a midmorning flight to save hundreds.
- Use one credit card for everything, and keep receipts so you know how much you are spending. Use cash only at a bar or for tips or emergencies.
- Pack meals that do not necessitate stopping at fast-food places. Pick up travel guides/discounts when you enter each state.
- Pick one hotel/motel chain, and join the loyalty club.

- Pack powdered lemonade to add to water and save on buying soda.
- If you think that it will end up in a yard sale, do not buy it.
- Check out menus and prices before being seated at a restaurant.
- Use Priceline to reserve your rental car.
- Never buy new clothes before a trip. Nobody knows you anyway!
- Check out the national trusts for discounts for Red Hatters.
- Use a travel agent. The services are free except for airline tickets.
- Carry your own bags; you will save money on tips.

on some attractions. If you are not sure what to see at your chosen destination, review the CityPass package and you will have a good idea of a pretty solid itinerary (www.citypass.com or 888-330-5008).

Travel and tourism offices. Travel and tourism offices, also referred to as convention and visitors' bureaus of your chosen destination can be a wealth of information. One of the most valuable lessons I learned while writing *The Red Hat Society Travel Guide* was about these offices. All these years I have been calling or writing the Chamber of Commerce for city information when I should have been writing or calling the local tourism board. These offices are likely to have knowledge of or access to discounted tickets and/or recommendations for local shows and suggestions for restaurants. They usually know the most Red Hat–friendly places to visit as well. If you are Internet savvy, go to the visitors' and conventions site for your destination. You will be amazed at what is available. If you are not Internet savvy, call Information to get the number and follow up with the office. (See Tourism Offices Worldwide Directory, www.towd.com.)

LUGGAGE

Ahhh . . . the joys of shopping for luggage. It is another one of my favorite reasons to travel! Now, if it has been a while since you embarked on your last adventure, you might want to dig out that old suitcase and check its zippers and snaps. (You might even find a lost treasure or two in the side pocket!) Starting off your trip with your favorite purple pants twirling about the baggage belt as a result of a broken luggage zipper really isn't a lot of fun.

There are several things to think about when shopping for a new suitcase. I look for the wildest, craziest-looking bag in the bunch. Not only does that make it easy for me to spot at the baggage carousel, but it is also easier for me to notice when someone else accidentally walks off with it. One very important point is that red luggage is much more available than it once was. It has gained in popularity but is still easier to spot in a crowd than the old standard black. I strongly encourage you to check the ID tag because some bags *do* look alike. I like to tie a small ribbon or a bright-colored tag to my bag, *just* to make sure I know which one I am grabbing. You may want to use a red and purple ribbon on the top of your bag.

I once got into a tug-of-war with a gentleman who had, I am sure, the only other piece of luggage with my chosen pattern. It was *so ugly*. I had it at my side as I was watching for my other pieces (totally unmatched), and he reached for it! I grabbed the handle and held on tightly, never taking my eye off the baggage carousel while watching for my other bags. He tugged; I tugged. He tugged; I tugged. Finally he politely said, "I think this is my bag." I turned and, laughing, said, "Now what other crazy person would buy a piece of luggage this ugly?" He just laughed, smiled, and said, "This one," as he pointed to his name on the ID tag attached to the handle. *Wham*, just then, my ugly bag went gliding by. So, even if you think you have the only purple-and-red rhinestone-studded, zebra-striped bag on the planet, check the ID tag before you leave the baggage area.

Buying Baggage . . . (I mean luggage; nobody needs to buy baggage)

Watch your weight! Ahhhhhhhhhhhhh, I know these are dirty words to those of us with Hattitude, but always, always, always lift it before you buy it. There can be as much as a five-pound weight difference in bags. Five pounds may not seem a lot when you are in the store and in love with the purple-and-red polka-dotted fabric of the bag, *but* when you are five pounds over the weight limit at the airport scales and they want to charge you $80.00 for the overage, it *does* make a difference. If you are buying a carry-on (or roll-aboard as the airlines call them), definitely check the weight. No, an airline doesn't typically weigh your carry-on, but there is a forty-pound limit on most carry-on items. You very well may have to lift that bag over your head and wrangle it into the overhead compartment.

I suggest picking that puppy up right there in the store to see if you can maneuver it. If you cannot, then you will need to check it with your other bag. Counting on some young person to lift it for you could hold up the boarding process. The flight attendants are discouraged by their employers from assisting with luggage. Too many back injuries. Luggage with a fiber-glass or aluminum frame will be lighter weight, yet very strong.

Test the zippers. I completely zip and unzip every zipper on a bag before I buy. If it sticks the least little bit, it's a deal breaker! Broken zippers are just one part of an adventure I would rather not have to face. And sticky zippers are an added frustration that doesn't need to be there. Double-stitched zippers can be one indication of the luggage's quality. Also, think about the zipper pulls. I have one carry-on bag with a helper strap on top that I love and the 360-degree wheels, but the little loop that held the zipper pulls was not completely closed. I had to get the pliers and squeeze the zipper pulls holder closed to keep them from coming off every time I tried to zip the zippers. What a pain!

Splurge on wheels. If you have not been luggage shopping in the last ten years, this is your perfect excuse to go. The luggage in your attic, even with that lifetime guarantee you got when you bought it, may not be up to the newest, latest, and greatest prototype. For instance, if any piece of luggage that is larger than an oversized purse doesn't have wheels on it, consider doing yourself a *big* favor and go luggage shopping. The last five years in luggage development have resulted in ultralight carry-on bags with 360-degree turning radius wheels that can serve as a chair should you need to rest. I highly recommend, at a very minimum, splurging for luggage with wheels. Even if you are staying at the nicest hotel in town with the best bellmen available, I can just about guarantee that at some point during your journey, *you* will be schlepping that suitcase and it is so much easier to do with wheels. I prefer the 360-degree wheels because they are much easier to maneuver. If you don't get 360s, at least choose the "in-line skate" wheels.

Check out the bag's interior. I look for a couple of things. Even in a small roll-aboard bag, I want a hanger hook. Although I may not intend to use it, I like to know it is there. If I need to pack an extra change of clothes for emergencies, having that hanger holder keeps it secure. The other nice feature is the little straps that hold the clothes in place once you have packed. They really do help keep clothing from getting wadded up and wrinkled in the suitcase.

Count the number of handles. Make sure there are at least two attached handles on the outside of the bag: one on the top and one on the side. An added bonus is one on the bottom. This may sound crazy, but if you are trying to drag a suitcase out of a car trunk that has been put in top side first, and there is nothing to grab onto, that is a broken fingernail waiting to happen.

Evaluate the telescoping handle. As for the telescoping handle on the wheeled bags, test it in the store. Practice extending it and sliding it up and down a few times. Some have release buttons to allow the handle to go up and down. They can be in various places. If you are unfamiliar with your luggage and have not practiced, you may have quite a battle trying to figure out how to collapse that handle. Also notice where the telescoping handle goes. If the casing for the handle is inside the bag, it may take up a bit of precious room. If the casing is not enclosed or at least covered in some way, you can pretty much guess that at some point during your travels, it is going to take quite a beating.

Choose luggage with straps. I like to have luggage with a snap-on strap that lets me attach my super-duper, extra large purse or backpack to my luggage. Then I have a free hand for my Diet Coke, preflight frozen yogurt, or whatever. I look for the ones that are detachable so I can unclip them and stick them in the front pocket before I check the bag. That protects the strap from being jerked off in the baggage carousel. If I am looking for a carry-on I am really going to carry, I choose one with extra wide, extra padded straps. Shoulder straps, like bra straps, can be annoying if they cut into your shoulder. As with most things, I like to follow a two-option strategy. If it has a shoulder strap, I also like to have an alternate handle that will allow me to pick it up and carry it should my shoulder get tired or the bag not hang comfortably.

Examine hanging bags. In a hanging bag, pay close attention to the way that the hanger is attached to the bag. Remember, this hanger, which sometimes consists of a very flimsy link chain, will be holding the weight of the entire suitcase and its contents. Make sure it is securely attached to the bag. Also, notice whether you can use your own hangers. I haven't seen one yet that came with enough hangers for everything I wanted to put in it.

TSA Locks

Never check an unlocked bag. The new regulations for screening checked luggage have made this a little bit trickier than it once was, but as with all other travel issues, there is a solution! The Transportation Security Administration (TSA) screens every passenger's luggage before it is placed on an airplane. In most instances, your luggage will be scanned electronically and may never need to be opened. However, there are occasions when the airport TSA agents may need to open your checked bag. This determination usually comes well after you have merrily made your way to the security area and are heading for your gate.

Immediately after 9/11 a TSA agent's only option was to cut off your lock, wrap it neatly in plastic wrap, and stick it in your bag with a little note saying he was the culprit. Since then, TSA has worked with several companies to develop a TSA-approved lock, and several luggage manufacturers now put these locks on their luggage. These locks bear a special red logo that identifies them as locks that will work with a TSA master key. Some locks also have a device in them that allows you to tell whether the lock was indeed opened or not.

If you choose to use a standard luggage lock on your bag, you must leave it unlocked, hoping that TSA will lock it once they have finished their inspection. If you do by chance lock your luggage with a standard luggage lock, TSA will cut the lock off, wrap it up, and place it inside your bag.

Instead of locks, you may choose to use plastic cable ties. Then if TSA cuts them off, you haven't lost much. Just be sure to carry something with you to cut the ties off your bag once you reach your destination.

TSA-approved luggage locks are available in most airports and travel stores or at the following Web sites: www.safeskieslocks.com; www.travelsentry.org; and www.amazon.com. TSA-approved luggage locks cost between $8.50 and $25.00.

Consider different fabrics. Luggage these days presents many fabric options. Remember the days when all you had to think about was genuine leather? Well, that stuff is *heavy*! Go for the ballistic or Cordura nylon. If you plan to hit the road a lot, the ballistic nylon is a little more expensive, but it wears like iron. If you are going to the Red Hat Society conference once a year, and that is the extent of your planned travels, Cordura will probably serve you just as well and be a little cheaper. You will sometimes see the word *denier* to describe fabric durability. Typically the higher the denier, the stronger the fabric. Shoot for a minimum of 400 denier.

Consider a set vs. individual pieces. Even if the set comes with seven pieces, choose a set with individual pieces that really suit your needs.

Check size of carry-on luggage. Carry-on luggage should be small enough to slide under the airplane seat or in the overhead bin. It also has to be large enough to carry your absolutely, positively most important stuff that you cannot do without for twenty-four hours. Most carry-ons are less than twenty-two inches in size. Yet many department and luggage stores state that a suitcase is "carry-on" size, even though in the real world, it will not fit in the overhead bin. Keep in mind that the carry-on that will fit in the first-class overhead bin of a 777 may not fit in the space of the economy section of an M80. No, you do not have to be able to identify the aircraft overhead bin size by the plane model; just be sensible when buying your carry-on bag.

For the majority of air carriers, a good rule of thumb is a total size of forty-five inches. That translates to twenty-two by fourteen by nine inches, and these measurements are the inside compartment size. They do not take into account the little pocket in the front where you stuff that extra pair of shoes. This is assuming you leave all pockets empty and flat. If you unzip the little magic zipper that increases your space "by one full inch" and

Ruby's Roundup

- Remember space and weight constraints. Consider trunk space and airline restrictions.
- Buy what you need. There are very few places in the U.S. where there isn't a Wal-Mart just down the street. Pack what you think you need but be aware, if you forget something, you can probably buy it on the road.

pack the bag full, it is highly unlikely your roll-aboard will fit into the over-head bin.

Limit the number of bags. Most airlines are beginning to limit to two the number of pieces of luggage you can check. You can check two gianormous suitcases (as long as each weighs less than forty-five or fifty pounds, depending on the airline) and carry on a roll-aboard and one small personal item that can be a purse, a small backpack, or a hatbox not to exceed thirty-six inches.

PACKING

What to Pack

One of the biggest chores in the pretrip is the packing. It can be daunting! It can take days—and the agony! But one of the oldest solutions known to woman can truly make a difference. You "kiss" it. Yep, keep it simple, silly! Let's face it. The majority of us are not planning a trip to the wilds of Africa. If we really, really forgot something that was necessary, just how far away can the closest Wal-Mart be? With a little planning and preparation, packing can go smoothly, and you will end up at your destination with all the necessities of life.

CARRY-ON OR CHECK?

You do need to make a few decisions before determining your approach to the dreaded deed. The biggest and possibly the most pondered question known to the occasional traveler is, do you carry on or check your luggage? It is kind of like asking, paper or plastic? Coke or Pepsi? In the grand scheme of things, how much difference does it really make?

I am an admitted die-hard Diet Coke drinker. However, on those mornings when I wake up in a Marriott where Pepsi has the contract and I have a need for something cold, wet, and caffeinated, I can drink a Diet Pepsi. It may not be my preferred choice, but it beats heading off to the local Pic-and-Tote to buy one. It all comes down to how much you want to focus on "to check" or "not to check." What is peace of mind worth over the physical strain of lugging your bags between gates and the mental anguish of packing your favorite purple gown and hat in a valise not much bigger than your turkey fryer?

There are certainly strong arguments in the "if at all possible, carry it on" arena. The strongest is that about six out of every one thousand bags end up with some kind of difficulty reaching their destination. This doesn't mean that six out of every one thousand bags are lost, never to be found again; they just suffered some type of delay or destruction *or* ended up in never-never land. What it means to you is that there is a six out of one thousand chance that you will end up spending time on your vacation filling out a luggage incident form (see the "Lost Luggage" section of chapter 7). Amazingly enough, the majority of bags are not really lost, just delayed. Very often, your bags will be located within twenty-four hours and delivered to your destination.

Do you really want to try to become a professional well-practiced traveler who can pack two weeks' worth of clothes "and Toto too" in that little roll-aboard bag? You can buy books written on the art of the carry-on traveler. If this is your desire, it is certainly doable. I almost never check my bag when I travel for business. I can get five business days' worth of clothes, cosmetics, and my computer into my backpack and roll-aboard. I've been packing that same bag with the same stuff almost every week for six years. It is an art form.

Now, take the same five days and call them vacation when I may wear shorts, jeans, swimwear, or formal wear; tennis shoes, flip-flops, heels, or (gasp) two pairs of heels. I've never mastered getting that grouping into my roll-aboard. I still follow the "less is best" rule and try not to overpack. However, when I pack for vacation, somehow it just doesn't all fit the same way.

The length of the trip is a consideration, and most of us can pack all we need for a long weekend trip into a bag that meets the carry-on requirements. The reality is, unless you have practiced and planned very precisely, have *no* plans or money to shop with, and are really *very* determined not to check a bag, realize there is absolutely no shame in checking luggage.

Just in case you are still pondering the check or carry-on question, here are a few considerations, with pros and cons:

- Is this a direct flight, or do you change planes? Logically you may think the opportunity to lose your bags is increased if you have connections, so you would want to use a carry-on. This may be true. The consideration is, are you up to schlepping your bags from gate

EQM Sue Ellen and I are the same size (except for shoes), and we have made a vow to one another that we will stay that way. We hold ourselves accountable, too. The reason for this is simple; when we travel together, especially to conventions, we can pack lighter because we can share clothes. You may have noticed that the dress one of us wears one day is worn by the other on a different day. We choose different outfits by checking with one another before packing. EQM Sue Ellen may tell me that she is bringing two purple dresses and two purple pant suits. I will reply that I'll pack two purple skirts and tops that go together. We mix it up when we get to the convention. We are quite familiar with one another's wardrobe, as you might imagine. It works with hats and jewelry too.

—*Linda Murphy, Esteemed Vice Mother*

to gate? Remember, if you are trying to make a connecting flight, chances are you will include a restroom stop and possibly a snack stop. You will always have a small carry-on with medicine, your book, and your emergency overnight stuff, but if you have checked luggage, this bag tends to be a bit lighter than when all you own is in the roll-aboard and your carry-on.

- If you are on a tight schedule and timing is a factor immediately upon your arrival somewhere, you may want to work hard to get everything into your carry-on luggage. Let's say that you are flying into New York for a long weekend and are planning on making an 8:00 PM show. Waiting for your luggage could be the difference between being there when the curtain goes up and being there at intermission. I've waited up to an hour for my bags to come off the baggage carousel. That was not really a *big* problem—after all, they did arrive—but the delay can affect your plans.

- Checking baggage takes time at the airport. If you are a JIT (just in time) traveler and are one of those holdouts who doesn't believe in getting to the airport the suggested two hours prior to takeoff, you may want to carry on your bags. Standing in line for baggage tags and security for your checked luggage adds time to your airport stay.

Packing List

Try to keep everything under the three-ounce liquid limit even if you are not flying. It takes up less room in your bag. Then, if you need extra room for treasures you have found along the way, you can throw it away the last day of your trip. If you are flying, either pack your liquids in your checked luggage or put them in three-ounce containers in a one-quart baggie to carry through security.

Toiletries

Toothbrush

Toothpaste

Hair brush

Moisturizer

Facial soap (if you use it)

Medication (take three extra days' worth just in case)

Make-up (just the necessary stuff)

Deodorant

Shampoo and soap (unless your are staying in a hotel that supplies it)

Hot rollers or curling iron as necessary

Portable stain removers (Shout wipes or a Tide pen)

A book or your knitting

Red hat and/or purple scarf

Clothes for the weekend

1 pair of black or khaki slacks

1 pair of jeans or casual pants (wear these)

2 blouses or T-shirts

1 sweater

3 sets of undies

1 pair of black shoes

3 pairs of socks (wear one)

1 pair of walking shoes (wear these—it will leave more room in your suitcase)

1 pair of pajamas

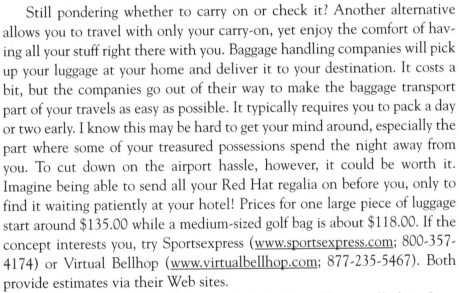

Clothes for a week (take the above lists and add the following)

1 more pair black or khaki slacks

4 to 5 blouses or T-shirts

5 more sets of undies

5 pairs of socks, knee highs, or hose

1 pair of pajamas

If you are willing to wash a few things out, you can go to 3-4 blouses and 3-4 sets of undies and socks. Be sure to take some laundry soap if this is your plan.

Still pondering whether to carry on or check it? Another alternative allows you to travel with only your carry-on, yet enjoy the comfort of having all your stuff right there with you. Baggage handling companies will pick up your luggage at your home and deliver it to your destination. It costs a bit, but the companies go out of their way to make the baggage transport part of your travels as easy as possible. It typically requires you to pack a day or two early. I know this may be hard to get your mind around, especially the part where some of your treasured possessions spend the night away from you. To cut down on the airport hassle, however, it could be worth it. Imagine being able to send all your Red Hat regalia on before you, only to find it waiting patiently at your hotel! Prices for one large piece of luggage start around $135.00 while a medium-sized golf bag is about $118.00. If the concept interests you, try Sportsexpress (www.sportsexpress.com; 800-357-4174) or Virtual Bellhop (www.virtualbellhop.com; 877-235-5467). Both provide estimates via their Web sites.

Another option to the "How the heck do I get all my stuff where I am going?" question—and perhaps my favorite—is to use DHL, FedEx, UPS, or overnight mail. Pretty much, that is the way the baggage handling companies get your stuff where it needs to be; they just add the advantage of service into the mix. But you can set this up on your own. You can even schedule UPS, FedEx, or DHL to pick up your packages at your house.

Something to remember when using the pack-and-send method is to alert the hotel that you may be getting a delivery there before you check in. Also, require a signature when your goodies are delivered. You can track your belongings online every step of the way and take comfort in knowing they have been delivered to your destination. Oh, and one other thing, be sure to throw packing tape and labels in the boxes before you close them. You will need them for the return shipment home, and you don't want them taking up room in your carry-on.

I realize I have not given you a definitive answer to the check or don't check question, but you do have a few things to think about. If you have decided that checking a bag is in your future, my philosophy is that you might as well check two. Now, this may sound crazy, but once you check one bag, several of the "I can get it all in my carry-on" arguments go out the window. You now have to check in at curbside or the ticket counter or kiosk, you have to stop at baggage claim, and TSA may go through your stuff anyway. The main reason I say that if you are going to check one, you might as well check two is that I cannot count how many times I have been at a ticket counter and watched some person digging through her bag and cramming things into her carry-on to try to get below the fifty-pound limit. (If this is you, pull out the shoes; they drop weight faster than anything.) It is much better to take two smaller, singularly manageable bags than to pack one monster bag that you have to use a forklift to get into the trunk.

OUTFITS

Once you have decided whether or not to check a bag, the fun really begins. First, claim your staging area. I use my bed because it is close to the closet and lets me lay out everything. This is a good plan if you are a one-day packer. If you need several days to mull over what is going in the suitcase and what is going back in the closet, you may want to consider an alternate site. It is very frustrating and counterproductive to lay out everything, then have to clear off the bed so you can climb in it at night.

Before you place even one thing in that suitcase, organize everything. Lay out each outfit, along with the accessories and shoes, for each day. Now, step back and determine which outfits you can combine. You probably don't need three pairs of black pants and two pairs of black shoes. Combine the outfits to end up with one pair of black pants, three tops, and one pair of black shoes. Do this with your other outfits as well. Gather all but one set of your undergarments, and put them in zip-top bags. You can roll the bags up to squish the air out of them, and they will take up less space. Put the one set in a zip-top bag by itself, and lay it aside for your carry-on.

One thing you never want to forget is your Red Hat regalia. Now, you may not be heading for the National Conference or some other official RH event, but you never know when the opportunity will arise to mingle with other members of our awesome sisterhood. My crushable red hat stays in my roll-aboard bag right next to my toothbrush and makeup. There is always room for my purple T-shirt. My red baseball cap lives in my computer briefcase/backpack. (More than once I have been on a business trip and dining alone, only to see a chapter dining out. I do not hesitate to whip out my red hat and introduce myself; they always make room at the table).

As you weed out the clothes you are not going to take, remove them from the staging area. If they stay there, they will somehow wiggle their way into your suitcase. While you have your clothes laid out everywhere, think about your travel day outfit. It should be, above all, comfortable. You should plan on wearing comfortable walking shoes for two reasons. Number one is obvious: they are your comfortable walking shoes. Number two is that your comfortable walking shoes are probably your bulkiest shoes. So, less space is taken in the suitcase! Your travel day outfit should consist of layers. Unless you are driving your own vehicle alone, you can bet that the climate control knob will not always be within your reach. Be prepared to shed or add a sweater if necessary.

COSMETICS AND TOILETRIES

Now that you have figured out your daily apparel, consider your cosmetics. *Under no circumstances* should you pack your medications in a checked bag. No excuses or rationalization can make this all right. Medication, prescription or nonprescription, belongs in your carry-on bag. (See chapter 9, "Travel Health," for more on packing medications.) Your checked luggage *is* the place for your 4.2-ounce jar of Lancome or other very expensive night cream. You cannot take liquids over three ounces in your carry-on luggage, even if the jar is only half full. If the container says four ounces and you have two ounces left, you will not be able to carry the last two ounces on the plane with you. Pack the jar in your checked luggage. You can choose from all sorts of travel bottles on the market so that you can transfer your Sam's size bottle of shampoo into a smaller one to save space. Do not fill the bottle completely to the top, though. The cargo area is not pressurized, and bottles sometimes leak as a result.

This leads to your next task. Separate your toiletries into two sizes and/or categories: those that go into your carry-on and those that go into your checked bags. Your carry-on should have anything that you cannot live without for twenty-four hours. These items (if they are liquid) should be in containers under three ounces and then placed in a quart-sized zip-top bag. For example, your economy-sized tube of toothpaste can go in your checked luggage. Bring a little travel-sized tube for your carry-on. This bag needs to be in an easily accessible outside pocket so that it will be handy when you reach the security checkpoint. Place the other items, especially liquids, in another zip-top bag, the size depending on your needs, to protect your clothes in your checked luggage in case something leaks.

Okay, you have clothes and toiletries scattered about the staging area. Some order has been restored because you have separated your toiletries into your carry-on zip-top bag and your checked zip-top bag . You have organized your clothes into combo outfits with your travel day outfit and shoes set to the side.

ESSENTIALS FOR THE CARRY-ON

It is time to pack your carry-on bag, which can be your best friend. It should be easy to maneuver, so I recommend a small wheeled suitcase. It doesn't have to be stuffed; in fact, keep it as light as possible so you can lift it into the overhead bin, but make sure to place the following essentials in it:

- A change of underwear. If your flight is diverted or delayed and you have to spend the night in an airport or an unplanned hotel room, you will not be able to get your suitcases off the plane. The same applies if you accept an offer to take a later flight or fly the next day in exchange for a travel voucher. Most likely, they will not take your bags off the plane. Your bags will be waiting for you at your destination.

- Any medication you may need for the next forty-eight hours at a minimum (I personally have *all* medications that I could ever possibly need in my carry-on).
- Your money, traveler's checks, and credit cards. Keep them in your carry-on. You may need them sooner than you think.
- Travel itineraries with confirmation numbers, hotel phone numbers, and addresses of places you will be staying.
- Any other travel documents, including cruise ship tickets, train tickets, and so on.
- Toiletries you absolutely cannot do without for twenty-four hours. This should include a toothbrush and toothpaste.
- Small containers of liquids. Remember, you may not carry on any liquid in a quantity over three ounces. All liquids must be in a quart-sized zip-top bag. Toothpaste, hairspray, mascara, and moisturizer count as liquids. You can put these items in larger sizes in your checked baggage, so get the sample size for your carry-on and pack your full-sized bottle in your checked bag.
- Any valuables. I strongly urge you to leave as much as you possibly can at home, but if you bring jewelry, computers, or cameras, place them in your carry-on.
- Your Red Hat regalia. Never be without your crushable red hat, baseball cap, or even red ribbon or topper. A purple boa takes up almost no room. When you are stranded with only your carry-on, there is nothing more comforting than knowing that your Red Hat regalia is safely tucked inside.
- A list of the items in your checked luggage. If you lose your luggage, it will help you file a claim form.

Once you have finished packing your carry-on bag, zip it up and lift it over your head. You will have to be able to do this to put it in the overhead bin of the airplane. Just so you know, the flight attendants cannot help you with this task. A few may offer, but for the most part, you are responsible for being able to place your carry-on in the overhead bin. You may get lucky and some nice young man or woman may help you out, but I would not bet money on it.

Now for your other bag.

Packing Methods

There are three primary methods of packing. All require some mastery and practice. As I mentioned before, there are entire books on different methods, but they all pretty much boil down to the following:

1. Roll packing. Many of you are familiar with this type of packing. It was one of the top five suggested packing tips submitted by fellow Red Hatters. Rolling your clothes decreases the number of creases. (I still think buying travel wear and non-wrinkle-type material works the best.) There are multiple variations on this theme and no magic one way to roll that works better than others. How you roll may depend on the type of clothing and the size of your suitcase. The basic premise is, the fewer folds, the fewer creases. I roll my T-shirts two at a time. I lay one on top of the other facedown. I fold the sleeves in to make the T-shirt into a rectangle. Depending on the size of the suitcase I am carrying, I adjust the length of my roll by folding in more or less of the sides. I then fold up the tail to shape the rectangle in half. Next, I roll the shirt from right to left (it doesn't really matter) to make a tidy little roll. I roll jeans one pair at a time. I lay them out as I would if I were going to hang them on a pants hanger, fold the legs in half, and roll them from the fold to the top.

Some people think that the roll method not only saves clothes from wrinkles but also saves space. I am not completely convinced of the space-saving aspects. It seems to me that my flat socks take up less room than my rolled ones, but I have found that certain rolled clothes seem to gather fewer wrinkles.

2. Bundle packing. This packing method is by far the most revolutionary, and I *do* think it makes a difference in both wrinkle control and space. Judith Guilford, the cofounder of Easy Going (a travel store) and the author of *The Packing Book*, developed this method, and I consistently use some variation of it every time I travel. It is a layering method that decreases wrinkling, but it is a bit difficult to explain.

Red Hat Regalia

Stranded in an airport with a long layover or delay? Take your Red Hat regalia out of your carry-on and don your hat and boa. You are almost assured to be chatting with another member of the Red Hat Society within minutes!

You start with your largest garment, say, your jacket, and lay it in the bottom of your suitcase with the collar against the back side, and arms and tail flowing over sides and bottom. Gently smooth out the jacket, pressing it down into the bottom of the bag. Next, take your pants and layer them lengthwise. Alternate which end you place the waistband, and let the legs flow over. Next, lay your shirts in the bag, using the width of the bag, alternating the band side with the overflow side. Once you have placed your clothes in the bag with the sides overflowing, fill the little nest you have made in the center of the bag with your toiletries, shoes, and accessories. (This is where you put all those things you have collected in the zip-top bags.) Now, fold in the tails and sleeves, creating a bundle in your bag.

3. Traditional folding method. Believe it or not, you can still fold your clothes like you see them in stores (and wish they would stay like in your dresser), put them in a suitcase, and reach your destination. Really! I use this method too. A few things can make this more effective, though. One is a simple folding board that helps you get that nice crisp, folded look. You can buy them at www.nu-era.com. A simple flat board is about $9.00. My favorite is the Flip Fold Shirt Folder that sells for $18.00. (I originally bought mine when my daughter saw one being used in a store where we were shopping. She told me that if she had a board like that to help her fold the laundry, she would take on that job. Well, you can only imagine how long it took me to figure out how to order one.)

When I pack with the traditional folding method, I tend to combine it with handy dandy zip-top bags. I use this method when I take a larger suitcase and when my travels require combo dressing (business, casual, and beachwear). If I have a certain outfit and accessories that need to be worn together, I use the traditional folding method. I place each outfit, along with the accessories that go with it, in its own individual two-gallon zip-top bag. It helps me with the quick, last inventory before I close the suitcase, and it also keeps things neat and tidy should TSA have to go through my suitcase.

The moral of the "how to pack" saga is this: There is no right or wrong way to pack. Each method has pros, cons, and multiple variations.

PACKING AIDS AND ALTERNATIVES

Zip-top bags. Okay, if there is only one packing tip I could give that would suit every trip length, suitcase size and type, and clothing need, it would be

Red Hat Recommendations
for Packing

- Lay out what you think you need, then take half.
- Layer for plane trips.
- Take good walking shoes.
- Pack enough in your carry-on to get you through if your luggage doesn't show.
- Roll your clothes.
- Keep your meds with you at all times. Pack extra to cover travel delays or unplanned detours.
- Use zip-top bags to separate and compress types of clothing.
- Seal your cosmetics and lotions in a zip-top bag before packing.
- Use two smaller suitcases rather than one large one due to the airline weight restrictions; doing this also helps you in case one is lost.
- Pack clothing you can mix and match using two main colors (purple and red, of course).
- Pack things inside other things (stuff undies or socks into shoes).
- Check with your hotel to see if hair dryers are provided; if they are, leave yours at home.
- Separate delicate items with tissue paper.
- Take extra batteries and/or film.
- Pack a laundry bag for dirty clothes.
- Take a travel umbrella.
- Pack a flashlight.
- Pack a travel candle or air freshener for that not-so-fresh room.
- Pack old underwear, and throw it away after every use so you have room for your new stuff.
- Pack way ahead of time, then take out what you realize you won't need.
- Pack your suitcase, then place it inside another suitcase if you are a shopper and buy souvenirs.

- Wrap breakable items between clothing.
- Never check your laptop, digital camera, medicine, jewelry, or traveler's checks.
- Pack less and do more laundry.
- Don't forget to take a wig if you wear wigs.
- Write down your contact information and phone numbers; do not just store them in your phone.
- Start out with no carry-on and pack a tote in your suitcase.
- Bring snacks.
- Follow the traveler's code: one to wear/one to wash.
- Invest in traveler's clothes that do not wrinkle.
- Always take a nightlight.
- Take an eyeglasses repair kit and a little sewing kit. You may also want to take a copy of your eyeglasses prescription.
- Think disposable.
- Tie a bright ribbon or large colorful luggage tag on your suitcase so you can easily identify it on the baggage carousel.
- Pack each outfit complete with accessories in a zip-top bag to make things easy to find.
- Pack your suitcase and carry it to the car. If you can't carry it, it's too heavy. Repack.
- Pack nylon underwear. It dries quickly.
- Keep a list of your medication names, dosages, and doctors' names available.
- Pack a "wrinkles free" spray.
- Always put a large piece of paper with your name, address, cell phone number, and destination in each checked bag. If it gets lost, your luggage just might find you.
- Bring one red hat and headbands or feathers to change your look.

to buy zip-top bags. Now, not all zip-top bags are created equal. I definitely have my favorite, and because I have tried and tested many, I feel strongly that Hefty One-Zips designed for food storage are my favorite. Not all Hefty's are created equal either. Hefty sold a zip-top quart bag with airplanes on the side in a nice little pack that would fit into a suitcase. For some reason, this bag tends to split at the zipper easier than the ones made for food storage, so I am sticking with the basic food storage bags. I use everything from the jumbo size, which holds 2.5 gallons, to pack complete outfits to the one-quart size for my carry-on liquids. The bags that you just press together at the top are a bigger hassle than zip-tops, and you don't save that much money. Good quality zip-top bags will work just like the airtight bags you see on TV. You can smash them and roll out the excess air and maximize your suitcase space. But remember that maximized space may lead to overweight luggage, so just because you can fit all that stuff in there doesn't mean it has to go.

PART 2

Sleeping, Traveling, and Tipping

CHAPTER 2

Accommodations

Absolutely nothing can make a vacation more miserable than having a crummy place to lay your head after a long day of shopping and enjoying delectable desserts. My travels have introduced me to some of the nicest hotels you can imagine. They have also introduced me to places my mother warned me about. The Internet age has helped me to ward off what could have been long, sleepless nights in nasty hotels known for the size of their spiders and smelly sheets. The Internet has become a wonderful source of information when trying to determine what hotel room to book. It is great to be able to have someone's real experience—the "I've actually stayed there and . . ." input—but as with all opinions, they are subject to the bias of the reviewer. I try to read two or three reviews from one or two sites and then make my best choice. Tripadvisor.com, Expedia.com, Hotels.com, and AAA.com are a few of my favorites. If Internet access is not something that factors into your daily life or trip planning, all is not lost. AAA prints guide books with hotel recommendations and ratings that can give you a pretty good idea of what you are going to be getting once you walk through the door. You can view AAA online, request the guide books by mail, or go to your local AAA office where they are usually available.

Another way to pretty much ensure consistency and avoid most surprises is to stick with a chain hotel you know. A Marriott Residence Inn in

Washington, D.C., is going to have the same green couch and tan blanket as a Marriott Residence Inn in Waukegan, Illinois. You will get a small bar of bath soap, face soap, and combo shampoo and conditioner. There is something to be said for consistency. And I have to admit that more times than not, especially when traveling for work, I tend to stay with the familiar and just book a large chain hotel close to my work site. While writing *The Red Hat Society Travel Guide*, I did force myself out of my rut and into the unique world of boutique hotels. Places like Hotel Max in Seattle, Washington, and the Brown Hotel in Louisville, Kentucky, will make you a believer in getting out of your rut and enjoying something a little different. But again, please take a few extra minutes to do research and make sure you will be spending safe, restful nights wherever your next adventure takes you. Here are a few things to consider when booking accommodations:

Safety. *Never*, under any circumstances, compromise safety for savings. If it is not a place you would stay alone, it should not be a place you would stay with your traveling buddies. You never know when circumstances, such as a headache or a treasured nap, would place you there alone, so just don't do it.

You will notice that I did not include motels in my list, and I will tell you why. Motels, for the most part (and by definition), are hotels that offer rooms with direct outside access and free parking adjacent to the rooms. That sounds convenient, and in some cities, say, Branson, Missouri, it probably wouldn't be a problem. But in the majority of cities, I just cannot stress enough the safety compromise that occurs with direct outside access. Give me a lobby and front desk that the bad guys have to walk past any day.

Location/transportation. Location is a key factor. Location and transportation options have to be factored in to where you want to stay. The convenience factor comes into play here as well. Light rail access in large metropolitan areas makes staying in less expensive digs, and taking the train into the city, an interesting option. I have actually saved more than $100.00 a night in hotel costs by staying in New Jersey and taking the train into New York City every day. When the $100.00 was coming out of my pocket alone, it was worth the extra hour to commute into the city. Had I been splitting that three or four ways among my Red Hat chapter sisters, well, I might have spent the extra bucks to stay in the city. If you are attending a conference and foresee that frequent trips to your room will be necessary, it would probably be worth your while to stay in the conference hotel. If walking a few blocks or waiting for shuttles doesn't bother you, then you can probably save a little money staying in a hotel a little farther away from all the hoopla.

One location not to overlook is an airport hotel; that holds even more true if you have a very early flight. On more than one occasion I have spent the last night of my adventure at an airport hotel, especially if I have a rental car. I check out of my "location preferred" hotel (which tends to be more expensive than the airport hotel) and spend my day sightseeing, shopping, or doing whatever my day's play involves, with my luggage safely stowed in my rental car. That evening, I check into an airport hotel that has a free shuttle to the airport. After I unload my bags, I return the rental car to the airport (at a savings because I didn't keep it those extra hours), take the rental car bus (without having to schlep my bags along with me) to the airport, and catch the free hotel shuttle back to the hotel. The next morning, the free hotel shuttle drops me off at curbside check-in and I have a virtually hassle-free morning of departure.

Type and desire. There are all sorts of places to spend the night, from a room at the local YMCA to house swapping, but for the purpose of the masses, I am going to focus only on four.

> It's a once-in-a lifetime trip, and I go to enjoy it. If not on tour, I do use middle-rated motels/hotels to economize. I'm there only to sleep so why pay big bucks? I do check the rooms to make sure they are clean.
>
> —Georgean Kruger, Queen Boop-d-Doop, Red Zippity Do Dahs

TYPES OF LODGING

FULL-SERVICE HOTELS

A full-service hotel usually offers an extensive array of guest services, including valet or bell service, room service, concierge, dry cleaning, Internet (usually at an extra charge), an on-site restaurant with three meals, and a workout room or arrangements with a nearby gym. It also has in-room amenities such as an iron, an ironing board, and a hair dryer. A few examples of full-service hotels are the Marriott, Sheraton, Hilton, and Hyatt.

LIMITED-SERVICE HOTELS

If the main focus of your adventure is something other than life in your hotel, a limited-service hotel is probably something to seriously consider. These hotels tend to be less expensive ($10.00 to $20.00 a night less on average) and will not have valet service for your car, but the value is certainly not limited. Although there probably will not be a bellman, they may have a luggage cart you can use to move your things to your room. Very often a free continental breakfast is available (included in your rate), but room service and three-meal restaurant service are not likely. The comforter is unlikely to be quite as plush as the one in a full-service hotel and the mattress is not on the level of a "heavenly bed," but the room is usually clean and comfortable. You may have to request an iron and ironing board, but the hair dryer is usually in the room.

SUITE HOTELS

Suite hotels have anything from a studio-type single room with a microwave and a fridge to a two bedroom, two bathroom, living room, and dining room affair that would rival many of our homes. Some suite hotels have both standard hotel rooms and suites. When you reserve your room, be clear about what you prefer.

BED-AND-BREAKFASTS

A bed-and-breakfast is usually operated out of a large single-family residence where guests can be accommodated at night in private bedrooms. There may or may not be a private bath. Breakfast is served and may be full fare or continental. They're usually run with a very small staff, who may or may not be available at your leisure. Just as with hotels, online services enable you to locate bed-and-breakfast lodgings. One is www.bedandbreakfast.com, which includes locations and ratings. The Web site www.bnbfinder.com provides pictures and links to the B&B sites. For those of you who want something in hard copy, the *North American Bed-and-Breakfast Directory* is available in most bookstores. You can also call a state's Bed-and-Breakfast Association. The theme and atmosphere of each home add to the spirit of your adventure. Staying in a B&B can sometimes present a significant cost savings; however, if you are used to falling asleep with the TV on every night, be advised that there may or may not be one in your room.

BOOKING THE LODGING

Once you have determined what role your accommodations play in your adventure, you can determine the type of accommodations to seek and the amount of your travel budget you are willing to devote to them.

You can't turn on your TV or listen to the radio without hearing the Priceline negotiator jingle or watching the Hotels.com crew basking by the hotel pool. I really do like those Web sites and appreciate the service they provide with the hotel reviews. Some of my friends never make reservations any other way, and they get awesome deals on hotels. They also are very experienced travelers and pros at rolling with the punches. My luck has not been so great. Twice I have gone to my hotel to check in—only to be told they are full but they have graciously made arrangements for me at a lesser hotel down the road. Yes, twice. Another time, and most recently, I showed up with my printed reservation in hand, only to be told that the hotel did not have my reservation. The desk clerk contacted the online service, which faxed the reservation to the hotel, and the issue was resolved within thirty minutes. But I was tired and cranky after a long travel day and did not want to have to deal with the hassle.

While doing research for this book, I checked the rates on www.expedia.com, www.travelocity.com, www.hotels.com, and a few other discount hotel booking sites. Frequently I found a super-duper rate for a particular area and excitedly tried to book it. The rate ended up being good for only one day with the rates on either side of that date so high that there was no true bargain. Or when I tried to reserve the room, it was no longer available. The other issue with booking hotels this way is that I really do not like to prepay for my hotel room because it is a whole lot harder to pick up your toys and go somewhere else if you have already paid for a week's worth of lodging. In many cases, I was able to find the same rate via AAA or the direct hotel Web site and did not have to prepay for my room.

Once again I don't mean to discount the value of the discount Web sites. Deals are out there. I admit that I have not had a lot of luck finding them, but I know people who have. So, if a good enough deal comes up that you don't mind prepaying for your hotel bill and if you are game for a little possible hassle occasionally, go for it. However, if you are a novice traveler just spreading your wings, my recommendation would be to (1) check out the hotel's propriety Web site and scope out the rates, (2) consider using AAA, and (3) explore the discounters and see whether you find significant savings. If you don't find a big difference, make a reservation through the hotel. If you *do* find a big difference, pick up the phone and call the hotel directly. Ask the reservation taker if there is a AAA rate available and what it is (if you are not a AAA member, you will need to be by the time you check in). Ask whether there are any packages or weekend specials. Then be sure to ask the magic question, "Is that your best available rate?" Very often you will end up with a rate that is very close to the one on the Internet site and you will still have the confidence of booking directly.

Still not getting close to that super-duper Internet special rate? Well, you can try one more thing. Call the hotel directly and ask to speak to the general manager. Tell the GM about the rate you found on the discounted site, and let him know that you would prefer to book directly through the hotel. Ask him if he can match the rate. You may end up with a great room rate *and* the confidence of having booked directly with the hotel. Make sure you get the GM's name, and request an e-mailed or written confirmation with your quoted rate. This method tends to work best when the hotel is not booked full, so if there is a convention in town, you are probably out of luck.

Make sure you have a credit card available to secure your reservation. In most cases when you book directly with the hotel, you will not be charged until you check out of the hotel.

UPON ARRIVAL

Upon arrival, check that you got what you paid for *before* you unpack. If you check into your room and discover that "lake view" means you can see the pond in the neighboring cow pasture, request a conference with the hotel manager immediately. There is a very good chance he will move you to another room and possibly upgrade you in the process. Scope out the bathroom and beds to make sure they appear clean and tidy. If the room has large carpet stains or smells musty, ask to be moved to another room. If you asked for a nonsmoking room and your room smells like an ashtray, ask to be moved elsewhere.

Do not unpack until you see that your room is satisfactory and you will feel safe and comfortable there. It is much easier to switch rooms *before* you unpack. If your room is not what you expected and you want to be moved but there is not another room available until tomorrow, unpack the minimum. Then be hopeful that the hotel will assist you tomorrow and throw in an upgrade or some compensation for your inconvenience.

UNDERSTANDING HOTEL PHONE COSTS, INTERNET PACKAGES, AND OTHER HIDDEN CHARGES

Before you pick up the hotel phone to call your sister—locally at that—make sure you read and understand how much that call will cost you. It may be worth your while to make the call from the hotel lobby. I've seen connection fees alone that cost as much as $3.00 per call. Many hotels have Internet and phone bundled packages that include both services for a flat rate. If you choose this route, call the front desk and confirm that the phone service is included and noted on your bill. Review your bill before you leave to make sure there are no miscellaneous charges.

Oh, and those handy dandy bottles of water they put in your room now—look around for the obscure little piece of paper that tells you to "enjoy" and states how much will be added to your daily bill for the "refreshing enjoyment."

The minibar is another "danger zone" that can skyrocket that great hotel rate. Read the fine print. Some places not only charge you a ridiculous amount for the Snickers bar, but they also add a restocking fee.

CHECKING OUT

When checking out of the hotel, make one final sweep of the room. Open the drawers, and look under the bed. You may not have put anything there, but your roommate may have. She will thank you for pointing out that lost penny loafer! Although you should never, never hang anything on the hook on the bathroom door, always, always check behind the bathroom door before you leave—just in case. Review your hotel bill before you leave the hotel if at all possible. It is much easier to have mistakes taken off the bill before the final checkout than it is after the paid bill reaches the accounting department.

CANCELLATIONS

Hotel cancellation policies vary, and you should find out what yours is. The old standard of 6:00 PM day of arrival has changed in some places to anywhere from twenty-four to forty-eight hours prior to expected arrival. Should it become necessary to cancel your hotel room, write down the cancellation number. Keep it on hand so that if you inadvertently are charged by the hotel as a no-show, you can supply your cancellation number.

Travel Safety

T raveling safely is a top concern for Red Hat Society members. More and more women today are hitting the roadways and airways and traveling. When most of us grew up, a woman traveling alone was almost a scandalous thought, and certainly no good could come of it. Today, more than one-third of the business travelers are women. Now you see women, many of them members of The Red Hat Society, traveling together or alone for leisure travel as well. Traveling safely should be a primary concern for all travelers. You can keep yourself and your treasures safe and secure by following simple guidelines and planning ahead.

Most of us feel somewhat safe in our homes. We tend to transfer that feeling to wherever we are laying our heads at night. Feeling safe and secure can certainly play into whether your current adventure is a restful one or one where you are trying to sleep with one eye open. Feeling safe in your hotel room, the hallways, and the lobby can play a big part in your level of enjoyment of your vacation. Feeling your belongings are safe while you are out gallivanting about is almost as important. Whether you travel with a partner, companion, sister Red Hatter or alone, first and foremost, stay safe.

Red Hat Recommendations
for Safe Travels

- Make your hotel reservations using only your first initial and your last name. That way, you are not identified as a man or a woman, and unnecessary hotel staff (the maintenance man, delivery people, laundry service) are not aware that a woman is in the room.
- Always, always make your hotel reservation for a party of two. I have yet to check into a hotel in the United States that charged any more for one person than it did for two.
- Stay in hotels that have interior entrances to the rooms.
- Ask the desk clerk to hand you your key or key folder and not state the room number aloud when you check into your room. You do not want the entire lobby to know your room number. (I am always surprised that when many people check in instead of looking at the number in the key folder, they verbally ask the desk clerk, "What's my room number?")
- Request a room change as soon as possible if you lose the room key and the key ring has the number on it.
- Keep your key card separate from the sleeve with your room number on it. If you do lose your key card, ask the front desk to reset the code.
- Don't store your key card next to your cell phone. For some reason, this can wipe out the code on your key card and leave you standing in the hallway much longer than necessary.
- Get your room key out of your purse while you are still in the lobby. This is a good idea for two reasons: (1) if you have lost it or left it in the room, you are right there at the front desk and can take care of the issue immediately; and (2) it just isn't a good idea to stand in a hallway with no one else around while you dig for your room key.
- Never open your door without verifying who is there. Most doors have a peep hole. Use it. If there is an unexpected knock at the door and someone identifies himself as a hotel employee, unless you are very comfortable with

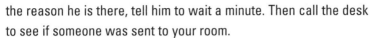

the reason he is there, tell him to wait a minute. Then call the desk to see if someone was sent to your room.

- Use the safe in your hotel room. If there is not one in the room, leave your valuables in a sealed envelope at the front desk and ask that it be put in the safe there.
- Lock your luggage even in your hotel room.
- Notify your bank that you will be traveling. Some banks track your credit card activity, and if they see charges coming in from places other than your normal haunts, they may block your card.
- Use all the locks on the hotel door. I fell asleep one night without flipping the dead bolt. I was awakened in the middle of the night by a man coming into my room. The hotel had booked both of us in the same room.
- Don't put your room number on your bar bill. Pay with cash or a credit card.
- Go back into the room and call the desk if you see someone in the hall who makes you uncomfortable. If you are going to your room, turn around, walk back to the lobby, and report the person to the front desk. If you want a member of hotel personnel to walk you to your room, request it.
- Put out the Do Not Disturb sign if you have items in your room you do not want anyone to bother. You won't get maid service, but neither will anybody go in your room.
- Request that security walk you to your room and wait while you unload your car if you check into a hotel that has exterior entrances to the rooms and you arrive late in the day.
- Check and double-check that your doors and windows are locked. Check the sliding glass door anytime you come back to the room, even if you have not used it.
- Pick up one of the hotel's business cards when you leave to go sightseeing or shopping. That way you will have the street address and phone number, just in case you need them.
- Take a nightlight.

IN GENERAL

Let your friends and family know where you are and when you will be back. Check in frequently.

Do not carry large amounts of cash. Use traveler's checks.

Leave your bundle of credit cards at home. Narrow it down to two. If you use American Express, take a Visa or MasterCard (better yet, your Red Hat Society Platinum MasterCard) with you as well. Not every place takes American Express.

No matter where you may be—on a subway, on an airplane, or in your hotel room—be aware of your surroundings. Know where the emergency exits are, and watch for places where you could become vulnerable.

Leave the bling at home. Attracting attention to yourself can bring both good attention and dangerous attention.

Always carry a flashlight.

Never volunteer the fact that you may be traveling alone.

Photocopy all your identification, driver's license, passport, and credit cards, and keep the photocopy in your locked suitcase or hotel safe. In case of theft you have the numbers ready to identify for replacement.

Carry a traveler's purse around your neck that you can tuck under your clothes. Keep your extra cash and credit cards there. Before you leave your room, take out only what you will need at the time, and put that in an easily accessible place.

AUTO SAFETY

Make sure all tires (including the spare) are inflated to standard pressure when traveling by car.

Pay the few extra dollars and get the GPS system when renting a car. Maps are great, and you should always review your route before taking off. The GPS will correct your route if you don't make it across those four lanes of traffic to your exit ramp.

AIR TRAVEL

Use luggage tags that do not reveal your name, address, and phone number to all passersby. If it is a full-display luggage tag, put only your first initial, last name, and a cell phone or business phone number.

Do not leave your purse or money in your seat while you go to the lavatory on the airplane.

Always, always look and act confident. If you are going to walk somewhere, review the directions before you leave. Write them down on a piece of paper, and tuck the map inside your purse. If you do get lost or need to consult your map, do so in a safe, well-lighted area.

If you are traveling alone, walk with a crowd and act as if you are part of the gang.

CHAPTER 4

Girlfriend Travel

There is just about no better feeling than getting the giggles at midnight with your best girlfriends after a long day of shopping and sightseeing. As much fun as that is, there is something about the third or fourth night of living in one room with these same girlfriends that can sometimes set your teeth on edge. Traveling with friends, especially more than one, adds depth and breadth to any adventure. Experiencing art, music, shopping, and dessert through someone else's eyes is always interesting. Advance planning for traveling with friends is almost as important as planning the trip itself. By thinking about and planning a few things in advance, you can ward off the discomfort of little issues that often arise.

IN GENERAL

Understand expectations. Understanding your expectations and those of your traveling companion can ward off many a squabble. Some people travel with the expectation that their companion will be by their side 24/7. You will eat together, sleep at the same times, and enjoy each and every activity that is planned together as the dynamic duo, trio, or so on. Others travel with the idea that "we are sharing a room," and other than possibly running into each other for a quick change of clothes, your contact will be only in passing.

Understand up front your expectations of your companion and her expectations of you. Be very honest with yourself and your fellow traveler about your desires and/or limitations. Knowing *before* your trip that your traveling companion would rather spend the day by the pool and you would rather spend your day shopping will lead to a happy compromise and better planning. And remember, it is more than okay to go your own ways for part of the time.

Understand the roles. In most groups, a leader will emerge, as will a planner, a navigator, a photographer, and so on. If your group is diverse, with specific talents, recognize that, and assign jobs. I know a group of Red Hatters who are great at traveling together. One of them is a good driver, and one of them just isn't. When they are on road trips, pretty much Lou is the designated driver. On the other hand, Katy is a logical, methodical thinker. She is the one who digs out the maps, plots the course, and acts as the navigator.

Being the leader can become wearing, both on the leader and on the others. One way to handle a group where everyone wants a turn to lead is to assign days. Then each person gets to do the one special thing she wants to do on the trip. If Anna wants to go to the Hearst Castle, she should be in charge of obtaining all the information, checking transportation options, and overseeing the activities that day. If Sarah's goal in life is to go to SeaWorld, she should be in charge of that outing.

One thing that should *not* be designated as a one-person job is picture taking. It is very frustrating to the one person who has to view the entire vacation through a view finder. It is also a huge disappointment to all if that one camera ends up lost or misplaced—or is in the hands of someone who "waits until November the fourteenth every year and *then* uploads or develops all her pictures from the entire year because that way they are such a nice surprise."

Discuss money issues. Money can quickly become an issue if you haven't devised a way to deal with problems *before* they come up. All of us have been in situations with that one friend who never has anything smaller than a $20.00 bill so we end up paying for every bus fare, tip, bellman, and Diet Coke along the way. Get it out in the open! I know one group of girlfriends who travel together, and each puts a set amount into the trip kitty before the trip. This money is used for cab rides, tips, and group incidentals. What's left at the end of the trip is split up as an added bonus. This can really make a difference in awkward moments, such as sitting in the taxi with everyone handing out a $10.00 bill or $20.00 bill, and the English-as-a-second-language

Discount Tips

I have made many trips to Walt Disney World with my Twisted Sisters. We get a discount on rooms by having one member in each room with an annual pass. That way we get up to half off our room. We also share rooms, and that also cuts the individual cost. We dine at the fancy, expensive restaurants for lunch when the meals are cheaper. Our best memories are usually the silliest. Two of us use wheelchairs/scooters. One day it was raining and all of our group were wearing the Disney yellow plastic rain ponchos. Another Disney guest saw us zipping around the park with our walking sisters and thought we resembled a duck family because we were having such a good time. We have also played checkers in the rain in Frontierland while waiting for the parade. We had that section of the park to ourselves because of the rain. All those so-called able-bodied folks had chickened out and gone back to their hotels. We have also gone on private tours behind the scenes and enjoyed those tremendously.

—Katherine Bibber, Queen, Twisted Sisters of Cyberspace

taxi driver is trying to figure out what the heck these women waving bills at him are thinking.

Have more money discussions. Be aware of your spending habits and budget constraints, and be sensitive to others. You may be fortunate enough to be able to splurge on that extra $155.00 theater ticket without a second thought. Your roommate, on the other hand, may not be quite as fortunate. This doesn't mean you have to miss the play. Just be aware that your companion may not be able to join you, and be sensitive to her decision, especially if it involves a big ticket item.

ROOMMATES

Find out whether everyone is a smoker or nonsmoker. A smoker in the group will step outside for a smoke after each meal, upon awaking, and probably right before bed. Some hotels still allow smoking in hotel rooms. Others, such as Marriott, are smoke free. Finding out you are rooming with a smoker in a smoking room, when you are allergic to smoke, can put a damper on a trip really quick.

Compare sleep habits. If you are a total darkness sleeper and your roomie is a bathroom light kinda person, it can be a very long week for both of you. Discuss your sleeping habits! Are you an early riser? Do you go to sleep with the TV on? Do you snore? Discussing these things in the early stages of trip planning can really help in making a long weekend a pleasant one. If you are traveling in a group, try paring up the snorer with your friend who uses hearing aids. Team up those early risers; they can get up, dress, and go read the newspaper. Let the late sleepers close the blackout curtains and sleep till noon if they want!

Plan the bathroom schedule. One of the great mysteries of the world is how many women can actually share one bathroom and survive. Team up the morning bather with an evening soaker. Above all be flexible and considerate. Be honest about how much time you need in the bathroom, when you need it, and then stick to it.

Remember that all fellow traveling companions are not created equal. You may be a bathrobe and slippers kinda gal while your fellow traveler may have no qualms about dashing (or not) naked from the main room to the bathroom. If this is likely to make you uncomfortable, let it be known early. It just isn't worth stewing about, and if you discuss it early on, you can prevent the problem or at least understand that it may be there.

Establish ground rules for settling disagreements, and then use them. Knowing how you are going to approach a problem or issue can sometimes be the hardest part of settling it. Figure it out. Are you going to talk it out, draw straws, or Farkle for it?

Set ground rules for borrowing or lending items. In many cases it makes sense to share things on a trip. You bring the hot rollers; I'll bring the curling iron. If you are uncomfortable sharing your sunscreen or toothpaste, let everyone know that up front. With five kids in the family, we all used the same toothpaste tube. I will never forget one trip when my traveling companion forgot her toothpaste. I readily offered mine, never thinking twice about it. She was *appalled*. I had to ask why it was such an issue. As she explained, I understood. The way she applied her toothpaste to her toothbrush, the toothpaste tube touched the toothbrush bristles, contaminating the end of the tube. Therefore, there was no way she wanted to use my tube of toothpaste because she assumed I applied my toothpaste the same way. I showed her the way I applied toothpaste to my toothbrush, which did not involve any touching of the toothpaste tube to the toothbrush, and she was much relieved. We shared toothpaste the rest of the trip.

Determine whether neatness is an issue. Now, this may not seem like a big deal, especially on a short trip, but you may be used to lining up your shoes alphabetically by color in your closet and your traveling buddy kicks hers off at the door and never seems to mind tripping over them all week-end. Sometimes the little things can add up to big irritations if you do not discuss this difference.

CHAPTER 5

Train Travel

Traveling by train is definitely an experience where getting there is part of the adventure. If you have never taken a train trip, you should. When I was growing up, my grandfather worked for Kansas City Southern Railroad. As a very young girl, I don't remember where we were going or even what we did when we got there, but I remember the ride.

We were escorted onto the train by a redcap, who showed us to our compartment and stored our bags. We ate dinner in the dining car, zipping along the tracks. We went to the observation car and looked out at the night sky. Lulled to sleep by the clickety-clack, clickety-clack of the train on the rails, we slept in bunks. It was wonderful.

Passenger trains are alive and well in the United States today. The dining cars, observation cars, and even the redcaps are still a big part of the experience. If you are not in a big hurry to reach your destination, and you are not bound to a tight time schedule, such as catching a plane or a cruise ship, consider taking the train.

Unlike bidding on rental car rates on Priceline or checking endless Web sites for airfare, there is only one place to find and book your train: www.amtrak.com. Discounts are available through your Purple Perks membership on select routes, AAA, and there are other senior discounts as well. Most discounts are taken off the "rail" price only, which is the base price before you add in the sleeper cars and other services. Train travel is not necessarily a bargain, especially if you use it as a way just to get to where you're going. However, if you factor in that the ride *is* part of the adventure, the cost can be justified. Now, when I speak of the "cost," I am not really talking about the basic, standard coach seat. It is about the same as an advance fare airline ticket. The sleeper cars add a significant price increase, but they come with certain perks (meals are included and so forth). You can purchase Amtrak tickets online or call 800-USA-RAIL (800-872-7245).

Amtrak provides accessible accommodations by reservation. You cannot book accessible accommodations online, but you can call and make your reservations. Amtrak offers discounts to passengers with disabilities if you provide a letter from your physician, a transit system ID card, or a membership card from a disabilities organization.

I consider myself somewhat Internet savvy and travel wise. However, I have yet to master the Amtrak Web site. That may be because I do not live in an area with direct access to a train and I had difficulty determining which stations were closest to me. The stations are listed by state, but I had no idea which station was on one side of the state or another. I also seemed to pick routes that entailed getting off the train to spend several hours traveling by bus. I even called Amtrak to help me pick a route, which the agent did. But she *never* mentioned that for part of the trip, I would be aboard a bus. Only hours later, while I continued to pursue various possibilities, did I notice a footnote about the bus trip.

Check the Web site, and if a route looks good to you, go for it. But scroll over each city point to make sure the footnote does not say "bus." I do not really recommend that a first-time train traveler make reservations online without at least calling Amtrak for advice.

Perhaps the best way to enjoy a vacation by rail is to pick a preplanned Amtrak vacation. Seasonal specials and packages include everything from Broadway shows in the Big Apple to jazz clubs and gumbo in the Big Easy.

The Amtrak Web site provides great floor plans and explanations about the types of accommodations. There are bedrooms with bathrooms that are handicapped accessible. This in itself can be a huge bonus. Be aware that not all trains have all accommodations available. Some trains do not have sleeper cars, so before you set your heart on an overnight train ride, be sure you are not setting yourself up to spend it in a coach seat.

Packing

Packing for your train ride may take a little planning. The storage space in the bedroom compartments can be limited. You will have plenty of room for a small suitcase or two, but if you packed "big bertha," you may need to check it. Keep your smaller suitcases, with a change of clothes, makeup, medications, and other necessities, in the cabin with you. Amtrak limits your carry-on luggage to two bags with a fifty-pound weight limit per bag. This limit does not include your purse, laptop, or briefcase. The bags you carry on may not be larger than 28 x 22 x 14 inches.

There is a three-bag limit for checked baggage. The fifty-pound weight limit is the same, but the bag can be a bit larger: 36 x 36 x 36 inches. Check luggage at least thirty minutes prior to departure. You must have a valid photo ID to check and to claim your luggage. Do not be in a big hurry to claim your luggage after your trip. It can take thirty minutes to one hour for them to unload your bags, especially if you brought along a golf bag or skis.

Just like the airlines, Amtrak has a list of items prohibited in carry-ons or checked baggage. For the most part, it is the standard list: no guns, knives, clubs, axes, ice picks, or swords. For a complete list of prohibited items, check the Amtrak Web site.

At the Station

Amtrak recommends that you get to the station at least thirty minutes before departure time. I recommend an hour, especially if you are going to an unfamiliar station or one that could be busy and crowded. Once you get to the station, check in, and ask for a redcap. Redcap service is the best thing going because it is free (be prepared to tip). You are assigned a service person (wearing a red cap), who will assist you with your luggage and help you get situated on the train. That means you board before the crowd, and if you do not have a reserved seat, this is definitely a bonus.

Whereas I had experienced being escorted onto the train by a redcap as a child, it was not until I was an adult and actually traveling on my own that I truly learned what the redcap advantage was. I learned about the true advantage of redcap service from a businessman whose only carry-on was a briefcase. He was in front of me in line and asked for a redcap. A few minutes later, the redcaps came into the waiting area and gathered their assigned passengers. The man with the briefcase handed the redcap his briefcase, and off he went. The man sitting next to me told me about the extra service and advantage provided by the redcap. I immediately went to the check-in desk and asked for a redcap to assist me with my roll-aboard. Prior to the general boarding announcement for my train, the redcap found me in the waiting area and escorted me onto the train. I had my seat, stowed my carry-on bag, and was ready to read my book before anyone else boarded.

On the Train

Whether you are traveling coach or in a sleeper car (they are not just for sleeping), train travel is for the most part very comfortable. The ability to get up and roam around certainly helps ward off the kinks. Remember that you are moving at a significant rate of speed, and bumps and lurches do happen. Hold on to handrails, and be aware of your surroundings. The fact that you can roam around means that other people can roam as well. Be smart about where you stow your luggage, particularly if you are in coach and likely to take a snooze during the ride. If your roaming takes you far and long, keep your valuables with you. On most long-distance trips, a full-service meal car is available. Some trains require reservations for mealtime. Once again, a little planning can ward off both hunger pains and frustration.

Delays and cancellations do happen. At times the railroad cancels a sleeping car or two, depending on track availability or some other reasons I never quite seem to understand. Flexibility can be a strong factor in determining whether the train is the right way for you to travel. Amtrak shares the rails with freight trains, and they sometimes determine whether a track is open or under repair. It is not as if they can change altitude and look for smoother air. When there is a problem with your track, you are pretty much going to have to sit back, relax, and get there when you get there.

Red Hat Recommendations
for Train Travel

- Go ahead and splurge! Buy a roomette.
- Get a redcap to help with your bags.
- Reserve a sleeper car early, and call back to confirm.
- Don't make tight connections.
- Check with the conductor before departing about what sights you can see along the tracks.
- Keep a small tote bag with all essentials within easy reach. Include your red hat and purple boa and see if you don't run into other Red Hatters along the way!
- Have your binoculars and camera ready.
- Try the Empire Builder Train from Milwaukee to Glacier National Park in Montana. The scenery is spectacular.

CHAPTER 6

Car Travel

Oh, the call of the open road! For some of us, there is no better way to travel than to jump in the old Oldsmobile and take off down Route 66. For others, there is the five-hour rule: if it takes more than five hours to get there . . . we fly. My husband and I come from two very different camps. He is quite content to drive—and in fact *loves* the idea of driving. In his youth, his family vacations involved camping and hiking, and the journey to the destination was part of the adventure. I, on the other hand, tend to be of the mind-set that the vacation starts once we get where we are going. Over the years, I have come to understand the allure in making the journey part of the adventure. We started out with a compromise. We would fly to a "base camp" and take one- or two-day car treks from there. One year, base camp was Las Vegas. We flew to Las Vegas (back then it was a cheap flight), then took day trips to Bryce Canyon and Mount Zion National Park. We went back to Vegas for a day, and then went the other direction to the California coast to play in the ocean. We did a similar trip by flying into Boston, renting a car, and visiting seven New England states in five days. Even with gas prices soaring, driving or a combo trip can be a great way to get there.

As with most adventures, you will come out ahead if you do a bit of preplanning. Granted, car travel lends itself to spontaneity more than most other means. But if you take the time to plan, you can save yourself potential headaches and perhaps even add a little something to the trip.

Before You Go

I stand by my number one rule of the road: join AAA (www.aaa.com). You can check out other automobile clubs and their benefits. I am not saying that others fail to provide good service. However, I do not leave some things to chance, and this is one of them.

Rent a Car

One option is to rent a car or a van. Doing this relieves one person from having to bear the ultimate responsibility of being the entire group's ride home. You may want to consider the following:

Is there an off-airport location for your chosen rental car agency? If there are off-airport locations where you can rent a car in your city, check them out. Very often the airport charges a fee for having the rental car agency located at the airport. By renting at an off-airport location, you can save a few dollars.

What is the daily rate and the weekly rate? Even if you do not plan to keep the car a week (say the trip is five days) you may actually come out ahead by renting at the weekly rate. Beware: if you take the car back early, they may charge you the daily rate, so make sure there is no penalty for returning it early. Worst case, park it in your driveway for an extra day.

Do you have a credit card with rental car benefits? Some credit

> ### Options
>
> I use Priceline for the rental car. I look at menus outside of restaurants before choosing one for a meal—seeing if they have what I like and what the prices are. Do they offer a la carte? This way I get what I want to eat for the most reasonable price. I stay in condos instead of hotels.
>
> —Chris Maston, Queen Chris, Gold Country Mad Hatters

cards have perks that include extra coverage or discounts with certain rental car companies. See if you have something you can use.

Comparing rental car rates on Priceline.com or Travelocity.com is helpful. You can also go directly to the rental car agency Web sites. Remember that rental car rates, like hotel rates, change as a result of supply and demand. You will be more likely to get the type and style of car you want at a reasonable price if you make your reservations in advance.

For more information about renting a car, see chapter 8, "Ground Transportation."

Take Your Own Car

If you decide to take one person's car, figure out the ground rules before you leave. Here are a few discussion points to mull over:

Who pays for gas? When I have traveled in a group, the car owner was exempt from pitching in for gas to compensate for the added miles and wear and tear on the car. This may or may not be the best way to approach this issue, depending on the length of the trip, but it can open the discussion.

Who drives? When I was growing up, nobody, I mean *nobody*, was allowed to drive our car except my father. He did not loan it out, nor under any circumstances, did he allow us children (once we were of driving age) to let anyone else drive. If you are the car owner and the driving is presumed to be a shared responsibility, do a gut check. Are you really comfortable with your travel companions driving your car? And think about this: If you are all in your nighties and comfortable for the evening and a few of the gals want to hit IHOP, is it going to be okay with you that they take your car without you in it?

Who pays for repairs? What happens if you have a flat while tooling down the highway? Does everyone pitch in to get the tire fixed, or does that become the sole responsibility of the car owner? A flat fixed? No real biggie. Split it and move on, but what happens if the transmission goes out? Who is responsible for coming up with the $1200.00 to fix that? I know nobody wants to think about this, but defining these issues on the front end can save vacations and, even more important, friendships in the end.

Are smokers allowed? Do you allow smoking in your car? Are you a smoker? If you are, are all your riders okay with your smoking in the car? This is a consideration whether your adventure is in a personally owned car or a rented one.

Does your insurance cover other drivers? Make sure you understand how your auto insurance covers other drivers. Does your insurance cover uninsured drivers?

Do all the designated drivers have a license? You might be surprised at how many people out there, for one reason or another, are driving around without a valid license.

Are you okay with people eating and drinking in your car? There are two factions on this: those who say, "No problem," and those who have never found a French fry under the floor mat. Just another thing to think about and hash out before you set out in the car with unexpected expectations.

Have you done a trunk space check? Picture this: you are packed and ready to go, and you head out merrily to pick up your other three passengers. You stop first at Abigail's house, only to discover that she has three large suitcases plus the golf bag in which she has packed her red hats. Hmmmm, if you are driving a Hummer, this may not be a problem. If you are driving a more conventional vehicle, and unless you have the packing skills of Santa when he loads his sleigh every year, getting her bags, your bags, the emergency car kit, and the bags of your other two traveling companions in your trunk may present a problem.

Plot Your Course

Once you have decided whose car or van you are going to take on your adventure, it is time to plot the course.

GPS. If you rent a car, by all means, cough up the extra $10.00 a day for the GPS (also known as NeverLost). No map you can print from Google, MapQuest, or any other map program has the ability to reroute your course should you miss a turn. GPS is awesome. If you do not know how to program the unit, fear not! When you check into the rental car agency, take the address of your destination, and ask the nice young man or woman at the counter to show you how to program it into the system while he or she illustrates the features of the GPS system. If a member of your group owns a GPS system, make sure she is using the most up-to-date data for the system.

Maps. *Even* if you have GPS, always, always, consult a map. Once again, here is where AAA can help you. As a member of AAA, you have access to Trip Tiks, which are hard copy maps with your route plotted for you. Order these well in advance of your trip. Also, use a minimum of two online direction services. I use Google maps or Yahoo maps and then MapQuest or AAA online. I always get the two online maps and compare them. There is a high possibility they will route you two different ways. With both available to you on your trip, along with the GPS, you should have a pretty good idea of where you are headed and the best route to get there.

Just in case you are not renting a car with NeverLost or Garmin and you don't have access to a GPS system, all is not lost. The key is to be very familiar with your route. If you have not practiced map reading lately, or if you are not accustomed to maps from www.mapquest.com or www.maps.google.com, I recommend you do a couple of trial runs before you strike out on the road. Before you leave town, look up and print out a few online maps to a destination with which you are very familiar. Occasionally there will be a street name that you have never heard of. It will be a street you are supposed to be on for less than .01 of a mile, and then you will see the street you are looking for. Once you have done this a few times in familiar territory, you can figure out, and expertly navigate, the directions provided online. This may seem to be a ridiculous suggestion, but try it and you will see what I mean. Some online map services (www.aaa.com, for one) will plot hotels, restaurants, and places to sightsee along the way. They also provide mileage and travel time approximations. All are helpful.

Gas prices. If you really want to get crazy about planning, you can even plot where gas prices are lower and factor that into your trip. GasBuddy.com is a good start. If you travel cross-country, most gas prices Web sites ask for the county name to drill down to the city. I personally don't know the county name of most places I am going, but you can find it on state maps, many atlases, and elsewhere. Just remember that price isn't everything. The five cents per gallon price difference may look inviting at first glance, but if that station is one mile off the interstate during rush hour in New Jersey where jug handles can boggle any mind, you probably should pay the extra few cents a gallon and stay close to the access road. Stations located close to the interstate generally are a bit more traveler friendly than local stations in town. By traveler friendly, I mean bathrooms that they expect people to use and therefore do not double as storage rooms for used automotive parts, tire rims, and supplies.

Red Hat Recommendations
for Car Travel

In the Trunk

- An automobile emergency kit. If you have one, wonderful! (If you do not, perhaps you should get one.) Check the expiration dates on the flat fix product and flares. Are the jumper cables there? Someone may have borrowed them, and they may not have made it back to the trunk. Make sure the flashlight has fresh batteries. If you don't have one, it is a worthwhile investment. They always go on sale right after Christmas, and you can get some pretty cool ones with lots of stuff!
- A blanket. Make it an old one that won't be missed, should it get grungy.
- Spare tire and jack. Check the air in the spare tire. Be sure that the jack did not disappear with the jumper cables.

In the Car

- Disposable hand wipes. Always carry a pocket pack of hand wipes in the glove box. It should go right next to the little pack of Kleenex.
- A small first aid kit. Check expiration dates on the aspirin and ointments. Add Dramamine (car sickness) and Benadryl (antihistamine) to the kit if they are not included.
- A travel blanket (not the one that is in the trunk) and/or pillow. A travel blanket can be a great equalizer if your hot flashes are out of sync with someone else's. Very seldom is everybody in the car comfortable at the same temperature. The driver should be the most comfortable. The rest can share the blanket or make adjustments. Be considerate of the other people and space in the car. Those king-sized pillows can take up the space of a small person.
- Audio books. Conversation is awesome and part of the allure of the car trip, but occasionally a diversion is in order. Audio books can be checked out of most libraries and can be a fun addition to the trip.
- Toll change. If you know you are going to travel on toll roads, count out the change in advance, and have it ready. If you are the driver and everyone else is asleep, you can continue in the tranquil peace and quiet if you don't have to scramble for toll change.

Rest stops. The U.S. interstate system provides rest and welcome centers along the way. They vary in service from a bathroom and vending machines to large pavilions with food courts, tourist information about the area, local artist displays, and Wi-Fi access. (I think Iowa has some of the most interesting centers.) You can find rest and welcome centers, listed by interstate number and direction, at www.roadnotes.com/interstate.

Public transportation. Another thing to think about is that there is no shame in parking the car at your hotel or destination and using public transportation. Take New York City, for example. If you choose to drive into Manhattan, park the car at your hotel and use taxis or the Metro for your inner-city travel. It doesn't cost that much more, and it will save you the headache of locating parking wherever you want to stop plus relieve the added danger and stress of driving in an unfamiliar area.

Air Travel

BUYING YOUR TICKET

Very few of us decide to take off on a trip with less than three days' notice, but then again there are those of us who do. With air travel, the further in advance you make your reservations, the better off you will be—up to a point. The magic cutoff for getting a decent rate is at least twenty-one days before you plan to leave. I try to make them between three and four weeks before I am supposed to leave. Anything less than that, the cost can really go up. Plan too far ahead and something always seems to come up. Then you end up paying that wretched $100.00 change fee. Try to shoot for twenty-one to twenty-eight days prior to travel.

While you are out there playing around on the different airline sites, sign up for their awards or preferred traveler programs. It doesn't cost anything, and it can definitely have its advantages. When I originally started traveling for work, I didn't think I would be making enough trips to make a difference; I was wrong. I probably was very close to a free trip before I finally took the time to enroll. Those trips can add up, and when you finally get to fly on that first free ticket . . . well, it is rather exciting.

There are so many ways to shop for discounts and best deals on airfares that you could spend days doing it. There are hundreds of sites so I have listed the top and most consistent ones to try. You should have more than enough information to determine whether or not you are going to be able to get the best price. My recommendation is that you start price searching as soon as the travel bug hits. Just surf the Internet every couple of days. You will soon determine which site is easiest for you to use and which is the most consistent.

While you are searching, don't believe that the rate being shown is the rate you can get. I don't know the exact percentages, but more times than not, when I click on the *incredible* rate that is shown on the screen, I get a little red warning that says, "Sorry, that rate is no longer available."

Once you have made the final decision about where to go and how to get there, have your credit card ready for the final search. More than once, with the airlines directly and with the other Web sites, I have found my dream rate, left the site to confirm with my six other comrades, then returned to the site only to find the rate gone. On the direct airline sites, some will allow you to put the flight on hold for twenty-four hours. If you are at a site that will allow this, grab that fare, put it on hold, and *then* call everyone else. I admit that I tend to surf my favorites to compare price, and then I almost always end up booking through the airlines. My rule of thumb is that if I can't save more than $50.00 (that is $25.00 each way) by booking with a discount agency, then I book directly with the airlines. I have found that when there is a problem with delays, changes, or lost reservations, it is easier to deal directly with the airlines than with the nonproprietary sites.

Now, this is not to discourage the use of the price-saving sites. I am all about a good deal. I just believe that at this point in my life, convenience and ease of issue resolution are worth a few extra bucks. Many of the airline Web sites now give you the option of searching not only the fares but also the schedule with the rate. You want to be in this mode when you do your research. You can save hundreds of dollars by picking a flight that might be an hour earlier or later than you would have chosen by random selection. For me, this has proven to be the most consistent way to make a significant impact on the price of my ticket.

Several of the sites mentioned also offer the option of searching airfares for alternate airports. These airports are usually sixty to ninety miles away from your first choice airport. Sometimes, you can find a fare that has a significant enough savings to warrant flying from an airport a few miles away. When you figure in the savings that this might offer, once again consider the convenience (or inconvenience) cost as well.

Even if the alternate airports do not provide initial savings, you should know about them. When the last flight to your city has had to cancel due to maintenance problems, you might be able to sweet-talk the airline into getting you on a flight to the alternate city. Again, you have to take into account the convenience factor, but sometimes reaching your destination or home is worth the extra effort that flying to the alternate airport might require. For example, you may be scheduled to fly into John Wayne Airport, and because a problem occurs for which the airline is responsible (something other than weather), your flight is canceled or you miss your connection. Then you may be able to request that they put you on a flight to Los Angeles (LAX) or Ontario. You may have to take a shuttle home or to John Wayne to pick up your car, but at least you can get home. The airlines don't usually offer this option up front, but if you know your alternate airport, you can request it, and they may be able to accommodate you.

Alternate airports should be a strong consideration when the choice is between taking a nonstop flight vs. making a connection. The minor inconvenience of driving a few extra miles could save loads of time and stress, should issues with connections or delays arise.

Here are my favorite Web sites for checking fares, booking flights, or even just finding out which airlines service your area:

- www.orbitz.com
- www.travelocity.com
- www.expedia.com
- specific airlines sites

Very few sites that display fares include the discount airlines such as Southwest (www.iflyswa.com or 800-IFLYSWA [800-435-9792]) and JetBlue (www.jetblue.com or 800-JETBLUE [800-538-2583]). If you are lucky enough to live in or near a city served by either of these airlines, check out their rates.

When you are fare shopping, pay close attention to the price being quoted. At first glance, what appears to be a cheaper fare may actually be the fare without taxes included.

Sites such as www.farecompare.com and www.kayak.com offer the opportunity to compare fares across several markets as well. Although they are not booking agents, they allow you to see what may be out there. Once again remember, the fare you see at first glance may not actually be the available fare. Be *very aware* that some flights originate on one date and end on another. Flying the red-eye on a nonconnecting flight may not be too bad, but the four-hour layover after the flight that landed at 5:00 AM may not be worth the $20.00 savings, especially if the shops are not even open while you have to wait.

Once you have made your decision when to fly and which airline to fly with, purchase the ticket. If you have a credit card that provides extra travel insurance or benefits for lost baggage, use that card when you purchase your ticket.

Setting an Alert

On several airline Web sites and on Orbitz you can set travel alerts that will notify you when your flight is going to be delayed or is canceled. This is an absolute must. You can receive them as text messages or as calls to your cell phone, and they are lifesavers. More than once my text alert let me know about a delay or cancellation before the board at the gate changed. Then I was able to be first in line to rebook or make changes if they were necessary.

Do you suffer from buyer's remorse? Afraid to book because a better deal might come along? The Yapta tracker (www.yapta.com) will keep an eye on that for you. Just download the program, and it will send you a notice if the flight you have booked has dropped enough to make calling the airlines and rebooking at the lower fare worth your while.

PICKING YOUR SEAT

Once I have made my reservations, the very next thing I do is to pick my seat. I do it based on a number of things.

Front or Back

HOW LONG IS THE FLIGHT?

This makes a difference, especially when accessibility to the bathroom (or "lav" in airplane speak) is a consideration. For a one-hour flight, this may not be worth pondering. For a flight lasting more than an hour—and there is the chance of the drink cart being between you and the lav for any length of time—this can be very important.

If access to the lav is a consideration, you may want to think about positioning yourself conveniently. In most aircraft, there is a lav in the back. In some, there may be one in the front, between first class and coach, as well. If you do not think the lav is a consideration, then don't sit close to it. It can get crowded back there at times. And often that "lav odor" can creep out during a long flight.

HOW CLOSE IS YOUR NEXT CONNECTION?

I've missed a flight because the 125 people on the plane in front of me did not move off the plane as quickly as I needed them to move. Invariably, if you have a close connection, getting the aircraft door open and all those other people out of your way will seem to take an eternity. If your connection is a close one, choose a seat toward the front. If your connection is longer than an hour and fifteen minutes, in most airports, this is not a key consideration. Anything less than an hour, it outweighs the lav consideration. Go before you get on.

Aisle or Window

FLYING FOR THE FIRST TIME?

If you have never flown before, even if you are going to fly at night, make it a point to sit by a window and look out. It is truly amazing to see the incredible earth from the sky. The lakes, rivers, and mountains are beautiful; irrigated crops and the patterns they make in the land provide a glimpse of the art of the earth. Just the expanse of undeveloped areas still in this great country of ours is something to see.

DO YOU HATE INTERRUPTIONS?

Are you easily annoyed when people step on your toes? Do you become disagreeable when disrupted or asked to get up once you are seated? If so, sit by a window. If you are in an aisle seat, the person next to you will have multiple opportunities to step on your foot, fall in your lap, and/or knock your coffee into your lap. And that is if he is careful and considerate.

DO YOU HAVE PHYSICAL ISSUES?

Are you really tall, or do you have a bad knee? Hands down, an aisle seat has the advantage of easy in and out and a little extra space without the airplane wall or a person on both sides of you. If you have a bad knee that needs to be flexed occasionally, an aisle seat can make a huge difference in the comfort of your flight. Just make sure you are on the side that will accommodate your bad leg.

If you do choose to sit in the aisle seat, wait until your window seat "roomie" has taken his or her seat before you get too comfortable in yours. You may want to stand up and step into the aisle to allow the window or middle seat person to quickly step into the seat. Also, if you are sitting in an aisle seat, stay alert until the overhead bin above your head is filled and closed. I've seen more than one person knocked in the head as the person hefting her roll-aboard carry-on missed the target bin, and well . . . you get the picture.

The Exit Row

Sure, the exit row may have more leg room, but are you ready, willing, and able to operate the exit door in case of an emergency? Have you read the instructions on the card in the seat back pocket in front of you? I mean *really* read them? Are you willing to stop your phone conversation or the conversation with your seatmate to look the flight attendant in the eye and verbally answer her when she asks you these questions? Are you willing to make that door your number one priority should you need to? If not, don't sit there.

I absolutely *hate* it when I see some frequent flier businessman become irritated because the flight attendant requires him to take out the viewing card and look at it, or he won't give her a verbal yes that he is willing and able to operate the emergency exit. What a snot! I don't want my life in the hands of anyone who is so inconsiderate that he can't acknowledge that he accepts that responsibility. I don't care if he has read the thing one thousand times before. If I am sitting around that exit, as a passenger, I want to hear his verbal yes and his commitment to opening that exit. If you want the extra comfort of the exit row, remember that with privilege comes responsibility.

CHALLENGES

Disability or medical challenge. If you have special travel needs due to a disability or medical challenge, discuss it with your airline. The easiest and quickest way to discover what the airline can accommodate is to go to the Web site. Most airlines have a page that details what they can accommodate and the arrangements that need to be made.

Northwest
Go to www.nwa.com.
Go to Travel Tools.
In the drop-down box, click on Traveler Services.
Click on Customers with Disabilities.

Delta
Go to www.delta.com.
Go to Planning and Reservations.
In the drop-down box, click on Special Travel Needs.
Click on Services for Travelers with Disabilities.

American Airlines
Go to www.aa.com.
Go to Travel Information.
In the drop-down box, choose Special Assistance.
Click on Customers with Disabilities.

I am not recommending one airline over the other as far as service, only that you read a few different sites to get a good idea of what may be required on your end and what is available on theirs. They all have a slightly different way of navigating to the site, but you can figure it out from there. If you do not have Internet access, give the airline a call and request a booklet with the information.

And while these pages should give you an idea of the types of accommodations that can be made, once you have an idea of your needs, *call* the airline and confirm the information. And then, three days before you travel, call again and confirm any arrangements that you have made.

For more information, see chapter 9, "Travel Health."

GETTING THERE

I have never been a JIT (just in time) traveler and when traveling with my friends, they have come to understand my obsession with this. I believe that the airlines advise people to get to the airport two hours before their flight because they have some experience in these matters. They recognize that lines never move as quickly as you would like them to move. I also believe that if you polled the people complaining about the length of the security or gate agent line or those panicked because they are afraid they are going to miss their flight, less than 1 percent of those people arrived at the airport two hours before their flight as advised by the airline. Hmmmm, go figure.

If you are lucky enough to hit the wave just right, you may soar through all the lines and end up with time to spare. Imagine that! A few extra moments to sit back, relax, buy a bottle of water to take on the plane, read a magazine, and in some airports, even shop! If you are flying at 2:00 PM, plan to meet your fellow travelers or Red Hat sisters at the airport two hours before your flight. There is a very good chance you will have time to eat lunch or enjoy a vacation kickoff toddy once you have cleared security. If you put your Red Hat Society luggage tag on your carry-on, you will probably find yourself meeting new friends before you ever leave the ground. I know I have. Just remember to get to your gate and hang close starting about forty-five minutes before your flight. You will be on hand should changes or cancellations occur.

Getting to the airport is something else to think about. If you are lucky enough to have someone who can drop you off at curbside check-in, then by all means that is the way to go. Just remember that someone will have to pick you up when you return. Although that doesn't seem to be a big deal, that service could easily turn into a little more effort than both of you bargained for. The prearranged time when she plans on picking you up is tentative. The possibility of flight delays requires you to take extra consideration. If you plan to rely on a friend who doesn't drive after dark or doesn't tolerate surprises easily, you may want to consider a car service or a taxi.

Planning on driving yourself? No worries, but depending on where you live and the distance to the airport, it may actually work out cheaper and be less of a hassle to use a taxi or car service. After all, it drops you off at curbside check-in and picks you up just outside baggage claim. And the added bonus is that you don't have to keep up with your car keys or remember where you parked your car.

If you drive yourself and park your car in the airport parking lot, slip the parking ticket above the visor in your car. It will be right there waiting for you when you need it. Take a few extra seconds to write down where you parked, and put the information in your purse. It may seem like a simple thing to remember right now, but several days of traveling and remembering room numbers, flight numbers, gate numbers, and countless sets of directions can scramble even the sharpest mind.

CHECKING IN

There are several ways to check in for your flight. Most airlines have online check-in available twenty-four hours before your flight. Doing this is advantageous even when you have luggage to check. Some airlines (Southwest, for example) give priority boarding according to your check-in time. Priority boarding means you get to go on first. If you are traveling with several people and you like them well enough to sit by them for several hours or want to make sure there is room in the overhead bin for your carry-on, you want to get on the plane and choose your seat in the first group of twenty-five that boards, not the last. Believe it or not, you can actually print out your boarding pass on your printer at home. If you don't have access to a printer or you're out of paper, it is still in your favor to check in at home.

Another advantage to checking in early or online from home is that *if* you have (as suggested) joined the airline's preferred customer plan and *if* you have completed your profile with some type of electronic notification method (cell phone or text messaging), the airline might just notify you if your flight is canceled for some reason. No promises on this, but it happened for me—only when I was checked in for the flight.

If you are not checking a bag and have just your roll-aboard and your purse, you can bypass the ticket counter and go straight to security with your photo ID and your printed boarding pass. Have your quart-sized zip-top bag containing your three ounces or less of liquids handy, should you go this route.

The number one rule before handing over your luggage to be checked is to confirm that your flight is indeed flying and on time. If you plan on curbside check-in, ask the skycap to confirm. If you plan on checking in at

Red Hat Society
TSA Story

Having worked as a security screening officer for TSA, I want to make sure all my fellow Red and Pink Hatters have a safe and pleasant journey. Most important when you book your flight, ask for the latest TSA information, or go to www.tsa.gov, and click on For Travelers for the most up-to-date guidelines. Always check the permitted and prohibited items lists and other important items under Additional Resources currently on the bottom left of the 3-1-1 for Carry-Ons portion of the Web page. It pays to double-check this information the day you travel to see if there have been any changes, so you won't be upset because you had to surrender something you packed unknowingly.

Please be gracious, use your best manners, and kindly do all the things each security screening officer asks of you. We ask you to do things some may think are silly, but I guarantee you it is for your as well as the flight crew's safety. If you don't like to walk barefoot, bring a little pair of footie socks to slip on your feet (there should be a chair nearby for you to sit on if needed), and bring a zip-top bag to place them in once you are done with them, so you don't get things dirty in your purse or carry-on.

It is best to clean out your purse at home before you leave for the airport, so there is not a pound or two of change in the bottom, or something in there you forgot about that might embarrass you in the security line, such as a pocketknife or lighter (always double-check the prohibited items list). If you feel you just have to take a lot of change or jewelry, put it into a zip-top bag, and at the security checkpoint take it out and put it into a bowl before it goes through X-ray, so it will be quick for us to examine and get you on your way sooner. If you are worried about someone seeing your valuables in the bowl, simply place another bowl (bottom down) on top of it, as the X-ray can see right through it, but no one else (except Clark Kent) will be able to.

If you are one of those lucky ladies who have had your hips or knees replaced (I have only run across one out of thousands of ladies I have screened who didn't say, "I wish I had this replaced earlier"), you may ask for your cleared valuables to be brought around and placed near you until we finish screening your person. Otherwise, if we have to take a look in your pocketbook, bag, or bowl, a security screening officer will be attending that bag, purse, or bowl until you get cleared and over to her for her to clear your items. Mind you, this could change at any time, so please be the wonderful representative of the Red Hat Society that I know you are, and don't be unladylike to the screener if she is not allowed to bring your valuables to you anymore, as rules change often.

And please, when someone is clearing you or your bag, do not touch or reach into your bag or other belongings. I know it is second nature to want to help, but hands to yourself, ladies, until told you may gather your items, or this will cause you more time and undue aggravation. I personally never wear my belt or jewelry to the airport. I stick them in my bag or purse, and I pull them out and put them in the bin separately, and put them on after I finish the screening process. If you are asked to step into one of the puffers at an airport, make sure to stick a comb in your purse because it will muss your hair and blow your skirt up. Just in case any of you ever wanted to be like Marilyn Monroe, here is your chance. Don't use hand sanitizer, as it could delay you.

To make your trip more enjoyable, always arrive at the airport at least two hours before boarding, and bring a good book or a good friend to pass the time. You have a better chance of a relaxing experience this way, as you won't be rushed at the counter, through security, and getting to your boarding gate.

And from experience: you ladies who arrive in or request a wheel chariot, always check at the airline ticket desk to make sure a wheelchair pusher has been notified to attend to your needs, even if you requested this when you booked your ticket. This should help keep you on schedule, so you don't miss your flight.

Also we see it every day. Flights do get canceled or delayed for mechanical or weather problems. If possible, take the earliest flight that day, so you can be put on the next one out. Flying the day before and prebooking a hotel room are really helpful if you are booked for a cruise the next day, so you don't have to pay extra for a helicopter or small plane to fly you to the first port of call because your original flight was canceled. Yes, I have seen it happen! *(continued)*

I have also talked to some passengers who have been delayed for one to three days, especially in very bad snow and/or ice storms, as all of the flights are normally fully booked the weeks of Thanksgiving and Christmas. If you can, prepare ahead for this unfortunate possibility during the winter months.

I have found it helps to place an extra airline baggage ID tag and/or a self-adhesive return address sticker inside your luggage just in case the one on the outside comes off. People leave cell phones and laptops behind at the airport every day, so put another one of those self-adhesive return address stickers on the item. This way instead of paging for someone who left an item at the checkpoint, ticket counter, bathroom, or restaurant, we can page you directly.

If you have special needs, be sure to let us know. We are always happy to assist you, which includes a sturdy arm to help you through the walk-through, and a private screening of your bags or your person. If you have the time, and have had a wonderful experience with a security screening officer, or feel someone was unprofessional, ask to speak to a TSA supervisor to report this. I hope this information helps you have a more relaxed and enjoyable travel adventure.

—Leah Durr, Bright Red Hats, Lawrenceburg, IN

the kiosk, look at the departure board, and make sure the flight is on time before you hand off your luggage. Once your luggage makes its way down that luggage belt, it is very difficult to make any adjustments to your flight. On the other hand, if you see that your flight is delayed and/or your connections are compromised, it is easier to make changes with your luggage still in your possession.

Contrary to popular belief, the airlines don't really want to torture you with the trials of air travel. If they can accommodate you by rerouting you, and your luggage can go with you, they just may do that. If your flight is running late, get in line to check in with the gate agent. If everything seems to be running smoothly, check in curbside or at the kiosk.

Curbside. Should you be lucky enough to depart from an airport with curbside check-in, this is the way to go. Many airlines have started charging for this convenience, usually $2.00 per bag, but the cost is well worth it. Just note that the $2.00 per bag charge is not the tip that you need to give to the skycap. For some reason the line at curbside check-in is shorter than the one inside at the electronic check-in *or* the ticket agent line. If you are traveling with someone else, one can check in at the curbside while the other hangs by the car; then you can switch places. After both check in, you can park the car and not have to drag the bags back to the terminal. To find out whether your airline has curbside check-in at your departure point, call the airline directly. Not all airlines offer the service. It also varies with airports.

Kiosk. More and more airlines use electronic kiosks to check people in for their flights. They are fairly easy to use and work even if you are checking luggage. To get started at the kiosk, you will be asked to swipe a credit card through the card reader. The information gathered from the credit card is for identification purposes only. You will not be charged anything. If you use the same credit card in the kiosk that you used to buy your ticket, there is a good chance it will automatically pull up your reservation information. If you don't have the credit card you used to purchase your ticket, never fear; you will still be able to check in at the kiosk. It is helpful to have your confirmation number or departing flight number, but it will find your flight even when you do not have all the information. If you checked in at home, pull out that boarding pass you printed, and all the information you need will be on it. If you checked in online, you will want to go to the kiosk to request your luggage tag. You will still have to show your ID to a gate agent and the gate agent will actually print your luggage tag and attach it to your bag, but that line is usually shorter than the one where you wait to check in with the gate agent.

Gate agent. Checking in with the gate agent will guarantee a wait in line. If you are more comfortable checking in with the gate agent than at curbside or at an electronic kiosk, be prepared to wait in line, and schedule your arrival at the airport a minimum of two hours prior to departure. You will wait in line at least twice, once at the ticket counter and once in the security line. Airlines tell you to arrive at the airport two hours before departure time because they know that there is a good chance it could take that long to maneuver the stops and starts of departure.

CONFIRMING GATE NUMBER

When you checked in (any time from ten minutes to one hour ago), you were probably given a gate number where your plane will depart from. You need to understand the gate number is only good for that particular moment. Gates change for any number of reasons. This is why your first stop on the other side of the security arches should be the departures display board. Locate the display board and your flight by flight number, and confirm your gate number. If the ticket agent told you just fifteen minutes ago that your flight was leaving from Gate 14A, and the departure display board now says your flight is leaving from Gate 27A, believe the departure display board and proceed to Gate 27A. Once you get to the gate, confirm via the sign at the gate or with the gate agent that your flight is indeed departing from Gate 27A. Then and only then should you take the time to make a trip to the bathroom, buy a magazine and bottle of water, or shop at the stores up and down the concourse. Once you have taken care of any wanderings that may be necessary, once again confirm via the departure display board or sign at the gate that your gate has not changed. Park yourself in the closest chair possible to the gate agent's desk, and keep your eyes and ears open.

Sitting next to the gate agent's desk is your insurance policy that you will stay informed if there are any flight changes, gate changes, unexpected delays, or other issues that may require your attention. For whatever reason, announcements regarding gate changes, cancellations, and delays are difficult to understand over the PA system. If you are sitting next to the podium, there's a chance you might be able to understand the announcement (or overhear the conversation regarding it) in time to act accordingly.

Always keep the phone number of your airline accessible. Mine is on speed dial. If you end up in a situation where your flight is delayed to the point of missing a connection or is canceled, you and everyone else on that flight are going to be queuing up to make alternative arrangements. If you are number four or more in that line trying to rebook, stay in line, and call the airline directly on your cell phone. You will gain the advantage of getting rebooked before all the really good options are taken. Stay in line so that the gate agent can switch out your boarding passes when you reach the desk. Something to think about while you are standing in that line is that gate agents do not control the weather. Weather-related delays are not their fault. They cannot make a plane or flight crew appear by just wishing. Believe me, if they could, they would. They do not want you there, delayed and upset, any more than you want to be there.

If at all possible, know your alternatives. Depending on your situation, you may be able to get where you are going just by knowing your options. For example, if your flight to San Francisco is canceled, but you know that Oakland is an alternative airport, you can ask the gate agent to put you on the flight to Oakland. She may or may not be able to do it, but it is worth a try. Checked luggage sometimes crimps this plan, but if you absolutely have to be somewhere, you may have a chance of getting there.

If by chance you are stranded overnight due to a maintenance problem or crew issue, the airline may offer you a discounted hotel room. I have to tell you, I have yet to know anyone who has had a pleasant experience with this option. If it is the only affordable way to get some sleep, then take it. But if you can at all manage to swing a room in the airport hotel, skip the discount and get your own room. My experience, and that of others interviewed, has been that the shuttle designated to take you to your "distressed traveler rate" hotel will take up to an hour to show up. You will be taken to a hotel that may be, but most likely is not, close to the airport. You will ride with a shuttle full of unhappy people for ten to twenty minutes to your destination. You will not have your luggage, nor will you be able to get it (this should not be a problem if you have carefully prepared your carry-on). It is usually already *very* late when this becomes the alternative, so you are very likely getting to your "distressed traveler discount" hotel way past your bedtime. *And* guess what? Your ride back in the morning will be at 4:30 or 5:00 AM. The hotels are not usually ones that you would choose to stay in, which is why they have the super-duper discounted rate. *And* you are stuck there. Once again, if it is your only alternative, take your chances and try to get some sleep. If you can make other arrangements, my recommendation would be to do it.

ON THE PLANE

Boarding the Plane

When you board the airplane, you will most likely do it by group number. Look at your boarding pass. Your group number will be listed there. Most airlines board the first-class cabin first, then the top tier of their loyalty program, followed by the other groups. Typically they fill the plane from the back to the front. If you are sitting toward the back of the plane, and you board when your group number is called, it is likely there will be room in the overhead bin for your carry-on bag. If you do not board with your group and wait until the last minute to get on the plane, you may have to check that precious carry-on bag.

As you board the plane, try to do so quickly. Keep your boarding pass out so you can reconfirm your seat number. The seat numbers are usually posted just over the seats by the overhead bin. If you need to grab a magazine, book, or needlework out of your bag before putting it in the overhead bin, try to have it out before you board or at least readily accessible. If you have to dig around for an item before storing your bag, place your bag in your seat and step out of the aisle so other people can board. Once you have retrieved what you are looking for, you can then move quickly back into the aisle to store your bag. I will caution you, however, to make this a quick task. Just because that spot for your bag was there when you found your seat doesn't mean it will be there a few minutes later. The area over your seat is free shared space, and although it is implied that is where your bag should go, it doesn't necessarily mean someone else won't park his there. Overhead bin space is a limited, treasured commodity; grab it while you can.

Do not count on the overhead bin to be a safe place for anything that is crushable or valuable. Your fellow passengers want their roll-aboards to fit in that space, just as much (or more) as you want your award-winning feather-adorned red hat to fit. They will not, I repeat *will not*, have mercy or show any consideration or hesitation about crushing it to half its size if it means getting their carry-ons in that overhead bin.

Never, ever, if you definitely want to see it again, put anything in the seat pocket in front of you. It is the cousin to the sock monster that gobbles up those missing socks that never are seen again. Books, magazines, needlework, and passports are just a few of the things that are left in the seatback pockets every day.

Touchdown

About twenty minutes prior to landing, your pilot or someone will give instructions regarding stowing electronic equipment, putting seat backs up, and so forth. This is the time to gather your belongings and get organized to disembark. And if you did not heed my previous warning regarding the dreaded seat pocket in front of you, now is the time to get everything precious to you out of and away from that monster. Just before landing, the flight attendant will provide two pieces of valuable information: (1) connecting gate information and (2) baggage claim information. For whatever reason, the location of the baggage claim area seems to be less accessible than many other tidbits of information once you get off the plane, so listen up.

If you do not have a connecting flight and have checked your luggage, you may want to consider sitting calmly in your seat and letting all the other people rushing to wait for their bags in baggage claim get off in front of you. This is especially true if it takes you a little extra time to navigate or walk up the ramp or a wheelchair is waiting for you. There is no sense in being trampled in the stampede if you don't have to be.

If you waited to go to the bathroom until you got off the plane, now is the time to go. However, you may want to consider *not* going to the bathroom closest to the gate where you just deplaned. Every other woman on that plane will be in that first bathroom, and chances are the line will be a bit long. Try heading toward the exit or baggage claim. There is usually a bathroom somewhere, just down the hall, where the line is shorter.

BAGGAGE CLAIM

Most large metropolitan airports have skycaps available to help you with your luggage should you need it. They typically wear either a red cap or a red jacket and have a baggage trolley close by. If you need assistance with your luggage, signal the skycap and he or she will help you out. Remember, they work for tips, so be fair.

Some airports have luggage carts you can rent for $1.00 or so. If you are planning on needing this type of device, you will want to have some $1.00 bills in your purse. In the smaller airports, you may need to use quarters.

Jockeying to grab your bags off the luggage carousel can be a bit of an ordeal. It can be less so if you have marked your luggage with a specific identifier, such as a bright neon ribbon or luggage tag, so it can be spotted from a distance. (I use my Red Hat Society luggage tags AND a bright neon ribbin). Keep your baggage claim stickers available throughout the baggage claim exercise. Some airports have agents matching baggage claim numbers with your baggage claim checks as you exit the airport. It is always a hassle to have to dig them out at that point. Just in case the gate agent at check-in did not tell you, your baggage claim numbers are usually attached to your ticket jacket. (You know, the one you almost left in the seat pocket in front of you.) You need to hang on to it until you have either (1) exited the airport with all of your luggage or (2) made your way to the lost luggage desk where you will fill out a claim form that will ask for the numbers off your baggage claim stickers.

Lost Luggage

Don't panic. The U.S. Department of Transportation states that 98 percent of delayed luggage is returned to its owners within a few hours. Your mission right now is to beat the rush to the lost luggage counter. It is always a good idea to be aware of your surroundings. This is one of those times. While you are waiting for your baggage to come tumbling down the baggage carousel, check out where to find the lost luggage desk for your airline. If you flew on two different airlines to reach your destination, you will file a lost luggage claim with the airline on which you arrived.

The agent at the counter will key in your baggage identifier number and be able to determine the location of your luggage. More times than not, it will be on the next flight coming to your destination. Ask the agent to confirm that that is the case. If the "next flight" is within an hour of the one you came in on, *and* the agent can confirm it is on time, it is probably worth your while to hang out at the airport until the next flight arrives and get your luggage then. If you decide to do this, ask the agent for a meal voucher. It may help you pass the time until your luggage arrives. If you choose to leave the airport, even if your luggage is on the next flight, it may be several hours before it is delivered to your hotel. If your luggage is more than one to one and a half hours behind you, insist that the airline deliver your luggage to your hotel or home. The agent will give you a phone number to call and check the status of your luggage. Several airlines now give you the ability to track your lost luggage via their Web sites.

Remember, 98 percent of the luggage lost is returned to the owner within a few hours, or twenty-four to forty-eight hours at the most. This is why you packed your medications, toothbrush, a change of undies, and bits of Red Hat regalia in that carry-on bag! Vacations are too few and too short. Take a deep breath, consider it part of the adventure, and go have dessert!

STRANDED!

There is another great adventure waiting for you should you find yourself stranded overnight at an airport. This is not something I would wish on anybody, and in my many years of travel, it has happened about a half dozen times. In earlier years, I was much more likely to stick it out and find a spot to curl up. I now do my very best to recognize the situation early and get a hotel room. That is rule number one.

When you notice that the flights are beginning to cancel and being stranded overnight appears highly likely, book a hotel room as close to the hotel, or the airport hotel, as possible. If you are a member of a hotel loyalty club, book that one. If you have a hotel reservation at your destination, and it is past the required time to cancel your reservation or be charged for the night, book a reservation at a hotel in the same chain. When you book your hotel room close to the airport, ask the clerk what happens if you end up not getting there as a result of the weather. Most will allow you to cancel at any time. This way, if the weather suddenly clears and you *do* get to fly, you can cancel that reservation as you are boarding the plane and it seems likely you are going to take off. Also ask for the distressed traveler rate. The hotel may not have one, but you should at least ask.

If you do indeed end up needing the hotel room, ask the desk clerk, using his or her name, to please call the other hotel and let them know you have been delayed due to flight problems. Now, you should also call your destination hotel to make sure the desk clerk does not forget. This part is *very important*. When you call your original destination hotel, try calling the direct line to the hotel instead of using the 800 number. The on-site desk clerk may be more flexible than the call center. Then again, you may be transferred directly to the call center, but at least you tried. By following up no later than the next day, there is a good chance you will not be charged for both rooms. When you make the follow-up call, get the person's name you are speaking with, and use it in the conversation. If you have to repeat your situation to someone else or perhaps the person *did not* take the charges off after he told you he would, having the name of the hotel employee *always* increases the possibility of not being charged.

If you are staying more than one night at your final destination hotel, definitely call and make sure your entire reservation is not canceled as a no-show.

Okay, now you definitely have a room for the night.

After you have been successful at securing a room, you can cancel, should you not be able to get there (for instance, your flight is able to take off after all). You can still request a distressed traveler voucher from your airline. The airline *does not* have to give these out, especially if the delays or cancellations are weather related, so be sweet and charming when you ask. Most likely, the entire cost of your hotel room will not be covered, but the voucher will help. Once you have that in your hand, you can decide where you want to spend the night. If you end up taking advantage of the distressed traveler hotel provided by the airline, do not forget to cancel your backup plan.

The Distressed Traveler Hotel

If you decide to use your voucher as a distressed traveler, call the hosting hotel *before* you leave the airport and make a reservation; tell the clerk that you are coming and that you have a hotel voucher from the airline. When the airline gives you the voucher, it does not make a reservation; it does not guarantee the room—only the rate should a room be available. On one adventure with my sister Red Hatters we tried to take advantage of the distressed traveler rate after waiting what seemed like hours to take a shuttle bus fifteen miles from the airport. When we arrived, there were no rooms. The hotel found some rooms even farther away from the airport and at $10.00 more per night, but the extra hour or so it took to do that really took its toll.

Something to think about: If your travel plans are not time sensitive, and if airlines start canceling in the early evening, think about the wisdom of proactively asking the airline to book you on the first flight out in the morning. You can find a hotel close to the airport and be soaking in the tub, sipping hot chocolate or having a glass of wine, while thousands of other travelers are waiting to know their fate. So, you may not get there exactly when you thought, but there are advantages. If you change your flight plans early and rebook, you *may* have a chance of getting your luggage from the plane. Often when flights are canceled, the airline does not release the luggage. It goes onto the rebooked flight. If you rebook early enough, they may be able to get your things. Now, if you have packed with a plan, you won't really need anything out of your luggage, and you can leave it with the airline and not have to schlep it to the hotel for your brief overnight stay. The other advantage is that you will have made your decision early enough to be on one of the first flights out the next day. More than once I have heard of people who were stuck at the airport for two days because all flights were overbooked and full of passengers who were rebooked earlier.

When All Else Fails

These next few paragraphs are dedicated to the Mary Kay Convention in Dallas. Twice, not once, *twice*, I have spent the night on the floor of the DFW airport because every room in Dallas was taken by the Mary Kay ladies. There must be millions of them! They are such a gracious group that I am sure had I just known one to call, she would have shared her room, but alas, I did not. Just in case you are in a city where there is a Mary Kay (or some other) convention, here are a few things you may want to know.

Sleeping in an airport is not the end of the world. I know very few people who have died from it or had long-term detrimental effects. Take some deep breaths and embrace the adventure. In fact, some people actually plan to sleep in the airport. What a story this will make!

If it seems inevitable that you will be sleeping in the airport, you will want to do a few things. Before all the little shops start closing (and yes, they will close), buy water, snacks, and a deck of cards. If you are in danger of finishing your book, buy another one. If you have always wanted one of those little neck pillows, now is the time to make that purchase. If you don't have your travel blanket in your carry-on, you may want to buy one. (You can ask the airline for one, but do so early on. They run out.) Some airports have cots that they make available at some point. Go to the airport information desk and ask how you get one. Embrace the opportunity to meet new friends and Red Hatters. Get that red hat out of your carry-on and proudly display your membership to the sisterhood! Chances are you will find a fellow Red Hatter to share in your adventure.

If you are one of those people who sleeps soundly anywhere, be prepared to protect your belongings. If you are a really sound sleeper, you may want to consider bringing an extra belt or a locking bike wire to secure them to your seat. Bring Post-it notes or an alarm clock. If you don't have an alarm clock handy, stick a Post-it note on your blanket, forehead, or whatever, that says, "Wake me at 5:00 AM," or the time you choose. Someone usually will wake you up.

CHAPTER 8

Ground Transportation

When I started my traveling adventures many years ago, I had very little experience with various types of ground transportation. Having grown up in a city of 77,000, I knew of only one taxi that I occasionally glimpsed when I happened to go by the Greyhound station. City buses were a complete enigma to me since there was none in my city at that time. A subway was something I'd only heard about in tragic news stories. And the only rental car companies were Hertz and Avis.

My inspiration for venturing out and gaining experience with public transportation came after my first two-week stint in New York City. I reserved my rental car, because I thought I *had* to have a car, picked it up at LaGuardia Airport, and proceeded to drive into Manhattan. Discovery #1: there is *no reason* to drive in Manhattan unless you just want to be able to say you did. Next, I parked my car in the parking garage provided by the hotel. Discovery #2: parking in New York City costs almost as much as the daily car rental rate. I had to pay $35.00 per day for parking! Discovery #3: I never moved the car. I could have returned it to the rental agency, which I later discovered was one block away. But in my little world at the time, I didn't know I could return the car to different offices in the same area. I thought that all the rental car offices were at airports. More about that later.

TAXIS

Hailing a Taxi

Standing quietly on the street corner with a load of shopping bags and hurting feet wishing for a taxi will not get you a taxi. You have to let it be known that you want one. Taxi drivers look for a signal to let them know you want a ride. A quiet raise of the hand on a crowded corner will probably not get the taxi driver's attention. The "raised arm wave" is the preferred method. A nice loud whistle can help; just be aware of the guy standing next to you and don't blow out his eardrum. If other people were waiting on the corner before you got there, be polite and defer to them in the order that seems appropriate.

Don't waste your time or precious energy waving at a taxi that does not have its light on. If the light on the top of the taxi is off, it means the taxi is unavailable. *Look for the light on the top of the taxi.* It usually has numbers and letters on it, which are the taxi's identification letters. If the letters and numbers on the top of the taxi are illuminated, the taxi is available and looking for a fare. If you see a taxi with the *off duty* light on, he is *not* available.

Ordering a Taxi

In some cities you can prearrange your taxi pickup service. When you do this, always ask how long the dispatcher thinks it will take to get to your destination. Then, take the dispatcher's recommendation. Because I do not enjoy the plights of the JIT (just in time) traveler, I take the dispatcher's recommendation and then add ten minutes.

Never *Do This*

Never, never, never get in a car that is not licensed or sanctioned by the airport or hotel you are leaving. You may be standing at the baggage claim area when some person approaches you, quietly picks up your suitcase, and asks, "Do you need a taxi, ma'am? Let me get that for you. Just follow me. My car is just out here . . . a good price . . . no waiting . . ." *Don't do it!* The person may look respectable. It sure is nice that he wants to carry your luggage, but

I have not been in a U.S. airport that allowed people to solicit passengers directly to provide transportation.

On one of my early Red Hat adventures, my Red Hat sisters and I actually fell for this. A man approached us inside the airport asking if we needed a taxi. Before we could even blink, the guy picked up our luggage, and at a pace that seemed to be set by a speed walker, instructed us to follow him—which, like sheep to slaughter, we did. We followed him down the escalator, past the sign that said, DO NOT ACCEPT RIDES FROM INDEPENDENT DRIVERS, through the underground tunnel and through the underground parking garage. (Oh, yes, by this time we were spooked, but *he had our luggage.*) *And* like even bigger fools, we got in the car! Well, not to drag this out any longer than necessary, we reached our hotel safely, and he was a reasonably safe and courteous driver, that is one lesson learned I will never repeat or forget.

Some Rules for a Safe Taxi Ride

Ask the driver or dispatcher for an approximate fare amount before you enter the taxi. Also ask approximately how long it will take to get there. That way you will have no surprises.

Always ask for a receipt, even if you are not on business. It should include the driver's name, driver's ID number, taxi company name, and taxi number. Now, most likely you will get a blank receipt with none of this information on it, but try to remember to jot down the taxi number and/or at least the taxi company. This comes in very handy when you discover you left your new cell phone or prescription sunglasses in the seat as you exited.

Notice whether the meter has been turned on *before* you enter the taxi or *after*. It should be turned on *after* you enter the taxi.

The fare on the meter *may not* be the fare the driver quotes to you. It is not unusual for surcharges to be added to the fare you see on the meter. In New York City, Chicago, and many other cities, toll charges and bridge tolls are added on top of the metered fare. If you are from Oklahoma where tolls are usually $1.50 or so, this may not seem to be a big deal. The first time I was levied the $7.00 plus bridge toll on top of the metered fare in New York City, it took that poor driver more than a few tries to explain to me that it really does cost that much to go across that bridge! Some cities also have peak time surcharges for trips during morning and evening rush hours. These are typically $1.50 or so but can add up if you are not expecting them.

Taxis are supposed to take the most direct route to their destinations. Occasionally a driver will propose an alternate route to avoid traffic, an accident, or construction. Typically this is okay. Always trust your gut feeling.

Traveling as a group via taxi has different rules in different places, but a good rule of thumb is that if you are traveling in a preformed group, you may be considered a "party." The fare is computed from the first point of origin to the final destination. This often comes into play when you fly into a destination together but stay in different hotels. You can still share a taxi, but the fare will be collected at the final destination, and if you are the final destination . . . collect from your friends when they exit the taxi. The driver will *not* split the fare. An extra passenger charge is typically collected for this type of fare.

If you are graced with a driver who is friendly and accommodating, provides great service, and speaks either your native tongue or English so that you are comfortable with what he is saying, ask him for his card. In some cities, you can prearrange rides with the driver. While working in San Francisco, I met Ali, who became my number one taxi driver. I prearranged all my airport pickups, drop-offs, meeting transportation, and dinners through Ali. When my parents went to San Francisco, I gave them Ali's phone number, and he provided the same wonderful service for them the entire time they were there. If you run across such a driver, tip him well. It is worth it. I must stress that while you can do this in some cities, New York City is not one of them. There, it is illegal for the driver of a yellow cab to prearrange rides.

A good standard for tipping the taxi driver is either $1.00 to $2.00 or 15 to 20 percent of your fare. You should figure this on the fare, minus any tolls. If the driver gets out and helps you with your bags, you should tip more. If the driver doesn't get out to help you with your bags and you need help, don't be afraid to ask, but tip him for the extra service. If you do not receive good service, then do not tip. New York City actually publishes a Taxi Cab Rider Bill of Rights that recommends *not* tipping if any of your rights are violated.

BASICS

- Fasten your seat belt.
- Speak up and speak clearly to the driver.

- Know the address or cross streets of your destination. Telling the driver, "the Marriott downtown," could get you to the Marriott Courtyard, Marriott Residence Inn, Marriott Marquis, Marriott Eastside, or any number of places that may or may not be your destination.
- Do not smoke in a taxi; it is not allowed.
- Always get a receipt.
- Get out of the taxi at curbside. Even if you have to scoot across the seat in your best dress, it is better than getting the door knocked off the taxi and you knocked to the ground.
- Recognize that tipping is customary.

RENTAL CARS

Although much of the discussion on ground transportation is about getting from the airport to your next part of the adventure, I don't want to neglect the beauty of the driving experience. Many of you live within a comfortable driving distance to your next adventure. At this time in our lives many of us have turned in our minivan keys, but one would certainly come in handy for a nice little drive. Consider renting a minivan or passenger van for your next outing! You can travel in the style and comfort of a new, clean vehicle. And with most major rental companies the oil changes will be up to date and the tires will be in fairly good shape.

Renting a Car

Before renting a car, think about the size and type of car you require. Rental agencies refer to cars as midsize, compact, or luxury. However, different agencies do not view these classifications in the same way. Most agencies list online which type of car they classify according to size. Some consider the Toyota Camry a full-sized car, while others regard other models as full sized. The information is available online as well as by phone, but it is a good idea to know what type of car you reserve.

Whether you book your rental car through a travel agent or on your own, ask for specials that might be available. Rates on rental cars fluctuate almost daily. There are often price breaks for week-long rentals or weekend specials. Be aware that if you reserve the car for a week-long rental and bring it back early, you may be charged the standard daily rate, resulting in a higher charge. Also, advertised specials and the discount coupons you receive in the mail have blackout dates and restrictions. Read the fine print before you count on the third day being free or 20 percent off.

One phrase you must remember in reserving any type of travel is "the best available rate." This should be your mantra. Most major rental car agencies offer specials for drivers aged fifty or fifty-five and over. There are discounts from AAA as well as AARP. If you book on the Web, enter the code for each special for which you may be eligible. They may vary from 10 to 20 percent. A special promotion, weekly rate, or weekend rate may offer an even deeper discount. If you book via phone, ask the agent whether there are any specials. If the answer is no, be specific and ask for senior discounts.

Once you have decided which car rental agency to use, consider joining its preferred customer club. Some agencies charge for this, but others do not. As a member of the preferred customer club, often you can go directly to your car instead of standing in line to get your contract. If you have to stand in line to add a driver or request a different car, a special line may be designated for preferred customers.

If you have concerns regarding your driving record, ask the agency or your travel agent whether anyone screens or checks a renter's driving records before renting the car. You may want to be preapproved to rent. Some agencies reject customers whose driving records don't meet company standards, even if you have a confirmed reservation. Having driving violations, such as seat belt violation or driving with an invalid driver's license are triggers that may impact your ability to rent.

Ask the rental car company about special fees or assessments that may be charged on top of the base rate. Airport surcharges, drop-off fees, fuel charges, mileage fees, taxes, and out-of-state charges are a few of the little surprises tacked on the back end that can add up in a hurry. Clearly understand the fuel option plan described by the rental company. Such plans can be different at each company. A standard rule of thumb is to return your rental car full of gas. In about 99 percent of the cases this will work out best for you. If pumping gas is not something you want to do, ask the agent about the gas option plans, and choose the one that fits your needs the best.

The one thing you do not want to do is to return your car without having filled up the gas tank and without having designated a fuel option plan. You will be charged for the most expensive gas price this side of the Atlantic if you do that.

Rental Car Terms to Know

Required documentation. All rental car companies require a valid driver's license. As I mentioned before, if you have a concern regarding your driving record, make sure you have been accepted by the rental car company. Just because you have a reservation does not guarantee the company will rent you a car if you do not meet the driving standards. Most companies also require a major credit card number. If you do not have one, you may want to enlist the help of a travel agent to secure your car. Vouchers and other prepaid options may be available.

Collision damage waiver (CDW). Some states allow rental car agencies to offer collision damage coverage at a charge of roughly $9.00 to $13.00 per day. This coverage is *not* collision insurance. It does not cover bodily injury or personal property loss. It covers damage only to the car. If you have auto insurance, check with your agent to confirm that your policy would cover you in case of an accident. If it does, this waiver is probably not necessary.

Personal accident insurance (PAI). This rate can be from $1.50 to $4.00 per day. It pays a limited portion of medical expenses or a death benefit if you are in an accident. Once again, your insurance agent can shed light on your need for this insurance.

Personal effects coverage (PEC). This covers your luggage against damage and may cost $1.25 per day. If your homeowner's policy covers your belongings while you are traveling, this is probably not necessary.

Refundable charge. Some agencies impose what they call a refundable charge at the time you pick up the car. It can often be hundreds of dollars. Rental car agencies charge this amount to your credit card but do not process it unless you do not return the car on time or there are other issues. The problem arises in that your credit card spending limit may be affected by this action even if the company does not process the charge. If you plan on shopping or charging your hotel stay, you could run into problems. Check your credit card limit; you may want to leave a cash deposit or put

Car Rental Agencies

- Alamo: 800-832-7933
- Avis: 800-331-1212
- Budget: 800-527-0700
- Dollar: 800-800-4000
- Enterprise: 800-736-8222
- Hertz: 800-654-3131
- National: 800-227-7368
- Thrifty: 800-367-2277

the deposit of the car on a different credit card. Some agencies take this deposit in cash.

Airport surcharges and drop-off fees. Airport surcharges can bump up the base rental rate considerably. Airport authorities impose this fee even though the rental car agencies shuttle you off-site to pick up your car. In some airports it is so significant, it makes sense to rent a car at an off-airport site. This can especially be handy if you are visiting family or friends. Check on the proximity of the closest off-site location where you are staying, and weigh the difference. Remember, there is a price for convenience, but if a rental car agency has a desk in the hotel where you are staying, and a free shuttle to the hotel from the airport, you may want to rent a car at the hotel. (That also makes it handy when returning to the airport. No rental car to drop off!)

Fuel charge. Some rental car companies give you a half tank of gas and charge you $15.00 or $20.00 or so, telling you to return the car empty. Others fill the tank for you and charge you for the amount of gas that you use. Companies that send you on your way with that first tank of gas typically require you to return the car full. If you do not, they will charge you for the gas that you used. This charge will be considerably higher than what the local station just outside the airport charges. Understand the fuel policy before you leave with the car.

Mileage fees. Mileage fees are usually based on a cents-per-mile basis. Some companies have a set amount of miles you can burn up and then begin with the cents-per-mile fee. Shopping around can make a big difference with this fee. If you are going for a week-long drive, look for the company offering unlimited mileage.

Taxes. Oh, yes, you can count on taxes, and they can greatly impact that daily rate. If you are really trying to watch the pennies, take into consideration that the taxes may be lower when you rent your car in a more suburban area than right inside the city proper. Both states and municipalities tax rental cars, so taxes can add up.

Additional driver fees. Inquire about fees and restrictions on additional drivers. The extra cost involved in the additional driver fee is not nearly worth the cost if an unlisted driver is driving and an accident occurs.

Out-of-state charges. Some rental agencies charge when you drive a car out of state. If you are going out of the immediate area from where you have rented a car, check on these restrictions. Also, if you are anywhere near a U.S. border, please note that there are restrictions on driving the rental car across the border, especially into Mexico.

Picking Up the Rental Car

Keep your rental car confirmation with you to facilitate your car pickup. It should show a confirmation number, the type of car requested, and estimated time of pickup or flight information. (When you provide your flight information, remember to give the number of your *arriving* flight.) The confirmation should also have a telephone number for the rental car agency if it is an off-airport company. Some agencies track your flight via the flight information you provided. That way if your flight is delayed, the agency recognizes that you *will* arrive—but later than anticipated—and it will continue to hold your car.

Read your rental car agreement before you sign on the line. You need to understand the liability you are undertaking and know exactly what you will be paying for when you return the car.

Before you leave the lot, walk completely around the car, and look for dents. *Seriously* walk around the car. I once rented a car, and had my traveling companion not noticed the huge dent on the right side door as he was getting in the car, there is a good chance I would have been held responsible.

Also, take a few extra minutes to familiarize yourself with the car. Make sure you know how to turn on the lights and the windshield wipers, adjust the mirrors, and locate the release for the gas tank.

Returning the Rental Car

Rental rates are usually based on a twenty-four-hour period. If you keep the car for, let's say thirty hours, you will be charged for the twenty-four hours plus an hourly rate. It may be cheaper to extend the rental by one day than pay the hourly rate for the six extra hours. Just ask at the counter, and they will usually figure it both ways for you.

AND JUST SO YOU KNOW . . .

As the renter of the car, you are responsible for any and all parking tickets, traffic violations, and toll charges that are levied against the car while you rent it. And yes, they will find you.

LIMOUSINE SERVICE

Limousine service or chauffeured Town Car service can often be a convenient way to get to or from an airport. Prices for limo service can vary almost as much as the prices in airfare, so you have to do a little research before you can decide whether it is the best way to get to your destination.

You can often reserve a stretch limo for $20.00 or so more (once again the price varies greatly, but it may not be as much as you think). If several people gather in one car with multiple pieces of luggage, you may find it costs about the same as a van. Anyway, it is worth checking out, and it sure is fun if you have never ridden in a limo before!

Limousine services, like most other services, vary in quality. Often companies that belong to industry associations must abide by certain rules, insurance requirements, and service standards. The National Limousine Association (NLA) has liability insurance requirements and a peer review application process. You can access the Web site (www.nlaride.com) to search for limousine services in the area where you will be traveling. If you already have a limousine service in mind, you may want to ask whether that service is a member. Your best reference is your travel agent or a friend who has used the limousine service before.

Most limousine services provide two types of pickups: curbside pickups or baggage claim greeting (also referred to as "meet and greet"). Once again the fees vary from a token $10.00 to a more considerable $30.00 or so. Ask about this fee when you make the reservation. *If* you do not have a cell phone or your cell phone does not work outside your calling area, ask the limo reservation service whether there are call phones in the baggage claim area and how you can identify them.

Good to Know About Limos

If you do not arrange for the "meet and greet" service with the limo company, you will have to contact the company by phone upon your arrival. If you do not have a cell phone or if your cell phone does not work outside your calling area, ask the limo company whether there are dedicated paging phones or other phones located in the baggage claim area. Get the 800 number, and carry it in your travel documents—not packed in your suitcase.

Some airports require that the limousine services use "meet and greet" for all pickups. If this is the case where you are arriving, your limousine driver will meet you at the baggage claim with a sign stating your name, the group name, or the name of the limousine company. At these airports, the limousine drivers will usually assist you with your luggage to the parking garage where the limo is waiting. These drivers are not allowed to do curbside pickups so you may have a short walk to the nearest parking garage.

Curbside pickups. In most cities, airport ground transportation will not allow the limousine services to wait for passengers in the "active loading only" areas. They provide a holding area for the limos somewhere close to the airport so they can be there within five to ten minutes. Typically they give you a phone number to call when you have collected all of your baggage from baggage claim. When you call that number, they will give you a car number, and they may ask you what you are wearing so your driver can recognize you. You take your luggage, proceed to the "active loading area," and wait for your driver. Your car will have a number or your name on the window. When you see your car, wave your arm, and make eye contact with the driver. He will pull over to the curb and pick you up.

Don't call the number before you and all the members of your party have gone to the bathroom and collected your baggage. The limo driver cannot wait for you if you are not standing on the curb ready to go. In peak traffic times, it can take as much as thirty minutes for him to make the entire airport loop and get back to you. It will take him much less time to be dispatched from the limo holding area than to get back to you after a false start.

Baggage greeting. This works a couple of ways, so clarify with your limo company whether your driver will assist you with your luggage. Some will; some will not. Once he greets you, he will escort you either to the curbside pickup area or to the parking garage. Most likely he will greet you and assist you with getting your luggage to the curb, and then he will go to the parking garage, retrieve his car, and pick you up at the curb. *If* your limo company tells you that the drivers do not assist with luggage and you need to get a skycap, there is very little reason to have a baggage claim greeting. The skycaps are good about gathering your luggage, getting you to the curb, and helping you locate your limousine.

Group Arrivals

If you arrive with a group and have coordinated your trip to share a ride, remember to wait until all members of your party have arrived, collected their luggage, bought an extra bottle of water, and/or gone to the bathroom before calling the limo. It is very frustrating to have the driver arrive to pick you up and have to watch him leave to make the loop while you wait for others. I promise, this does *not* save time.

SHARED RIDE GROUND TRANSPORTATION

Shared ride ground transportation is an economical way to and from the airport or train station. Shared ride services combine the point of origin or destination with several other patrons in the same area to provide a clustered approach to transportation. Usually provided in a passenger van, shared ride services pick up several passengers at one point (the airport) and disperse each to her doorstep or the other way around. Rates are per person, and you may have to wait up to thirty minutes for your van to depart the airport.

SuperShuttle

SuperShuttle is a leading force in shared ride, door-to-door airport ground transportation. Since opening its doors in Los Angeles, California, in 1983, the company has continued to focus on customer service and quality. With a goal of turning every new customer into a repeat customer, the company stresses reliability, responsiveness, cleanliness, and great customer service. SuperShuttle provides service to twenty-three airports around the United States. Reservations can by made by calling 800-258-3826 or going online to www.supershuttle.com. SuperShuttle suggests twenty-four-hour notice to make reservations. If you are staying in a hotel, you can ask the hotel concierge to arrange for your pickup.

A SuperShuttle ride to the airport from your home, office, or hotel is by reservation. This means that you call (or reserve online) your ride to the airport from your home or your hotel preferably twenty-four hours in advance. All reservations are prepaid to reduce the hassle of collecting money and/or using credit cards at van side. SuperShuttle now provides a ride reminder service much like your doctor or dentist does. Twenty-four hours before your scheduled pickup, they will call to remind you of your pickup time. The van usually arrives within fifteen minutes of your scheduled pickup time. For example, if your pickup time is 8:00 AM, your SuperShuttle van will be there between 8:00 and 8:15 AM. If you don't want to share a ride with multiple people glaring at you all the way to the airport, be dressed, packed, and ready to go by 8:00 AM.

SuperShuttle rides *from* most airports are by demand. You can make a reservation in advance, which will cut down on the time and hassle of paying van side, or you can use the SuperShuttle walk-up option. Please note that if you make a reservation, the van is not at the curbside waiting for you. Due to security issues, airports do not allow vans to sit curbside at passenger pickup. They are usually in a holding lot a very short distance from the airport and come to the curbside when notified by a SuperShuttle attendant that he has a load ready to depart.

When you get to the airport, you should check in at the SuperShuttle desk, which is usually located near the baggage claim area. The SuperShuttle attendant won't actually take your reservation until you have your baggage and are ready to go, but he will tell you that the next van will be heading to your destination in X minutes, which may help you decide whether you really want to browse around the newsstand a few extra minutes.

SuperShuttle luggage policy pretty much follows the airlines' policies. You can have two checked bags and one carry-on, plus your purse. If your luggage weighs more than fifty pounds, or you are carrying your golf clubs or surfboard, you may be subject to extra fees. I suggest calling 800-258-3826 to get answers regarding oversized items.

SuperShuttle offers special rates and arrangements for parties of fifteen or more. Check the Web site or call the SuperShuttle reservations desk for more information.

FYI: In many cities, car seats are mandatory for children under age four. You must provide a car seat for a young child traveling with you.

SUBWAYS

No matter what you call it—MARTA, BART, or Metro—a subway can be ominous to some of us. I grew up in Fort Smith, Arkansas, where subways (like Russia during the Cold War) were something your mother warned you about. I mean they're fast, underground, and take you places you probably have never been before. However, they're also the most practical way to navigate in a city. The subway can be your best friend. After all, the hotel doesn't have to be right on Fifth Avenue. It just has to be close to a Metro station!

Subways can be demystified with a few simple instructions, a little planning, and a map. Each subway system has a Web site that will allow you to print the subway map. In cities where subways are king, that map will be readily available in every hotel or subway station. Grab a map and look over it a few times before you take off on your adventure.

- New York City: New York City Transit (www.mta.info/nyct)
- Boston: Massachusetts Bay Transportation Authority (www.mbta.com)
- San Francisco: San Francisco Bay Area Rapid Transit District (www.bart.gov)
- Washington, D.C.: Washington Metropolitan Area Transit Authority (www.wmata.com)
- Atlanta: Metropolitan Atlanta Rapid Transit Authority (MARTA; www.itsmarta.com)

- Miami: Miami-Dade Transit Service (www.co.miami-dade.fl.us/transit)
- Baltimore: Maryland Transit Authority (www.mtamaryland.com)
- Chicago: Chicago Transit Authority (www.transitchicago.com)
- Los Angeles: Los Angeles County Metropolitan Transportation Authority (Metro; www.mta.net)
- Philadelphia: Southeastern Pennsylvania Transportation Authority (SEPTA; www.septa.com)

You have to know only three things before getting on a subway: (1) where you are going; (2) which direction you need to go to get there; and (3) what color line will get you there. The first step in figuring out which train to take is to determine which direction you want to go. There must have been a woman on the board who came up with it because you *do not* have to know whether you are going north or south. Subway directions are determined by the last stop on the line. Just determine which stop you want to get off, check the last stop on the line, and that will be the name of the train you want to take.

Subway etiquette is as follows: when you get on, move to the center of the train, or find a seat as soon as possible. If you stand just inside the doorway looking for a seat during rush hour, you could be harmed in the process. Keep moving until you find an empty seat or grab bar, or take a seat quickly. Be aware when your stop is coming up, and gather your belongings to be ready to exit the train quickly. The seats just inside the subway door are supposed to be reserved as handicapped seating. If you need to use one of the seats and there is someone in it who appears *not* to need the seat, politely ask the person to move. Typically people will let you have the seat.

A subway can get crowded, and groups can be separated. When I am traveling with a group and we are getting ready to go into the subway area, we line up like ducks with me typically at the back of the line. It is easier to help someone from the outside of a subway turnstile than the inside, and believe me, someone will have a problem sticking the card in the right way or finding her card just as you get to the turnstile.

Before getting on the train, *have a plan* about what to do if you are separated. Determine whether everyone will meet at the next stop or at your destination. Your cell phone may or may not work underground, so know this before it happens. Also, know where you are going to meet. Each subway

Other Little Tips for the Subway

1. On some entry gates, you will slide your ticket into the slip, and it will pop up on top of the turnstile. Don't forget to grab your ticket!

2. On others, you will slide it in and out, just like you do your credit card at an ATM. Once again, do not forget to take your ticket.

Please note that if you have used up the fare on your card, the little elf inside the turnstile keeps it. If you are into collectibles and want your subway ticket for your scrapbook, you will need to buy a day pass or be sure to put a few cents extra on your card so that you get it back when you are finished with it.

station has at least two exits. If you head to the Thirteenth Street exit and your other travelers head to the Fourteenth Street exit, you could be very far apart. I recommend that you meet just as you get off the train. Move out of the way of the crowd; it will dissipate quickly. Wait for the next train, and then meet up and go on your merry way. It will be a fun story when it is over with and another adventure to post on the Red Hat Society Web site.

When you exit the train, have in mind which way you are heading. Exits will be marked typically by the street where the train leaves you. If you know which street that is, it will be a plus, especially if the weather is something other than perfect. You can end up a block or two away from where you wanted to be if you head to the wrong exit. Again, it is not difficult. There are few subway mistakes that cannot be fixed by just heading in the other direction.

Navigating a subway was one thing that I never thought I would do. After I did it, I felt a great sense of accomplishment. Now, when I am traveling, I still get a warm and fuzzy feeling that I am able to look at a subway map and figure out how to get where I am going.

CHAPTER 9

Travel Health

Travel is often a challenge for many of us. Sometimes we think it is more of a challenge than we could possibly handle. Red Hatter Liz Bebo of the Beehatitudes tells a wonderful story on the next page of travel and the challenge that health issues can present. The outcome of her "therapeutic" travel with a supportive friend is inspiring at the least.

BEFORE YOU GO

Well, let's face it. Health concerns are important, and we all have to consider them. Not only are many of us on some kind of "maintenance" program, but there is always the concern of "what if I get sick?" while I am traveling. There are some basic health tips that can keep you in your best shape on the road as well as a few that fellow travelers and I find helpful.

If you have health concerns or questions, discuss them with your physician. Problems or issues that you may think would be very difficult to manage on the road have probably been managed before. Your physician and the nurse may have suggestions or recommendations that make your trip easier to manage.

Be honest with yourself about your current physical conditions and limitations.

The Liz Bebo Story

From an early age I appreciated the value of vacations, as my family took one every year, usually during the summer and mostly by car. I can still remember aspects of all of them even now (at age sixty-five!).

Until the late 1980s, I was either a student or a teacher, often both, and continued the tradition of taking vacations, mostly by car, with my two sons. However, by the late 1980s, my sons were both working and university students, and I was felled by complications of multiple sclerosis. I got around via scooter, which could be loaded into the van and driven places. The spirit was willing, but the body and physical challenges kept me close to home. No vacations for me.

With a supportive team (including friends, family, and doctors galore) I pushed limits, trying to find ways to get around "no." I maintained involvement in church (including choir) and Toastmasters. My belief that if I thought about it enough, I could figure out a way to accomplish what I wanted, drove me in 2003 to ask a friend whether she'd be willing to push a lightweight wheelchair around say . . . France. She was facing some life-changing situations herself and believed the timing was serendipitous. Not really fully understanding what we were getting ourselves into, we signed up for a two-week Elderhostel to study art and artists of Paris and the Riviera.

Our Parisian guide, Guy, took us aside the first day (in our "accessible" hotel, where our room—and *all* the others—was down a flight of stairs) and said he just didn't think I could possibly keep up. I looked him squarely in the eye and said, "Just watch me!" (Only three weeks before the trip, after I had fallen in a parking lot, my rheumatologist ordered some physical therapy to strengthen my ankles. One of the exercises was stair-stepping, something I had not done for about twenty years!) I won't say getting around was easy, but the adrenaline (endorphins) caused by being in Europe for the first time in my life, seeing the sights, and absorbing the ambience that is Paris fueled me. I found myself using the wheelchair as a walker, as much as I could, then appreciated being pushed. Day by day, museum by museum, I pushed myself more and more (the twenty-three-step spiral staircase in Saint Chapel, the Metro, in and out of a motor coach, and of course down to bed every night and up for breakfast the next day).

On day eight, we flew to Nice where we met a new guide, Ute. She just couldn't believe I'd be able to get around the ancient cobbled streets and was very worried. I caught my fellow Elderhostelers smiling as I assured her it would be all right. I confess that first day "walking" all around the old city of Nice I had maybe a few doubts. I needn't have. Again, there was so much to see and do (early every morning, my friend and I went down to the market to see the produce and flowers and a certain artist, from whom I bought a painting; eventually three others in our group bought paintings when we would introduce them to Paz). We ate most of our meals at neighborhood restaurants within a few blocks of the hotel. On the last night I was about two blocks from the hotel when I realized I'd left the wheelchair there. My Elderhostel friends urged me to keep going and promised they'd go get it if I needed to use it. I didn't. In fact, the only time I used it ever after that night was in the airport, where the officials insisted I ride rather than push it!

I gladly returned the rented lightweight wheelchair on my return to Phoenix. I also figured out how to wedge the scooter into the closet of a spare bedroom. And a few months later I went shopping for a new car: one without hand controls, without a lift. The salesman even made me test drive it (a scary moment, though my neurologist had assured me I'd be all right) before signing the papers. I was thrilled to sell my accessible van to a woman for whom it became the freedom she'd never had!

The next fall I participated in an Elderhostel to Vienna and Salzburg, and the following spring I traveled all by myself to England and Scotland! I never forget my twenty years in a scooter and I take nothing for granted. And I still believe in the value of vacations.

If you can't run a mile in your neighborhood, you probably won't be able to finish that 5K run at Pike's Peak.

If you need a nap or rest daily at home, plan your trip to include rest time.

If walking more than twenty minutes at a time is uncomfortable, make arrangements for a scooter or wheelchair before spending the entire day at a museum.

At least a week before you pack to leave, review your prescription medications. Do you have refills on order at the pharmacy? Do you need to contact your physician's office to make sure that when you do call for refills, they will be available to pick up? It is no fun to think you are going to whip through the pharmacy drive-through to pick up your prescriptions on Thursday before you leave on Friday only to find out that you don't have refills ordered and your physician is off until Monday. If you use some medications only on an "as needed" basis, order refills of them. The old Boy Scout motto of "be prepared" works well in trip planning.

If you will be gone during that little period of time when it is too soon to get a refill (for insurance purposes) but you won't have enough medication to last the duration of your trip, sweet-talk your pharmacist. There are a few ways around that situation. Some pharmacies allow you to pay for just the number of doses that you need to get you through until you return. They will then credit that amount and the number of doses to your next allotment. Most have ways to work with you, so do not hesitate to ask. If it is an issue with the physician, the law, and a controlled medication, you can make arrangements with the physician and the pharmacy regarding those situations.

Once again, this may be your first experience in dealing with

Prescriptions

Early in my travels I moved all my prescriptions to Walgreens because I thought they were everywhere, and they do have a multitude of locations across the country, except New York City. (I think they now have a store or two in Manhattan.) I had to scramble to get my hubby to FedEx my Synthroid to me once because I did not do my research or work my plan. Overnight mail services—U.S. mail, FedEx, DHL, UPS, and others—are awesome problem solvers for such situations.

these issues, but most pharmacies and doctors have dealt with them before. Some national chains allow you to refill your prescriptions at any of their pharmacies across the country. If this is your plan, then check with your pharmacy, and make sure there is a location convenient to your destination.

Once again, make sure you have enough medication to last your entire trip and a few days extra. You never know when you may be inspired to extend a visit by a few days, have unexpected delays, or drop a pill down a drain.

Depending on the type of medication, you may want to discuss with your physician the necessity of changing your doses or times you take your medication. You can do this with a brief phone call and alleviate unnecessary worry and concern.

If your medication requires you to check your pulse before you take it, make sure you know how. My grandfather always checked my grandmother's pulse for her before she took her heart medication. She had no idea how to do it. The same goes for monitoring blood pressure. If you currently monitor your blood pressure or blood sugar at home, be prepared to monitor it on the road.

If you plan to use a medication that you are not accustomed to taking, for example, Xanax for the air squirmies or some type of sleep aid, try it before you leave home. Finding out that a new sleeping pill keeps you knocked out for days may cause you to sleep away your entire vacation. If that tranquilizer releases more inhibitions than you want to be without, you should probably find that out at home rather than in a closed airplane cabin 30,000 feet in the air.

Place an envelope in your carry-on bag clearly marked "medical information." This envelope should contain the following:

- Your primary emergency contact information. You would not believe how forgetful your traveling companion can be in an emergency situation. After all, *you* know your buddy's husband's work phone number, don't you?
- A list of chronic or ongoing health problems, including diabetes, epilepsy, or others.
- A copy of your prescription for your eyeglasses or contact lenses.
- A list of all the medications you take and the dosage (many pharmacies can print this out for you, or you can access it online).

MedicAlert

If you are not a MedicAlert member, you may want to consider becoming one. MedicAlert provides twenty-four-hour access to your vital medical information. Emergency medical personnel are trained to be aware of MedicAlert bracelets and/or the MedicAlert emblem. Using the member ID number on the back of the bracelet, they can call a phone number that is manned twenty-four hours a day and immediately identify you and safely administer appropriate treatment. Current pricing for basic service is $39.95 for the first year and $25.00 per year after that.

For more information on MedicAlert, contact the following:

MedicAlert Services Contact Center
800-ID-ALERT (800-432-5378)
6:00 AM to 7:00 PM (Pacific time), Monday–Friday
8:00 AM to 5:00 PM, Saturday
www.medicalert.com

- The name, address, and phone number of your family physician. Include the after-hours emergency numbers.
- A list of allergies.
- Copies of your insurance cards.
- A copy of your latest EKG if you have a history of cardiac problems.
- Scan this information and e-mail it to yourself or a family member.

That way you will have access to it whenever you need it!

Traveling with Oxygen

If you travel with oxygen, you may be required to provide documentation from your doctor stating that you are healthy enough to travel. Some airlines require these doctors' statements to be dated within ten days of your trip.

By air. If you use oxygen, or your physician wants you to take it with you when you travel, you will need to notify the airline in advance. The federal air regulations do not allow you to carry your own oxygen unit on a plane. The airlines will, with notice, be able to provide it for you, usually for a fee. You will need to make arrangements at your destination and at any of your layover sites for oxygen as well. Some airlines allow you to take *empty* cylinders and other equipment in your checked baggage. Check with the individual carriers to determine extra arrangements or charges that you may incur. Try to arrange nonstop flights to avoid extra fees and hassles involved in a layover. It may be worth a few extra dollars to book a direct flight or find an alternate airport where a direct flight may be available.

By car. If you travel by car, the restrictions are fewer, and you have a little more freedom about how you transport your oxygen and equipment. As you pack your vehicle, remember that oxygen bottles must be carried upright and should not be transported in the trunk where they can overheat.

By bus. Most buses today do not permit smoking and thus do not carry a large threat to those traveling with oxygen. As with the airlines, there is no standardized policy for traveling with oxygen on a bus. Check with the individual bus line or tour group to find out their policies.

By train. Traveling with oxygen by train is not usually a problem, but as with the other methods of public transportation, you should make arrangements in advance. Also, be aware that booking a nonsmoking car is necessary.

Whether you are traveling by air or by car, your current oxygen provider can most likely help you with these arrangements. No matter how you travel, make sure to have plenty of oxygen for the duration of your trip plus 20 percent. Do not depend solely on the electrical supply of a train or automobile to power any of your equipment.

Health Insurance

Know the confines and constraints of your health insurance. Check with your health insurance provider about whether you are covered outside your immediate home area. If you are not, check with your travel agent or your insurance agent, and ask if they have traveler's insurance that would suit your needs. Take along your insurance cards, even if you do not have coverage outside your home area. Those little cards tend to open doors to immediate health care needs. In a pickle, you can sort out who pays for what later.

Dental Care

If you have been experiencing dental issues, go ahead and make that appointment. I promise you this: a toothache on the road *always* hurts worse than a toothache at home! Get it taken care of *before* you hit the road.

Inoculations

If you know you are going to travel during flu season, get your flu shot in time for it to be effective before you leave on your trip. Typically it takes at least two to three weeks. Find out when your local pharmacy is giving flu shots and coordinate with your Red Hat Chapter to make it an event!

Special Needs

If you require extra time to board an airplane or assistance to go from gate to gate, let the airline know in advance so the information can be noted on your record. Then check and recheck once you reach the airport.

If you travel with a service animal, make sure his or her vaccinations and necessary health exams are current. Let the airline, hotel, or train know you will be traveling with a service animal so that they can make adjustments to your accommodations.

Thoroughly research your destination to become aware of accessibility issues you may encounter. It is much easier to deal with them on the front end than to have unexpected surprises. You will have enough of them, no matter how well you plan. Make prior arrangements with the rental car agency, airline, train, and/or hotel prior to your arrival. Travel can be accessible, but you have to plan for it. The tourist board at your destination can be a wealth of knowledge about arrangements you may need to make at local attractions and about special services available for you. You might be surprised at the nifty ways that people approach accessibility these days.

ON THE ROAD

Wash your hands. If you don't remember anything else while you are on the road, remember that good hand washing has the greatest single impact on preventative health care today. If you wash your hands before you eat or drink, after the trip to the restroom, and after shopping or participating in other activities with the masses, you will be more likely to stay healthy. Use warm water and soap, and vigorously lather for at least twenty seconds. You can always use hand sanitizer in a pinch.

Get plenty of rest. Sleep is vital to maintain good travel health and to ward off the crankies. Ask your roommates before traveling with them about whether they snore, they like the bathroom light on or off, or they sleep with the radio on. You will be much happier determining solutions for any of these issues before trying to fall asleep after a long travel day.

Many people have had success taking melatonin for sleep when traveling. If you plan to take it, let your doctor know. Melatonin as well as many other herbal remedies may impact your current medications.

Drink plenty of fluids. Water is the preferred liquid, but any liquid is better than no liquid. Avoid caffeine and alcohol. Some of us have the tendency to restrict fluids on long car trips or plane rides so we don't have to go to the bathroom. Actually the trip to the bathroom serves several purposes. Not only is it a good indication of hydration, but it also forces you to move. Sitting for long periods of time can cause health problems. Get up and move to avoid getting stiff, and get the blood flow going.

Take your vitamins. If you currently take vitamins, keep it up. If you don't, you may want to try some before your trip. Remember to try them before you hit the road. Certain vitamins can upset your stomach. It is better to find that out before you leave than on the trip.

If you travel with a group or companion and need to take a day or afternoon to rest and recoup, don't be shy to say so. Be comfortable enough with your traveling companions to pick and choose the activities you enjoy the most and beg off the ones you don't mind missing. Just don't expect them to miss out on activities to stay around and watch you rest.

If your daily routine includes exercise, try to maintain it on your trip. Bring your walking shoes, and utilize the hotel workout room, walking track, or treadmill. Many hotels have measured walking routes and maps you can use. Do not forget safety, however; take a buddy with you. Some resorts have organized morning and evening walkabouts.

Airplane cabins and hotel rooms can dry the body's tissues. If you have trouble with dry sinuses, spend a few extra minutes in the shower deep breathing in the steam or breathe through a warm washcloth. Place extra moisturizing lip balm in your carry-on for the plane trip.

Beware of constipation. One of the most common traveler complaints is constipation. Listen to your body, and be sensitive to its needs. Drink plenty of water, eat fruits and salads, and when you feel the urge, take time to go. It can make a *significant* difference.

CHAPTER 10

Tipping

*T*ipping is one of those things, like algebra, that I have yet to master well enough to be comfortable with it. I always have to remind myself of the "rules": who gets tipped what, when, and so forth. I do know the number one rule is to carry plenty of small bills. In most places frequented by travelers, there is almost always someone willing to give you an extra hand if you need it.

EATERY TIPPING

I'll start with the most common tipping experience, which is dining. I have to admit, I am a bit conflicted about the restaurant industry and how restaurants rate not having to pay their employees minimum wage. The rest of us are expected to subsidize them! The conflict comes because when I was waiting tables a million years ago, I made a heck of a lot more each day because of the tips than I ever would have made had I been working for minimum wage. It was the tips and not the $2.30 per hour that kept me in a pretty comfortable lifestyle for a college kid.

I'd bet that most of us are aware that tipping with a dining experience is expected. However, I'd venture to say that there are those of us who have never really been in a situation where we had to consider or figure the tip.

I'll 'fess up here. It wasn't until a few years ago that I realized I was expected to tip on the total of the bill *before* taxes. I still catch myself figuring 15 to 20 percent on the total amount of the bill!

I worked in a small boutique restaurant where we were the greeters, the waitstaff, the busboys, and sometimes the sandwich makers, so it was a surprise to me to find out that the tip people leave on the table is often divided among the seater, the busboy, the salad maker, the chef . . . on and on. This creates a conundrum: If you receive crummy service from the waiter, do you refuse to tip and thus punish the whole crew? I'd say no. However, I also would not just sit there and accept crummy service. If your waiter is negligent, request the attention of the manager, and calmly and politely explain the issue. If he makes up for the poor service by removing a meal, dessert, or round of drinks from your bill, go ahead with the standard tip. However, if the manager does nothing, you are certainly within your rights *not* to leave a tip. Also be aware that for a group larger than five people, many establishments add the tip into the bill. The tip and its percentage rate will be noted, so look for that before you add yet another 15 to 20 percent.

QUICK TIP GUIDE

Tipping the valet took me a while to figure out. (I finally asked a nice young man about my son's age what was customary.)

Valet: $2.00. You tip the parking valet when he brings your car to you. If you have a special request, such as keeping your car at the front and handy, you should tip when you make the request.

Host/maitre d': $5.00 plus. Tipping is not usually required for the maitre d' unless you want to be seated without a reservation on a busy night, have a request for a special table, or want help coordinating a special event. In that case, anything from $5.00 and up is appropriate. Consider sending a nice thank-you note in the event you may return.

Bartender: $1.00 per drink or 15 to 20 percent of the tab before tax. If you are sitting at the bar and being served by the bartender, it is customary to tip him or her. If you want especially good service and close attention, tip the bartender after your first drink instead of waiting until you are ready to close out the tab. (You should tip then as well.) That will ensure closer

> My sisters and I used to be of the mind-set that walking is good exercise, and unless there was inclement weather, we really did not think that valet parking was something we would indulge ourselves in. After a few expeditions to California and New York, we realized that the distance from the parking lot wasn't really the issue; we were paying for the availability of the parking spot. Unless you can actually see a parking spot from where you are, take up the guy on the valet offer. Another consideration is safety. The unfamiliar neighborhood that looks bright and cheery as you park for an early dinner a few blocks away from your destination may look a bit more ominous after the sun goes down.
>
> —Michelle Harris, Royal Red Hat Sisters of the Road

attention and may even warrant a fresh bowl of munchies. (If it doesn't, ask for one; you never know where all those other people's hands have been. . . .)

Sommelier: 20 percent of the wine bill before tax. If you eat at a standard chain restaurant, you probably won't have to worry about how much to tip the sommelier. These guys (or gals) are usually in niche restaurants and do more than hand you the wine list. They are highly trained and specialized in buying, storing, and matching wine to the menu and your pocketbook. They arrive at your table separately from your waiter. Their tip should be based on the wine bill and not the entire cost of the meal. If the sommelier gives a great recommendation, you may want to add an extra 10 percent.

Coat-check attendant: $1.00 per item. Some restaurants in cold or rainy climates offer a coat-check service. It keeps people from trampling over your coat as they make their way between tables. If there is a charge for the coat-check service, then a tip is not necessary. If the coat-check is free, then tip $1.00 per item.

Washroom attendant: $1.00 to $3.00. In some places the items provided by the washroom attendant are purchased by the washroom attendant. She is an independent contractor providing a service, and her tips are her only repayment for the service. If you have been in need of hairspray, feminine products, a needle and thread, or a Tide pen, then you know what lifesavers these ladies can be. Please remember that these people may be working for tips only. My philosophy is: when in doubt, be generous.

Hotel Tipping

Years ago when I went on the road, I read a book on tipping, and it pretty much said that if the person touched your bag, you should tip him. I was always confused about whether to tip the doorman and the bellman. My research concludes the following:

Doorman: $1.00. The doorman is responsible for greeting you upon your arrival, helping you get your bags from your car, and hailing a taxi for you as necessary. The doorman is not the same as the bellman, so you will *also* tip the person *who actually delivers* your bags to your room.

Bellman: $1.00 per bag. Tip the bellman when he delivers your bags to your room and again when he helps you upon departure. If you have special needs or deliveries, tipping him $5.00 early in your stay will ensure attention. Don't underestimate the value of having someone come to your room after several days of vacation and assisting you with your bags. You may need to request the bellman fifteen to thirty minutes before you are actually ready to walk out the door.

Concierge: $2.00–$10.00. The hotel concierge can be your best friend if you will let him. To ensure that special friendship, you might want to consider a $10.00 to $20.00 tip upon arrival. The concierge can do everything from make reservations for you at an especially popular restaurant, secure opera or theater tickets, or give basic transportation tips and directions. If you are just arriving at your destination and you have spare time in your itinerary, toss your bags in your room and visit the concierge. You may have the best travel agent/planner ever, but there is something to be said for a local resource. The concierge will be more than happy to look over your planned itinerary.

Hotel maid: $1.00 per night. The hotel maid is an often forgotten service provider. If you stay more than one night, you may want to consider tipping your hotel maid. This is especially a good idea when multiple people share a room. You may find you do not have to call the desk for extra towels every day. If you do want to tip your hotel maid, leave the money in an envelope marked "Maid" on the dresser.

Skycap: $2.00 per bag. Curbside check-in disappeared after 9/11 but is now making a comeback with one difference. Many airlines charge a fee for the curbside service, and that fee *does not* include the tip for the skycap.

If you are going inside to check in, the skycap can be a lifesaver. Politely signal him that you are in a hurry and need assistance, and he will be attentive. Tip your skycap when the bags have been checked or placed on the belt to be checked.

Airport cart driver/wheelchair assistant: $2.00–$3.00. Airport cart drivers and wheelchair assistants can be absolute godsends if you need a little extra help getting through the airport. My parents often require a wheelchair assistant, and I can tell you that person has the power when it comes to making a transfer stressful or stress free. If your attendant pauses to let you go to the restroom, gets you a soda, or just tells you a great joke, tip extra. He is worth it.

Shuttle bus driver: 15 percent. When the shuttle service is free, such as the one provided by the rental car places, no tip is necessary. However, if the driver helps you on and off and assists you with your luggage, that is first-rate service. In that case I usually tip a dollar per bag. Or more if you'd like.

If you are on a shuttle service for which you pay, you should be prepared to tip the driver 15 percent. It can be in cash or be included in the credit card bill. I was on a shuttle service from Los Angeles (LAX) one time and the driver not only had ice cold bottled water in an ice chest for his patrons, but he also carried our bags to the door at each place he let people off. I asked him whether that was a company standard or his idea of good customer service. He said it was his personal idea of first-class service, and he enjoyed the responses he got as a result of his extra efforts. I tipped him extra just for coming up with the idea. I think that was one of the best bottled waters I've ever had!

Limousine or car service driver: 15 to 20 percent. When traveling with a limo or car service, you should expect that the doors will be opened for you and your bags loaded and unloaded. Some car services add the gratuity in the fare so you may want to ask about that when you reserve the car. As always, if your driver is especially nice and provides excellent service, tip more.

CONSIDER TIPS A THANK-YOU

Tipping is not supposed to be considered mandatory or automatic. Its original intent was a thank-you for good service delivered or a subtle bribe or insurance policy for special treatment. One steadfast guideline that will make the tip or no tip question an easy one to answer is this: when traveling in the United States, say thank-you *and* tip if someone provides good service.

PART THREE

Eating Out

CHAPTER II

Dining Guide

O h, how we love to eat! Many Red Hat functions take place in our favorite local dining establishments. We have compiled the restaurant reviews submitted by Red Hatters across the country. When you are eating out on a road trip or even in your hometown, look up a recommended eating establishment in the area.

We have tried to give you a guide to help determine the impact that each place may have on your pocketbook. It is based on the cost of a basic entrée. Remember that it is just a guide:

$: around $10.00
$$: between $10.00 and $20.00
$$$: between $20.00 and $30.00
$$$$: may impact your shopping budget

ALABAMA

KOINONIA KAFFE
$
11 Grove Street
Headland, AL 36345
334-693-3355
It has a chick-place menu with items such as Fiesta Salad, and drinks such as Mayan Mocha.

RIVER NILE BISTRO
$
2620 Montgomery Highway
Crepe Myrtle Shopping Center
Dothan, AL 36303
334-702-9111
Another chick place, it offers gourmet sandwiches, soups, and salads.

HUGGIN MOLLY'S
$–$$
1 West Depot Drive
Abbeville, AL 36310
334-585-7000
Huggin Molly's is a truly old-fashioned ice-cream parlor loaded with antiques and an upscale menu.

MULLIN'S DRIVE-IN
$–$$
607 Andrew Jackson Way NE
Huntsville, AL 35801
256-539-2826
The best greasy hamburger in town!

CAFE BERLIN
$$–$$$
964 Airport Road SW
Huntsville, AL 35802
256-880-9920
German food in a great atmosphere of casual outdoor dining.

ARIZONA

HONG KONG GOURMET BUFFET
$$
4909 East Chandler Boulevard
Phoenix, AZ 85048
602-785-0660
Great sushi! Fresh! Reasonable price. Drinks are not included in the buffet price.

THE TEE PEE
$$–$$$
4144 East Indian School Road
Phoenix, AZ 85018
602-956-0178
Mexican food in a fun atmosphere with endless chips and salsa.

Z TEHAS GRILL
$$$
10625 North Tatum Boulevard
Phoenix, AZ 85028
480-948-9010
Unique atmosphere with a Southwest style and great service.

ARKANSAS

GEORGE'S
$
2120 Grand Avenue
Fort Smith, AR 72901
479-785-1199
Best burgers anywhere. French fries are heaped on the plate with plenty to share. Save room for pie!

TALIANO'S
$$
201 North Fourteenth Street
Fort Smith, AR 72908
479-785-2292
This family-owned Italian restaurant is housed in a historic landmark. The Italian platter is a sure thing if you can't decide what to order. Service is always wonderful, and the owners greet you at the door.

CALIFORNIA

A MAAD TEA PARTY
$
4355 Town Center Boulevard
El Dorado Hills, CA 95762
916-933-2121
A nice variety of choices on the menu.

AMSTERDAM CAFÉ
$
10905 Magnolia Boulevard
North Hollywood, CA 91601
818-506-1938
A small cafe, very artsy, but also friendly. It serves an excellent panini with complimentary salad, as well as a large range of Italian sodas, coffees, and smoothies.

CHEF GEORGE'S
$–$$
40100 Washington Street
Bermuda Dunes, CA 92203
760-200-1768
Small, cozy surroundings, wonderful food, and personal service. The signature dish is Hungarian goulash.

HOG'S BREATH INN
$–$$
78-065 Main Street
La Quinta, CA 92253
760-564-5556
Excellent food, reasonable prices, and relaxing ambience.

KANE'S FINE FOOD
$–$$
120 East Main Street
Grass Valley, CA 95945
530-273-8111
Kane's in Grass Valley is an upscale bistro-style restaurant with great food and service.

NATIONAL HOTEL
$–$$
211 Broad Street
Nevada City, CA 95959
530-265-4551
The National Hotel is a registered historic landmark. You can dine in the ambience of the Gold Rush days.

CHEESECAKE FACTORY
$$
1771 Arden Way
Sacramento, CA 95815
916-567-0606
Best cheesecake around. Go for dessert. It can be crowded at times, but if you go late, it isn't too bad.

JOE'S CRAB SHACK
$$
1210 Front Street
Sacramento, CA 95814
916-553-4249
This restaurant is located in Old Sacramento, right on the Sacramento River, and has delicious food. Great view and wonderful food combined.

MULBERRY STREET
$$
114 West Wilshire Avenue
Fullerton, CA 92832
714-525-1056
Old Chicago, 1930s-style decor. Great Italian food.

THE OLDE SHIP BRITISH PUB & RESTAURANT
$$
709 North Harbor Boulevard
Fullerton, CA 92832
714-871-7447
The atmosphere is warm and friendly; the food is unique and very good. I recommend the Scottish Bridie with a Newcastle Ale and the Sticky Toffee Pudding for dessert.

PINNACLE PEAK
$$
269 West Foothill Boulevard
San Dimas, CA 91773
909-599-5312
Great steaks at very reasonable prices.

CHOMP SUSHI & TEPPAN GRILL
$$–$$$
181 East Commonwealth Avenue
Fullerton, CA 92832
714-738-3511
Unusual menu and sophisticated decoration.

GIRONDA'S RESTAURANT
$$–$$$
1100 Center Street
Redding, CA 96001
530-244-7663
Great Italian food, local owners, and great service.

GUADALAJARA MEXICAN
RESTAURANT
$$–$$$
435 East Cypress Avenue
Redding, CA 96002
530-223-2540
*Guadalajara has great Mexican food
served by the owners in a fiesta-deco-
rated dining room. Great margaritas too.*

ST. PAULI INN
$$–$$$
10120 Highway 50
Kyburz, CA 95720
530-293-3384
*St. Pauli's is a great restaurant for
lunch and dinner, located on the
American River in the foothills. Guests
can sit inside or outside on a deck
overlooking the river. It is the section
with some rushing white water, and
the view and sound are nice accompa-
niments to the delicious meal.*

TAHOE JOE'S FAMOUS STEAKHOUSE
$$–$$$
191 Blue Ravine Road
Folsom, CA 95630
916-335-8420
*Very good to my Red Hat group.
Always splits the checks, and takes
the pictures.*

THREE SQUARES BISTRO
$$–$$$
140 Hidden Valley Parkway, Suite A

Norco, CA 92860
951-272-9888
Great food at a reasonable price.

MAGGIANO'S LITTLE ITALY
$$$
3055 Olin Avenue
San Jose, CA 95128
408-423-8973
*On Santana Row with great Italian
food, it is a place for large groups.*

RUBY'S HIDEAWAY
$$$
12303 Folsom Boulevard
Rancho Cordova, CA 95742
916-351-0606
*Another fabulous eatery. They split the
checks, played with our mascot, and
took lots of pictures.*

TAM O'SHANTER
$$$
2980 Los Feliz Boulevard
Los Angeles, Ca 90039
323-664-0228
*Fun place where the waitstaff is in
costume. Pub food and prime rib!*

LA VIE EN ROSE
$$$–$$$$
240 South State College Boulevard
Brea, CA
714-529-8333
*French cuisine, great ambience and
service. Great for a romantic evening.*

MARITIME SEAFOOD & GRILL
$$$–$$$$
1600 California Street
Redding, CA 96001
530-229-0700
Pricey but good for special occasions. Private booth seating allows intimate dining, or eat in the bar for more action.

NAPA 29
$$$–$$$$
280 Teller Street
Corona, CA 92879
951-273-0529
Fine dining with an extensive wine list.

CORK TREE
$$$$
74-950 Country Club Drive
Palm Desert, CA 92260
760-779-0123
Restaurant with outstanding service and food—California cuisine. A little pricey but well worth the cost. Food is better than excellent.

THE FIREHOUSE
$$$$
1112 Second Street
Sacramento, CA 95814
916-442-4772
Exquisite, excellent food and ambience. Very romantic. There is outdoor seating, and unique things appear on the menu such as antelope topped with blueberry chutney.

LE FORET
$$$$
21747 Bertram Road
San Jose, CA 95120
408-997-3458
Elegant French dining with an elegant atmosphere.

SLOCUM HOUSE
$$$$
7992 California Avenue
Fair Oaks, CA 95628
916-961-7211
Excellent food and ambience. Very romantic. The appetizers, entrées, and desserts were all good. Our waiters were knowledgeable about the menu and took their time explaining things we asked about. Try to get a table by the fireplace for an extra nice touch.

THE SUMMIT HOUSE RESTAURANT
$$$$
2000 East Bastanchury Road
Fullerton, CA 92835
714-671-4111
Fabulous food, elegant atmosphere, and beautiful hilltop views.

COLORADO

CHAMPS
$$
8501 West Bowles Avenue
Littleton, CO 80123
702-922-7988
Great sports bar.

ELEPHANT BAR

$$

7111 West Alaska Drive
Lakewood, CO 80226
303-922-7907
Great desserts served in elephant-sized portions. Asian and American food. Fun atmosphere. Senior discounts.

ROCKSLIDE BREW PUB

$$

Snowy Mountain Brewing
405 Main Street
Grand Junction, CO 81501
970-245-2111
Taste locally made beer and great food.

RED CANYON GRILL

$$-$$$

2325 West Ridges Boulevard
Grand Junction, CO 81503
970-243-7736
Wonderful views of the valley on a nice patio; fantastic food.

DEL FRISCO'S DOUBLE EAGLE STEAK HOUSE

$$$-$$$$

8100 East Orchard Road
Greenwood Village, CO 80111
303-796-0100
Great steaks.

CONNECTICUT

AQUA TERRA OYSTER BAR

$$-$$$

253 East Street
Plainville, CT 06062-2917
860-793-1600
Fresh seafood and raw oyster bar.

CARMEN ANTHONY FISHHOUSE

$$$

51 East Marin Street
Avon, CT 06001
860-677-7788
Fresh seafood and Angus beef. Zagat rated.

FLORIDA

ANGELL & PHELPS CAFÉ

$

156 South Beach Street
Daytona Beach, FL 32114
386-257-2677
A charming bistro that serves a variety of food with different kinds of live music in the background. While you wait for your meal, take a tour of the chocolate factory and store.

BELLA SERA'S PIZZA & PASTA
$
222 ½ North Nova Road, Suite B
Ormond Beach, FL 32174
386-671-7488
*You can dine on wonderful homemade
pastas and pizzas surrounded by Old
World charm.*

SADDLE JACK'S BAR & GRILL
$–$$
1545 North U.S. Highway 1
Ormond Beach, FL 32174
386-615-8511
*The food is plentiful and always up to
standard, and you can enjoy twenty
television sets on different channels,
dine outside, or listen to karaoke two
nights a week.*

CRAB SHACK
$$
5430 Baylea Avenue
Port Richey, FL 34668
727-847-6300
*Best grouper basket and casual dining
on an outside patio overlooking the
canal.*

**PRAWNBROKER RESTAURANT &
FISH**
$$
13451 McGregor Boulevard, Suite 16
Cypress Square
Fort Myers, FL 33919
239-489-2226

*Fresh seafood. Great clam chowder
and crab cakes. Try the seafood
platter.*

TARPON TURTLE
$$
1513 Lake Tarpon Avenue
Tarpon Springs, FL 34689
727-722-9030
*Off the beaten path, but on Lake
Tarpon with a great view. My Florida
chapter really loves it! Great appetiz-
ers, salads, fish—and even gator!*

ZANTE CAFÉ NEO
$$
13 North Safford Avenue
Tarpon Springs, FL 34689
727-934-5558
*A different atmosphere—like going to
your grandma's attic. Combination of
Greek/Creole food, all very fresh. The
couple who own it, and their young
children, work there. He, the chef, is
from Louisiana; she, the waitress and
cook, is Greek. It's a hoot! Don't be in a
hurry. Just enjoy!*

BONEFISH GRILL
$$–$$$
10750 State Route 54
New Port Richey, FL 34655
727-372-7540
*Best place for outstanding fish dishes
with signature sauces.*

HELLAS RESTAURANT
$$–$$$
785 Dodecanese Boulevard
Tarpon Springs, FL 34689
727-943-2400
Greek food and music—and wonderful Greek bakery as well. Order the saganaki; it will be flamed right at the table. (It's an appetizer.)

LIGHTHOUSE WATERFRONT RESTAURANT
$$–$$$
14301 Port Comfort Road
Fort Myers, FL 33908
239-489-0770
Fresh seafood. Homemade daily Chocolate Kahlua Pecan Pie.

THE VERANDA
$$–$$$
2122 Second Street
Fort Myers, FL 33901
239-332-2065
Unique and upscale dining experience. Southern cuisine.

BONEFISH GRILL
$$$
11535 Hutchinson Boulevard
Panama City Beach, FL 32407
850-249-0428
It has a beautiful place to enjoy the service, and the food is fantastic. Camera time.

CARRABBA'S ITALIAN GRILL
$$$
13800 Panama City Beach Parkway
Panama City Beach, FL 32407
850-230-4522
This is a wonderful, pleasant restaurant, and the food is fantastic. The service is amazing. Great place for small or large groups. Bring your camera. You will want to take pictures.

THE COLUMBIA RESTAURANT IN YBOR CITY
$$$
211 East Seventh Avenue
Tampa, FL 33605
813-248-4961
Noted for a Cuban influence.

COSTA'S RESTAURANT
$$$
521 Athens Street
Tarpon Springs, FL 34689
727-938-6890
Costa's Restaurant at the sponge docks in Tarpon Springs is known for wonderful Greek cuisine.

ISLAND WAY GRILL
$$$
20 Island Way
Clearwater, FL 33767
727-461-6617
Nice view, great sushi. Good wine list. Great ambience, dining inside or outside on the patio. It has a sushi bar and island food.

LONGHORN STEAK HOUSE
$$$
15721 Panama City Beach Parkway
Panama City Beach, FL 32413
850-233-4980
This is a great restaurant to have a good time, and the service is great. This is another place for pictures. Enjoy.

BERN'S STEAKHOUSE
$$$–$$$$
1208 South Howard Avenue
Tampa, FL 33606
813-251-2421
Noted for steaks and a fabulous wine cellar.

IDAHO

HAPPY'S CHINESE RESTAURANT
$–$$
549 Park Avenue
Idaho Falls, ID 83402
208-522-2091
Among the Top 100 Chinese Restaurants in the United States.

SANDPIPER RESTAURANT
$$
750 Lindsay Boulevard
Idaho Falls, ID 83402
208-524-3344
Eclectic American cuisine.

WASABI JAPANESE RESTAURANT & SUSHI BAR
$$
415 River Parkway
Idaho Falls, ID 83402
208-529-3990
If you like Japanese food this is the best place in Idaho to get it. The sushi is really good.

WHITEWATER GRILL
$$
415 River Parkway
Idaho Falls, ID 83402
208-529-3990
Asian fusion and Mediterranean food. The service is great, and the interior design is pleasing and adds to the dining experience.

ILLINOIS

FRONTERA GRILL
$$–$$$
445 North Clark Street
Chicago, IL 60610
312-661-1434
Award-winning chef-restaurateur, cookbook author, and television personality Rick Bayless is the chef and mastermind at the Frontera Grill. Very authentic Mexican food.

RIVA

$$$–$$$$

Navy Pier
700 East Grand Avenue
Chicago, IL 60611
312-644-7482
The view is unbelievable, and the food is very good. Seafood, steaks, and pasta.

INDIANA

GOLDEN CORRAL

$–$$

5301 Pearl Drive
Evansville, IN 47712
812-423-4930
A buffet with two locations, east and west. If you want a steak, they'll cook it to your liking. There's no extra charge for steak.

OLD MILL RESTAURANT

$$–$$$

5031 New Harmony Road
Evansville, IN 47720
812-963-6000
On the west side of town. Older restaurant, great food, and a fantastic waitstaff. Good enough for Christmas dinner.

RED GERANIUM RESTAURANT

$$–$$$

504 North Street
New Harmony, IN 47631
812-682-4431
Great steaks and seafood.

OCEANAIRE SEAFOOD ROOM

$$$

30 South Meridian Street
Indianapolis, IN 46204
317-955-2277
Fresh seafood daily, excellent service in a downtown location.

ST. ELMO STEAK HOUSE

$$$

127 South Illinois Street
Indianapolis, IN 46225
317-635-0636
Best steaks anywhere in a rare atmosphere.

NEW ORLEANS HOUSE

$$$$

8845 Township Line Road
Indianapolis, IN 46260
317-872-9670
A destination to dine at leisure on seafood or ribs. Excellent service in a laid-back atmosphere.

IOWA

Asian Deli
$
117 East Broadway
Fairfield, IA 52556
641-472-2649
It has a lovely, clean ambience and delicious Asian food at a reasonable price. Quick service too!

FAIRFIELD FAMILY RESTAURANT
$
2311 West Burlington Avenue
Fairfield, IA 52556
641-469-3360
It is as close to a diner as you will find in the Heartland.

TOP OF THE ROCK RESTAURANT/RED ROCK TAVERN
$$–$$$
113 West Broadway
Fairfield, IA 52556
641-470-1515
It has great food, it's nonsmoking, and it has a great view of the city of Fairfield, Iowa.

LOUISIANA

ANTOINE'S RESTAURANT
$$$–$$$$
713 St. Louis Street
New Orleans, LA 70130
504-581-4422
Fine French dining.

ARNAUD'S
$$$–$$$$
813 Rue Bienville
New Orleans, LA 70112
866-230-8895
Elegant dining and classic Creole in classic New Orleans.

EMERIL'S NEW ORLEANS
$$$–$$$$
800 Tchoupitoulas Street
New Orleans, LA 70130
504-558-9393
Eclectic dining combining Southwest, West Coast Oriental, and New England cuisine with a splash of Creole.

MARYLAND

CHAMELEON CAFÉ
$
4341 Harford Road
Baltimore, MD 21214
410-254-2376
Offers seasonal menus using local foods and produce. Fine dining experience in a casual atmosphere. Nice wine list.

MINNESOTA

PANERA BREAD
$–$$
8601 Springbrook Drive NW
Coon Rapids, MN 55433
763-259-0046
Consistently good food, especially the soup.

CRACKER BARREL OLD COUNTRY
STORE
$$
17189 Kenyon Avenue
Lakeville, MN 55044
952-898-5151
My favorite all-time restaurant and gift shop.

OLIVE GARDEN ITALIAN
RESTAURANT
$$–$$$
150 Coon Rapids Boulevard NW
Coon Rapids, MN 55433
763-786-1089
Best Italian food I've ever had.

MISSOURI

SPRING CREEK TEA ROOM
$
107 South Third Street
Ozark, MO 65721
417-582-1331
Open for lunch only. Great lunch specials. Go early to avoid the rush. Eat dessert first!

STROUD'S RESTAURANT
$
5410 Northeast Oak Ridge Road
Kansas City, MO 64119
816-454-9600
Home of pan-fried chicken served family style with all the fixin's and homemade cinnamon rolls.

FISH
$–$$
900 East Battlefield Street
Springfield, MO 65807
417-886-6200
Food is good. Atmosphere is awesome. There is actually a martini and manicure night. Love the waterfall.

LAMBERT'S CAFE
$–$$
1800 West State Highway J
Ozark, MO 65721
417-581-7655
Home of the tossed rolls. And you'd better bring your catcher's mitt! Served family style with very large portions. The "pass arounds" are brought to the table by the servers at no extra charge to your regular order. Lambert's is something to experience. The wait can be very long, but the gift shop can help pass the time.

THE KEETER CENTER
$$–$$$
1 Opportunity Avenue
Point Lookout, MO 65726
417-239-1900
Good for a casual lunch or romantic dinner, the Keeter Center at the College of the Ozarks is a great place to try. There is entertainment Thursday through Saturday by the college students. They have a great bakery with all sorts of pastries, and you can get them with ice cream on top.

LANDRY'S SEAFOOD RESTAURANT
$$-$$$
2900 West State Hwy 76
Branson, MO 65616
417-339-1010
The atmosphere is good. As you would expect, the seafood is good, but the Bananas Foster is to die for. The service was prompt and able to keep my tea glass full at all times.

JESS & JIM'S STEAKHOUSE
$$$
517 East 135th Street
Kansas City, MO 64145
816-941-9499
The best steaks for the money and huge, fully loaded baked potatoes on the side.

CANDLESTICK INN
$$$-$$$$
127 Taney Street
Branson, MO 65616
417-334-3633
Great atmosphere, service, and quality of food. It can be a little bit pricey, but it is worth it. Very romantic.

NEBRASKA

LEE'S RESTAURANT
$
1940 W. Van Dorn Street
Lincoln, NE 68501
402-477-4339

Family-owned place, well known for its delicious chicken and homemade onion rings.

AHMAD'S PERSIAN CUISINE
$-$$
1006 Howard Street
Omaha, NE 68102
402-341-9616
Middle Eastern food served with a personal touch.

BUTSY LE DOUX'S
$-$$
1014 Howard Street
Omaha, NE 68102-2815
402-346-5100
Good food in the Louisiana style.

JAZZ—A LOUISIANA KITCHEN
$$
1421 Farnam Street
Omaha, NE 68120
402-342-3662
Jazz is a bit of New Orleans in the Midwest.

UPSTREAM BREWING COMPANY
$$-$$$
514 South Eleventh Street
Omaha, NE 68102
402-344-0200
Casual dining. Delicious food. Brew pub on the premises that brews its own beer and root beer.

GORAT'S STEAK HOUSE
$$$
4917 Center Street
Omaha, NE 68106
402-551-3733
Gorat's is a favorite of financier
Warren Buffett with properly aged
steaks, seafood, chicken, and Italian
dishes.

NEVADA

HASH HOUSE
$
2605 South Decatur Boulevard, Suite
103
Las Vegas, NV 89102
702-873-9477
Open for breakfast and lunch only.
Great food and tremendous portions;
best breakfast in Las Vegas.

ROSEMARY'S RESTAURANT
$$$$
8125 West Sahara Avenue
Las Vegas, NV 89117
702-869-2251
World-class chefs in a small, quiet
place off the Strip.

MIMI'S CAFÉ
$
1121 South Fort Apache Road
Las Vegas, NV 89117
702-341-0365

Great varied menu and friendly, warm
atmosphere. American comfort food.

NEW JERSEY

WASHINGTON STREET INN
$$–$$$
801 Washington Street
Cape May, NJ 08204
609-884-5697
Enjoy a day at the beach and then a
great dinner in a lovely setting with
fine food. Take a stroll down
Washington Street Mall after dinner to
the quaint shops.

NEW YORK

LA BONNE SOUPE
$
48 West 55th Street
New York, NY 10019
212-586-7650
Excellent French cuisine and incredi-
ble onion soup.

JUNIOR'S RESTAURANT
$$
Grand Central Station
New York, NY 10017
212-586-4677
Junior's in Shubert Alley. It's good food
at a reasonable price, in the middle of
Broadway.

OLLIE'S SICHUAN RESTAURANT
$$–$$$
411 West Forty-second Street
New York, NY 10036
212-868-6588
Asian cuisine near the theater district. Yum. Great food and fast service.

CARMINE'S
$$$
200 West Forty-fourth Street
New York, NY 10036
212-221-3800
Family-style dining at its best, and everyone gets to share the Italian food.

STARLIGHT RESTAURANT & DINER
$$$
211 East Forty-sixth Street
New York, NY 10017
212-754-2707
Waiters and waitresses sing and dance as they serve. Fun!

PETER LUGER STEAK HOUSE
$$$–$$$$
178 Broadway
Brooklyn, NY 11211
718-387-7400
It's the number one steakhouse in the city and the U.S. Cash only.

NORTH CAROLINA

K & W CAFETERIA
$
1175 Glenway Drive
Statesville, NC 28625
704-871-0191
Great home cooking, family atmosphere, and reasonable prices.

NORTH DAKOTA

SANTA LUCIA RESTAURANTE
$–$$
505 Fortieth Street
Fargo, ND 58103
701-281-8658
Great food and presentation. Greek and Italian.

POST OFFICE CAFÉ
$$
604 Ninth Street NW
Cooperstown, ND 58425
701-797-3545
The old post office in Cooperstown features great comfort food in a unique setting. Worth the drive.

BUFFALO CITY GRILLE
$$–$$$
101 First Avenue South
Jamestown, ND 58401
701-952-9529
Renovated building from the early 1900s featuring buffalo burgers, the

best walleye sandwiches on the planet, and a surprise about what a small town can offer.

OHIO

BLUE GIBBON CHINESE
RESTAURANT
$$
1231 Tennessee Avenue
Cincinnati, OH 45229
513-641-4100
Best Oriental food in town. Relaxing atmosphere. Carry out too.

MECKLENBURG GARDENS
$$–$$$
302 East University Avenue
Cincinnati, OH 45219
513-221-5353
A German restaurant and bier garden with wonderful potato pancakes and sauerbraten.

THE CELESTIAL STEAKHOUSE
$$$
1017 Celestial Street
Cincinnati, OH 45202
513-241-4455
Good food and a view of the city and Ohio River. Awarded 4 diamonds by AAA eight years running.

PENNSYLVANIA

LE BEC FIN
$$$$
1523 Walnut Street
Philadelphia, PA 19102
215-567-1000
Complete with sommelier; very upscale fine dining.

FOUNTAIN RESTAURANT
$$$$
Four Seasons-Philadelphia
One Logan Square
Philadelphia, PA 19103
215-963-1500
Enjoy a very delicious dinner overlooking the fountains and beautiful city. Service is excellent, and hard-to-pick desserts are treats to the eye—and palate. Surprise bag with the check. Very elegant.

TENNESSEE

ROTIER'S RESTAURANT
$–$$
2413 Elliston Place
Nashville, TN 37203
615-327-9892
Located near Centennial Park, it has some of the best burgers in town. It features a selection of beers, but the star is the old-time milkshakes. This is also a good place for an old-fashioned meat and two or three, and is quite reasonably priced.

ALTRUDA'S ITALIAN RESTAURANT
$$
125 North Peters Road
Knoxville, TN 37923-4908
865-690-6144
www.altrudas.com
Never had a bad meal. Comfortable, great service in a place for the family. Best known for salad and rolls. The restaurant serves an Italian menu with an emphasis on pasta. Open for dinner.

HOME TOWN BUFFET
$$
2151 Gallatin Pike North
Madison, TN 37115
615-859-2185
This is in the Rivergate Mall area, and I believe might be connected with a chain. However, this is the best place to get a wholesome breakfast, lunch, or dinner, whatever one is in the mood for, at a very reasonable price.

LOVELESS CAFÉ
$$
8400 Highway 100
Nashville, TN 37221
615-646-9700
A Nashville tradition. Great food, famous for biscuits, fried chicken, and country ham. Worth the drive.

MONELL'S
$$
1235 Sixth Avenue North
Nashville, TN 37208
615-248-4747
In an 1880 Victorian house, family-style dining with delicious bowls of country food.

THE STANDARD AT THE SMITH HOUSE
$$
167 Eighth Avenue North
Nashville, TN 37203
615-254-1277
It's the oldest boarding house in Nashville, refurbished, very quaint, lots of history, and good food.

AUBREY'S RESTAURANT— KNOXVILLE
$$–$$$
6005 Brookvale Lane
Knoxville, TN 37919
865-588-1111
Aubrey's offers entrées for the grown-up palate, such as Rasta Pasta and Peanut Crusted Catfish Fingers, plus a tasty selection of sides like Dirty Potatoes, Parmesan Spinach, and Burgundy Mushrooms. But don't forget the delicious salads and sandwiches, and of course, all in a comfortable, family-friendly environment.

TEXAS

BACKSTAGE CAFÉ
$
204 East California Street
Gainesville, TX 76240
940-612-2000
Good food, very filling.

FRIED PIE CO. & RESTAURANT
$
202 West Main Street
Gainesville, TX 76240
940-665-7641
Great chicken-fried steak and out-of-this-world fried pies that are not the least bit greasy.

FURR'S FAMILY DINING—EASTGATE CENTER
$–$$
1440 Northwest Highway
Garland, TX 75041
972-270-7631
Great service. The waiter is always the same; he keeps you smiling and never forgets you. Food has always been fresh and hot.

HUBBARD'S CUBBARD
$$
901 Main Street
Garland, TX 75040
972-276-4179
Family atmosphere, relaxed, friendly. Food is good and service is quick. No rush to leave.

VIRGINIA

LAMPLIGHTER
$$
4068 Jermantown Road
Fairfax, VA 22030
703-273-9300
Out-of-the-way restaurant with excellent food at reasonable prices. European menu.

LUCIANO ITALIAN RESTAURANT
$$
2946 Chain Bridge Road
Oakton, VA 22124
703-281-1748
Small Italian restaurant that serves fabulous food.

SERVIAN CROWN RESTAURANT
$$$
1141 Walker Road
Great Falls, VA 22066
703-759-4150
Russian restaurant with wild game on the menu and interesting decor.

WASHINGTON

ANTHONY'S HOMEPORT
$$
6135 Seaview Avenue NW
Seattle, WA 98107
206-783-0780
Waterfront location.

DUKE'S CHOWDER HOUSE
$$
2516 Alki Avenue SW
Seattle, WA 98116
206-937-6100
Great chowder and location on the lake.

IVAR'S
$$$
Pier 54
Seattle, WA 98119
206-624-6852
Seafood and waterfront view.

WISCONSIN

GORDON'S
$
110 West Commercial Street
Mazomanie, WI 53560
608-795-2330
Serves hearty breakfasts, lunches, and dinners at a reasonable price.

WATTS TEA SHOP
$
761 North Jefferson Street
Milwaukee, WI 53202
414-290-5720
Watts Tea Shop has been in downtown Milwaukee for years. Wonderful chicken salad and sunshine cake. Open for lunch and dinner.

OLD FEED MILL RESTAURANT
$$
114 Cramer Street
Mazomanie, WI 53560
608-795-4909
Old Feed Mill is a restored 1850s feed mill that features antiques, beautiful quilts, and great food for breakfast, lunch, and dinner. It includes a gift shop, Millstone Mercantile.

WEISSGERBER'S SEVEN SEAS
$$$–$$$$
1807 Nagawicka Road
Heartland, WI 53029
262-367-3903
Located on a beautiful inland lake west of Milwaukee. The food is outstanding. During the summer, the view from the outdoor patio is fabulous.

PART FOUR

Profiles of Twenty Cities

CHAPTER 12

City Profiles

*T*he *Red Hat Society Travel Guide* profiles the top twenty cities requested by Red Hat Society members.

We have tried to capture the highlights of the cities listed here. For more information and possibly great money-saving coupons and itinerary tips, a visitors center Web address and phone number are included with each profile.

ATLANTA, GEORGIA

Atlanta Convention and Visitors Bureau
233 Peachtree Street NE, Suite 100
Atlanta, GA 30303
404-521-6600
www.atlanta.net

Atlanta might be a modern city in every way, but most of its attractions have historical and/or history-making roots. From Civil War destruction to civil rights organizations to the first twenty-four-hour news networks (and don't forget the Olympic Games), Atlanta has seen it all. Everyone should enjoy exploring the unique path this city has taken.

Getting There

Atlanta's landlocked location makes it an easy to moderate drive for many people. However, the vast majority of visitors make their way through one of the busiest airports in the world.

HARTSFIELD-JACKSON ATLANTA INTERNATIONAL AIRPORT (ATL)

Hartsfield-Jackson Atlanta International Airport has been designated the world's busiest passenger airport since 1998. The airport handles almost 90 million passengers each year. If things seem busy when you arrive, they are.

Taxi. There is a lot of construction going on at ATL, and some of the regular ways of doing things are being changed. However, the airport management thinks it's very important to make your visit as painless as possible. Keep an eye out for airport employees, and don't be afraid to ask where to find the taxis. One thing that is not changing is the fare to downtown; the flat rate is $30.00. You can call for more information about taxis at 404-762-6087.

Shuttle. You will never want for a shuttle at ATL. Many companies serve the airport and keep rates reasonable. On average a shuttle will cost about $30.00 per person to drop you off downtown. The good deal comes when you buy round-trip, so ask the company about specials. Contact Airport Metro Shuttle: 404-766-6666; Atlanta Superior Shuttle: 770-457-4794; or Gwinnett Airport Shuttle: 770-638-0666.

Limo/sedan. More than two hundred limo companies serve ATL. However, all arrangements must be made in advance. One of these companies is Air Drop, which can be reached at 404-444-9539 or www.air-drop-limo-svc.com.

Rental car. All of the big guys have counters inside the airport terminal. The local companies are located off-site.

Amtrak. Atlanta is part of only one line in the Amtrak system. If you live along the Crescent, which runs from New Orleans to New York City, you should consider a leisurely train trip to town.

Getting Around

The Metropolitan Atlanta Rapid Transit Authority (MARTA) offers an alternative to fighting the traffic congestion around Atlanta. There is a MARTA station in the Hartsfield-Jackson Airport close to the baggage claim area. Visitor passes, available for about $12.00, are good for unlimited system-wide traveling. You can get more information, including a system map, at www.itsmarta.com. You can also call 404-848-5000 to speak to a customer information operator.

Attractions

Visiting Atlanta is like witnessing the birthplace of much of American culture. Coca-Cola, CNN, Martin Luther King, Jr., and more got their start here.

MARTIN LUTHER KING JR. NATIONAL HISTORIC SITE

450 Auburn Avenue NE | 404-331-5190 | www.nps.gov/malu | Hours: daily, winter, 9:00 AM to 5:00 PM; daily, summer, 9:00 AM to 6:00 PM; closed Thanksgiving Day, Christmas Day, and New Year's Day

Here's a list of several Martin Luther King Jr.–related attractions. All are located in the same area, and you can easily spend most of a day in the various museums and exhibits.

Martin Luther King Jr. Visitor Center. This is the place to begin your journey through this remarkable man's life and the history of the civil rights movement he led.

Martin Luther King Jr. Birth Home. This unique location in history could also be described as the hottest ticket in town. You can visit the house only on a national park ranger–led tour. And the tours are limited to fifteen people! The first thing you should do when you get to the historic site is to sign up for this tour at the Visitor Center.

Historic Ebenezer Baptist Church. The church is still active, but the services have moved to a new sanctuary across the street. As a result, the historic sanctuary where Martin Luther King Jr. learned to preach is open for the public to tour. On Sundays, visitors are encouraged to attend a service in the new sanctuary, but come early, the place is usually packed.

King Center. The King Center is considered to be a living memorial to Martin Luther King Jr., and in many ways it is, in fact, living. The King Center continues Dr. King's work and remains a focal point for the civil rights movement and the philosophy of nonviolence.

Martin Luther King Jr. Resting Place. Visiting the crypt of Martin Luther King Jr. is a moving experience. Take a moment to reflect on all that has been accomplished in this man's name. If you don't have time to visit any other King sites, a few minutes here can have a tremendous impact.

THE ATLANTA CYCLORAMA AND CIVIL WAR MUSEUM
800 Cherokee Avenue (in Grant Park) | 404-624-1071 |
www.bcaatlanta.com/index.php?pid=81 | Hours: daily, 9:00 AM to 4:30 PM |
Cost: $7.00

Ever wonder what movies were before there were movies? The answer is cyclorama. As a platform rotates, you observe the Civil War Battle of Atlanta as it unfolds on the world's largest oil painting. The history of the painting and its restoration is almost as fascinating as the event it depicts. You also get to visit a Civil War museum with many artifacts from Atlanta's Civil War past.

CNN CENTER AND TOUR
One CNN Center (Marietta Road) | 190 Marietta Street NW | 877-4CNNTOUR
(877-426-6868) | www.cnn.com/tour/atlanta | Hours: daily, 9:00 AM to 5:00 PM;
tour reservations recommended | Cost: $12.00

From a failed real estate concept to the world headquarters of the first twenty-four-hour news network, this building has an interesting, if short, history. The fifty-minute tour will take you behind the scenes at CNN. Visit a replica of the control room, learn how all of that fancy equipment works, and then visit the gift shop and record your own newscast!

JIMMY CARTER LIBRARY AND MUSEUM
441 Freedom Parkway | 404-865-7100 | www.jimmycarterlibrary.gov |
Hours: Monday–Saturday, 9:00 AM to 4:45 PM; Sunday, noon to 4:45 PM |
Cost: $8.00; $6.00 for 60+

Whenever I visit a town with a presidential library, I always put it on my list. I don't pay attention to whether I supported the person or not. There are few places you can wrap yourself up in contemporary history as our collection of presidential libraries and museums. The Carter Museum isn't the grandest of the presidential storehouses, but it does not disappoint. You can see a full-sized replica of the Oval Office as it looked during Carter's term. See gifts given to the Carters by other countries and luminaries. You can also gain a wider perspective of the Carter administration and the way it shaped our country. After the tour, relax in the Japanese Gardens. The cafeteria has above-average fare and isn't a bad place to stop for lunch.

NEW WORLD OF COCA-COLA

121 Baker Street | 404-676-5151 / 404-676-6074 | www.woccatlanta.com | Hours: daily, 9:00 AM to 5:00 PM | Cost: $14.00; $12.00 for 55+

The biggest name ever to come out of Atlanta is Coca-Cola. This super-mega-brand wants to show you just how popular it is with the new World of Coca-Cola. This place isn't for everyone—it can get a little crowded and noisy—but if Coca-Cola has had any sort of impact on your life, you'll probably want to take this trip down memory lane. There are countless Coca-Cola artifacts and memorabilia. There's also a fully operational bottle works to observe. The end of the exhibit features an all-you-can-drink free-for-all of Coca-Cola products from around the world.

GEORGIA AQUARIUM

225 Baker Street | 404-581-4000 | www.georgiaaquarium.org | Hours: vary by season | $23.50; $19.25 55+ (Group Rates)

The Georgia Aquarium, holding a paltry eight million gallons of water, is the largest aquarium in the world. Another point of perspective: it takes more than sixty-one miles of pipes to keep the aquarium's systems operating. That is enough piping to encircle Atlanta on the I-285 loop! More than one hundred thousand animals and creatures call the waters of the aquarium home. Featured exhibits include the world's largest fish, the whale shark, and the Arctic beluga whale. It is best to purchase your tickets online and print them out at home so that you can avoid long lines at the ticket booth. The aquarium is one of Georgia's most popular attractions and can be crowded during peak times.

Shopping

Atlanta is a great place to shop, and one of the best places is Atlantic Station. Atlantic Station has everything you'd expect to find in an upscale megamall and some things you can't find anywhere else in the region, such as Ikea. North Georgia Premium Outlets is a drive outside the city center, but it offers more than 140 name-brand clearance stores. Phipps Plaza and the Mall of Georgia have a wide selection of shops and experiences.

Entertainment

Atlanta has a vibrant and varied performing arts community. There is something to see here every night. Be sure to visit the AtlanTIX booths at Underground Atlanta and Lennox Square. You can get half-price same-day tickets to many of Atlanta's shows!

ALLIANCE THEATRE
1280 Peachtree Street | 404-733-5000 | www.alliancetheatre.org | Show times and prices vary

Alliance Theatre is one of the top regional theater companies in the nation. In fact, it won the highly coveted Regional Theatre Tony Award for 2007. The repertoire is extensive and diverse. In one season you could see a classic like *Glengarry Glen Ross* and the hilarious *Sister Act: The Musical*.

HORIZON THEATRE COMPANY
1083 Austin Avenue NE | 404-584-7450 | www.horizontheatre.com | Show times and prices vary

The Horizon Theatre Company is for those of us who want something decidedly contemporary and possibly risqué. The company presents modern works that often deal with specific hot-button issues in today's society. It's not all serious, though; there are plenty of laughs to be had in some shows.

THE NEW AMERICAN SHAKESPEARE TAVERN

499 Peachtree Street NE | 404-874-5299 | www.shakespearetavern.com |
Show times vary | Cost: $10.00–$20.00, not including dinner

The New American Shakespeare Tavern is Atlanta's favorite spot for dinner and a show. Eating is optional, but they start serving an hour and a half before the show. Get there in plenty of time to eat, because once that curtain goes up, the waiters sit down. The food is nothing to write home about, but it serves its purpose and the shows are usually fun to watch.

ATLANTA OPERA

Cobb Energy Performing Arts Centre | 2800 Cobb Galleria Parkway |
404-881-8801 | www.atlantaopera.org | Show times and prices vary

The Atlanta Opera runs a limited four- or five-show season, but each show promises to be spectacular. Atlanta Opera is opera on a grand scale, and the company regularly presents top names from around the world. By the time this book goes into print, the Opera will have moved into a spectacular new facility built expressly for the company.

FOX THEATRE

660 Peachtree Street NE | 404-881-2100 | www.foxtheatre.org | Show times and prices vary

The Fox Theatre regularly features major, direct-from-Broadway productions. It's also home to the Atlanta Ballet. The historic building itself is a show, and lovers of old buildings will do well to take a peek. There are regular tours for visitors. Call the Fox when you get into town to see what is playing and which days they will give the tour.

Eateries

MARY MAC'S TEA ROOM

224 Ponce de Leon Ave NE | 404-876-1800 | www.marymacs.com | $$

No trip to Atlanta would be complete without a visit to Mary Mac's. This Atlanta institution has been serving home-style southern cooking for more than sixty years. Open every day from 11:00 AM to 9:00 PM so it's easy to find the time for a quick bite.

BACCHANALIA
1198 Howell Mill Rd #100 | 404-365-0410 | www.starprovisions.com | $$$$

Pretty much everyone agrees that Bacchanalia is one of Atlanta's, if not the South's, top restaurants. The innovative and evolving menu is served in multiple courses with prix fixe pricing.

Hotels

HIGHLAND INN
644 North Highland Avenue NE | 404-874-5756 | www.thehighlandinn.com | Economy

The Highland Inn was established in 1927 and still retains the charm of that era. It has shared ups and downs with the neighborhood, but both are in an up-mode now. There are no frills here, just a classic hotel experience in a good location.

OMNI HOTEL AT CNN CENTER
100 CNN Center | 404-659-0000 | Moderate

A pretty good value for the price, the Omni Hotel at CNN Center puts you smack dab in the middle of one of Atlanta's busiest neighborhoods. Don't worry. None of that busyness gets in the way of a good night's sleep. You can walk to several attractions from the Omni, including the World of Coca-Cola.

GLENN HOTEL
110 Marietta Street NW | 404-521-2250 | www.glennhotel.com | Moderate/Luxury

A small boutique hotel nestled in downtown Atlanta, the Glenn Hotel has southern comfort with big city accents. It is within walking distance of several downtown attractions and is big enough to feel safe, but not so big that you get lost on the way to your room.

BOSTON, MASSACHUSETTS

Greater Boston Convention and Visitors Bureau
Two Copley Place, Suite 105
Boston, MA 02116-6501
888-SEE BOSTON [888-733-2678]: fax: 617-424-7664
www.bostonusa.com

Every time I visit Boston I'm drawn to the historic sites. There are few places in the U.S. where you will find such a concentration of objects so important to the foundation of the country. The Revolutionary War started in Boston, and amazingly many of the key sites still exist. Beantown is one of the best-looking 375-year-olds around. And now, with its revolutionary new highway that incorporates a landmark bridge, the city is ready to show off its new face.

Getting There

LOGAN INTERNATIONAL AIRPORT (BOS)

Logan International Airport is the transportation hub of New England. It is a large, modern, and busy airport. Light rail, bus, or subway can take you any direction after you arrive.

Taxi. Depending on where you're staying, taxis can be an expensive proposition. People staying in Boston city center hotels can expect a fare of $20.00–$40.00. The nature of Boston and the New England region surrounding it makes rental cars a good option.

Shuttle. A shuttle will generally be cheaper than a taxi, unless you have one or more friends along. There are a couple of shuttle options, but Easy Transportation, Inc., offers shuttles to Boston hotels for $14.00. You can even get a multiple-person discount! Call for more information at 617-869-7760 or go to www.easytransportationinc.com.

Rental car. You can find the major rental car companies here, but you have to take a free shuttle to the desks. I recommend getting a car because there is just as much to do outside Boston as there is in town. If you do get a car, you *will want* to get the GPS. Boston is an old city with one-way streets and confusing blocks.

Getting Around

Like most of the Northeast, Boston has several public transportation options to get you to various spots in and out of the city. As convenient as this is, the options can make things a little confusing. If you didn't rent a car, pick up a public transit map at the airport.

Subway. The Boston subway works a lot like subways in other major cities. It has a flat fee, no matter where your trip ends. You will ride the Silver Line into town from the airport. If you didn't rent a car, the subway is probably the cheapest and most convenient way to travel. Ask your hotel staff if you have any questions about which trains to take.

Commuter rail. The commuter rail runs from central Boston to various outlying communities. It is a good way to get out of town to visit neighboring cities. However, once you get there, your public transportation options will have significantly dwindled.

Boat. The city of Boston operates a few boat routes that can take considerable time off a traditional land-based trip. There are even a couple from the airport. These go to very specific destinations, and you should know ahead of time if you need to take one.

Attractions

There is plenty to do in Boston. The city is overflowing with history and excitement. There is also a lot to do just outside Boston. I have included a mixture of things in the city and a short drive away. Again, I really encourage you to rent a car (with GPS!) for this adventure.

OLD TOWN TROLLEY TOURS OF BOSTON

Central Wharf and Milk Street | 800-213-2474 | www.trolleytours.com/Boston | Cost: $28.80 (if you purchase online)

Take a tour on the Old Town Trolley, "Boston's best sightseeing tour." You will be entertained by knowledgeable tour guides while you get off and on the eighteen stops at your leisure. Some of Old Town Trolley's stops are exclusive—see the historic North End (Boston's Little Italy), North Station (where you can catch the commuter rail to Salem), Fenway Park, Boston

Convention and Exposition Center, and the Seaport District for the Boston World Trade Center and the Institute of Contemporary Art. Bring your walking shoes so that you can shop and explore each area.

If you prefer something on the spooky side, take a nighttime ghosts and graveyard tour. It is a ninety-minute journey that takes you through some of the same streets once stalked by the Boston Strangler, and the tour includes an exclusive walking tour of two of Boston's oldest burying grounds.

THE FREEDOM TRAIL
617-357-8300 | www.thefreedomtrail.org | Cost: free for a self-guided tour; $12.00 for a guided tour

The Freedom Trail is a Boston must-do. The 2.5-mile walking tour takes you to some of the most significant sites in American history. If you want to do a self-guided tour, you can hop on the route from any point. But I highly recommend a guided tour. The guides are knowledgeable professionals who aim to make your visit to Boston unforgettable. The tours are ninety minutes long and depart from the Visitor Information Center.

Here are some sites along the Freedom Trail:

Historic burial grounds. There are three historic graveyards on the Freedom Trail. Granary Burial Ground, King's Chapel Burial Ground, and Copp's Hill Burial Ground hold the remains of famous Americans. There are headstones as old as the city itself and as fascinating as anything else you'll see in town.

Old North Church. The Old North Church is Boston's oldest religious structure and where the American Revolution began. Visit the building where Paul Revere hung two lanterns and signaled his fellow patriots about the British incursion by sea. The church is still home to an active congregation and offers its own special tours. Go to www.oldnorth.com for more information.

The USS. *Constitution* (*Old Ironsides*). Setting sail in 1797, the USS *Constitution* is the oldest commissioned warship, still afloat, in the world. The vessel was one of the first half-dozen ships built specifically for the U.S. Navy. The navy still mans and maintains *Old Ironsides* to this day. Active duty sailors give free tours.

HYANNIS

This picturesque Cape Cod town is worth the seventy-mile drive from Boston. The atmosphere is relaxed, and the people are friendly. There is something for everyone, from the nautical-minded to the boutique shopper. There are even lively nightspots. Hyannis offers several unique things to do. Keep on the lookout for a good harbor cruise, and check out the scenic train ride (www.capetrain.com). You may also want to catch a fast ferry over to Martha's Vineyard or Nantucket for excellent shopping.

SALEM

Salem is just a short drive north of Boston but contains an entirely different sort of historical flavor. You can also get to Salem via the commuter rail. Salem is, of course, famous for its witch trials, and the legacy is very much alive. There are witch museums and the graves of some of those involved with that dark past. Salem isn't all witches, though; several other museums and attractions make the town worth a visit.

Shopping

The most famous place to shop in town is Faneuil Hall Marketplace. This center in the middle of town has all the common chain stores and a great selection of local wares. For a more upscale, Beverly Hills–style experience, spend some time on Newbury Street. The Shops at Prudential Center are also a good bet for great deals.

Entertainment

There is plenty of modern and engrossing entertainment to cap off a day of historic sightseeing.

THE HUNTINGTON THEATRE COMPANY

264 Huntington Avenue | 617-266-0800 | www.huntingtontheatre.org | Show times and prices vary

The Huntington Theatre Company, one of the country's larger professional houses, presents a wide variety of consistently above-par plays and musicals. You might not always recognize the name of the show, but it's doubtful you'll be able to question its quality.

STONEHAM THEATRE
395 Main Street (Stoneham) | 781-279-2200 | www.stonehamtheatre.org | Show times and prices vary

The Stoneham is another excellent professional company that presents big-name musicals and the occasional quirky show. For those of you who want a sing-along Broadway experience, the Stoneham is your best bet. Even if one of your favorite shows isn't playing, don't let that keep you from experiencing this remarkable troupe.

SYMPHONY HALL
301 Massachusetts Avenue | 617-266-1492 | www.bso.org | Show times and prices vary

Check on the performances at Symphony Hall. This place has the best acoustics in the country! It is home to the famous Boston Pops and the renowned Boston Symphony. The hall is also often used by visiting performers and other talented local groups.

PRO SPORTS
You have plenty of options when it comes to professional sports. There are five major teams in town. The storied Boston Celtics play NBA basketball at the TD Banknorth Garden. The NHL hockey team, Boston Bruins, also plays at the Garden. For baseball you can watch a Red Sox home game at legendary Fenway Park. The NFL's New England Patriots play at Gillette Stadium, which the team shares with the soccer ballers of the New England Revolution.

Eateries

DICK'S LAST RESORT
Faneuil Hall Marketplace–Quincy Market Building | 617-267-8080 | www.boston.dickslastresort.com | $$

Dick's Last Resort is a unique but casual place to eat where the food is good and the waitstaff will keep you on your toes. You never know what to expect next—or what might be written on your hat. Dick's is located in Faneuil Hall and has a varied menu from the Dolly Parton Chikky Breasts to the Livin' Large Lobsta. You will have great fun at Dick's! (Note: this place may be a little on the risqué side for some people.)

UNION OYSTER HOUSE
41 Union Street | 617-227-2750 | $$–$$$

Union Oyster House is a can't-miss historic landmark established in 1826. It's America's oldest restaurant, and it had a rich history even before it was a dining establishment. It is the former place of business of Hopestill Capen, an importer of silks and fancy dress goods. The first stirrings of the Revolution came from the building's upper floor when in 1771 printer Isaiah Thomas published his newspaper *The Massachusetts Spy*—long known as the oldest newspaper in the United States. It was later the head-quarters for the first paymaster of the Continental Army. John F. Kennedy was a regular customer of the Union Oyster House. You can see his booth upstairs where he often enjoyed lobster stew while reading his newspaper. The food and service are wonderful, and you feel that you are dining in a place that was once a part of history. Bring your appetite because the portions are hearty.

THE PALM
200 Dartmouth Street (inside the Westin Hotel) | 617-867-9292 |
www.thepalm.com | $$$–$$$$

The Palm is an upscale restaurant located in the Westin Hotel. The service is as impeccable as the food. Celebrities frequent the Palm because of its fine dining, casual setting, and accommodating service. Each of the Palm's walls is decorated with caricatures of local notables and national celebrities. At the Boston Palm restaurant, you will find a menu of wonderful salads, fresh, premium fish, prime-aged steaks and chops, Italian specialties, and vegetables served family style.

SEAPORT HOTEL

One Seaport Lane | 1-877-Seaport [877-732-7678] | www.seaportboston.com | Moderate

This is my favorite hotel in Boston. It has 426 luxurious guest rooms that combine exceptional views and tasteful decor with the latest technology. The property really turns most of what we think about big hotels on its head. The Seaport is a service-inclusive hotel; you have no need to worry about tipping when hailing a cab or having your luggage delivered. This takes away the hassle from traveling so you can start relaxing. Seaportal is a new in-room interactive Web portal that provides guests with access to e-mail and the Internet. "Print Me" service allows guests to print documents twenty-four hours a day and retrieve them in the business center. There is a full range of services for the business traveler as well, such as A/V setup and staffing, and preparations for meetings (e.g., making tent cards and name tags).

Seaport has an indoor lap pool with underwater music and panoramic views, a fully outfitted fitness room with personal trainers, a complimentary juice bar, steam rooms, and full-service pampering, such as facials, massages, and manicures. In addition, the hotel offers bicycles for sightseeing and complimentary harbor cruises on Sunday morning. The Seaport Hotel designates four allergy-friendly rooms for those suffering from allergies or respiratory illnesses.

BULFINCH HOTEL

107 Merrimac Street | 877-267-1776 | www.bulfinchhotel.com | Luxury

This charming hotel in Boston's West End is located in the historic Bulfinch Triangle District. The motto is "There's nothing square about us." The hotel is triangular-shaped with eighty guest rooms and junior suites. It is part of the Choice Privileges rewards program and is just minutes from Logan Airport. The Bulfinch has all the modern conveniences, such as a twenty-four-hour fitness facility, complimentary high-speed Internet access, room service, and many other amenities. The rooms are cozy and comfortable. Many area attractions are within walking distance, including Quincy Market and the Freedom Trail. They opened a wonderful new tapas bar in 2007—the Flat Iron Tapas Bar and Lounge. The atmosphere is casual, and the dishes I sampled were superb. For dessert, you must try the fried dough fritters served churro-style with a hot Valrhona chocolate. The Flat Iron also has a very good breakfast buffet if you would like to eat before you leave the hotel.

JURYS BOSTON HOTEL

350 Stuart Street | 617-266-7200 | www.jurysdoyle.com/boston-hotel | Luxury

I'll be honest and let you know that I have never stayed here, but I've heard nothing but raves from my friends who have. This hotel is one of a pair of the Irish Jurys chain in the United States. It is the epitome of elegance and service. Just like many of Boston's historic buildings, the structure housing the hotel has its own interesting history. It was originally the headquarters for the Boston police. Don't let the old building fool you, though. The hotel itself is pretty new and contains all the amenities you'd expect from a modern luxury property.

BRANSON, MISSOURI

Branson/Lakes Area Chamber of Commerce/CVB
P.O. Box 1897
Branson, MO 65615
800-296-0463
www.explorebranson.com

Branson is an entertainment oasis in the Ozark Mountains. I know some of you girls are thinking, *Branson? Uhhh? You've got to be kidding!* Well, you just hold your horses. There is a lot of fun to be had in Branson. It is a great place for a long weekend or fall getaway. This quaint little town of seven thousand people attracts more than seven million visitors each year. It's home to big-name entertainers who present everything from country music to comedy and magic acts in more than one hundred live shows daily. Branson is surrounded by three pristine lakes in the scenic, wooded mountainous region of southern Missouri.

Getting There

An easy drive from St. Louis (230 miles), Kansas City (220 miles), Tulsa (220 miles), or Memphis (300 miles), Branson can provide accessible shopping and entertainment without ever having to get on a plane.

SPRINGFIELD/BRANSON NATIONAL AIRPORT (SGF)

Springfield/Branson National Airport (SGF) www.sgf-branson-airport.com is located in Springfield, Missouri, about forty-five miles north of Branson. SGF is a self-proclaimed "hassle-free" airport served by several regional air carriers providing nonstop service to and from twelve destinations, including Atlanta, Chicago, Cincinnati, Dallas/Fort Worth, Denver, Las Vegas, Memphis, Minneapolis, St. Louis, Tampa, and Orlando.

Taxi. Taxi service is limited, but is available once you get into Branson. Call 417-862-5511.

Shuttle. A few shuttle companies will arrange to pick you up on your schedule, but rates will vary. TriLake Shuttle offers scheduled service to Branson at $79.00 for one to two people. You can also try Springfield Limo and Shuttle Service (417-831-2096). I strongly recommend that you just rent a car and drive yourself. That way if you want to get out of town to surrounding attractions, you won't have to pay for another shuttle or depend on the hotel's transportation.

Rental car. Here is your best bet. Alamo, Avis, Budget, Enterprise, Hertz, National, and Thrifty serve the Springfield/Branson National Airport. Get directions and a map, and enjoy the beautiful drive in the Ozarks.

Getting Around

Branson is definitely a "bring your own" transportation city. I typically drive to Branson, but if you fly in, renting a car will be your best bet. There are some private transporation services available, and you should check with your hotel to see which are the most economical travel options for you. Public transportation is minimal.

Attractions

Branson has loads of entertainment. Most theaters present shows in the evenings as well as matinees. On Sundays, many offer morning church services and revival meetings.

SILVER DOLLAR CITY
399 Indian Point Road | 417-336-7100 | www.silverdollarcity.com | Cost: $46.00

Silver Dollar City puts the *theme* back into theme park. It is an 1880s-style village with shops, craftsmen, shows, and rides. Silver Dollar City is consistently ranked among the country's top amusement parks. Included with park admission is a one-hour guided tour of Marvel Cave, the park's original attraction. The tour is slightly strenuous and has some uneven surfaces, so keep that in mind before going. Even if you don't visit Marvel Cave or like rides, there is still plenty to keep you busy. The themed areas are well done and the shows of very high quality.

TITANIC
3235 76 Country Boulevard & Hwy 165 | 800-381-7670 | www.titanicbranson.com | Cost: $20.00

So, where would you find a giant replica of the *Titanic* that contained a museum and allowed you to enter through an iceberg? In Branson of course! This museum bills itself as the world's largest museum attraction. I am not sure exactly what that means, but it is big. Don't worry about not being able to find it; it's the only large ship on Highway 76. The attraction includes a full-scale replica of the grand staircase and different classes of sleeping cabins. You can also stand on the bridge and listen to commands from the captain. If you feel so inclined, you can shovel coal into the furnace.

Shopping

Hands down the best place for upscale shopping in Branson is Branson Landing. The modern center has a little bit of everything and is far from a small town shopping mall. Here you will find Ann Taylor, C. J. Banks, J. Jill,

Chico, and more! Branson is also home to three outlet malls. The Tanger is located on West Highway 76, the Factory Merchants Mall is on Pat Nash Drive, and the Shoppes at Branson Meadows is located on Gretna Road.

Entertainment

Don't let Branson's somewhat obscure location in the Ozark Mountains fool you. This is what makes Branson a favorite. It was once known as the city where country music stars went to "retire," but nowadays it is home to big-dollar entertainment of all genres.

JIM STAFFORD

3440 West 76 Country Boulevard | 417-335-8080 | www.jimstafford.com | Cost: $35.00

Musical funnyman Jim Stafford has presented one of the most popular shows in Branson for more than seventeen years. His theater is a neon-covered palace of laughs. The show features some of Jim's hits such as "Cow Patti" and "Spider and Snakes" along with patriotic songs and a variety of other music. The Jim Stafford show is classic Branson—and in a good way.

DICK CLARK'S AMERICAN BANDSTAND THEATER

1600 West Highway 76 | 417-332-1960 | www.dickclarksabbranson.com | Cost: varies

Dick Clark's American Bandstand Theater brings you a rotating schedule of hit makers of the 1950s and 1960s. Permanent residents include Bill Medley, Paul Revere and the Raiders, Fabian, and Bobby Vee. The Comets, Peggy March, and Johnny Preston also appear regularly.

ANDY WILLIAMS

2500 West Highway 76 | 417-334-4500 | www.andywilliams.com | Cost: $30.00–$50.00

The King of Entertainment himself has a theater here in Branson. Andy Williams will entertain you with countless standards that he has made famous. He also asks other famous stars to sing on stage with him. Be sure to visit the Web site to see if he will be performing while you are in town and who will be on stage with him!

YAKOV SMIRNOFF

470 State Highway 248 | 866-55-YAKOV [866-559-2568] | www.yakov.com |
Cost: $33.00

Yakov Smirnoff will have you laughing until you can't say, "What a country!" The famous ex-Russian and now proud U.S. citizen is known for his take on the culture clash between his new home and his native land. The show is full of laughs, Russian dancers, and Yakov-isms.

SHOJI TABUCHI

3260 Shepherd of the Hills Expressway | 417-334-7469 | www.shoji.com |
Cost: $38.00–$42.00

When famed violinist Shoji Tabuchi built his theater in Branson, he set a whole new standard. Now, don't think me crazy, but when you go to Branson, you have to visit the Shoji Tabuchi Theatre bathrooms. I am serious. Do it. The show is good too and features Shoji with his wife and daughter. You will see that involving the whole family in a show has become a Branson tradition.

Eateries

CAKES & CREAMS DESSERT PARLOR

2805 West 76 Country Boulevard | 417-334-4929 | Dessert | $

Everyone with a sweet tooth, young and old, should stop at least once at Cakes & Creams. This is the sugariest and tastiest shop in town. The top-quality sweets here include all types and tastes.

BRANSON CAFÉ

120 West Main Street | 417-334-3021 | $–$$

When it comes to down-home cooking, the Branson Café is as good as it gets. This eatery is a great excuse to wander into Branson's downtown. After you eat, have a look around!

DOLLY PARTON'S DIXIE STAMPEDE
1525 West Highway 76 | 800-520-5544 | www.dixiestampede.com | $$$$

Dixie Stampede is dinner and a show. It is also one of the best deals in town. Choose your side, North or South, and see what Ms. Parton has in store. Dolly is not in the show, but her touches are everywhere.

Hotels

THE BRADFORD INN
3590 State Highway 265 | 800-357-1466 | www.bradfordhouse.us | Moderate

The Bradford Inn may be small as hotels go, but it is big on views. Its great location and quaint charm make it the perfect place to relax and enjoy your vacation.

SAVANNAH HOUSE HOTEL
165 Expressway Lane | 417-336-3132 | www.savannahhousebranson.com | Moderate

The Savannah House is a three-story luxury hotel with an amazing perch overlooking the Ozarks. It's a great value, and you'll leave feeling that you should have paid more.

HILTON PROMENADE AT BRANSON LANDING
3 Branson Landing | 417-336-5500 | www.promenadebransonlanding.hilton.com | Moderate/Luxury

Some say this is the best hotel in town. I would have a hard time arguing. There is a lot to do in the Branson Landing area. You might just forget to go to a show!

CHICAGO, ILLINOIS

Chicago Convention and Tourism Bureau
2301 S. Lake Shore Drive
Chicago, IL 60616
877-CHICAGO (877-244-2246)
www.choosechicago.com

Welcome to the Windy City, ladies! Chicago—it's my kind of town. Thanks to a couple of the busiest airports in the country, Chicago is just a short direct flight from almost any regional airport in the United States. Chicago also provides a little something for everyone: plenty of shopping, great museums, renowned performing arts groups, and second-to-none attractions. I've been to Chicago about a dozen times, and I still find great things to do. Chicago has been called the birthplace of modern architecture, and I highly recommend it for any building buffs out there. I would be remiss if I didn't mention another thing Chicago is famous for, and that's the good food. From its celebrated deep-dish pizza to four-star, five-course prix fixe, no one will go hungry here. Oh, and there is a reason they call it the Windy City. Be careful wearing your hats outside!

Getting There

Two major area airports serve Chicago. The city is also the Midwest hub of the Amtrak passenger train service. The cost of travel varies with the mode of travel. A train can take longer but can sometimes be significantly cheaper than a plane (and more fun for groups!). Don't forget to look for deals at both airports when booking your travel. The price difference between airports can be surprising. (Note: Find up-to-date information on Chicago airports at www.flychicago.com.)

O'HARE INTERNATIONAL AIRPORT (ORD)

You have plenty of options to get from O'Hare to the city core. Although it is only seventeen miles from downtown, the time it will take you to get from airport to downtown (and back) will depend on your mode of transportation.

    Taxi. Taking a cab to downtown will cost you between $35.00 and

$40.00. For wheelchair accessible vehicles, call United Dispatch at 800-281-4466.

Shuttle. It will cost about half as much as a taxi to take a shuttle. Remember, the shuttle charges per person while cabs are per ride. If you're in a small group, splitting the cab fare may save you money and time. Airport Express offers daily, door-to-door service to and from O'Hare Airport and the rest of the city. The hours of operation are 6:00 AM to 11:30 PM, departing approximately every five to ten minutes outside the baggage claim areas of the lower level of the domestic and international terminals. The fare to the city is approximately $25.00. Lift-equipped vehicles are available on request for passengers with disabilities. Advance notice is strongly urged. You can make reservations with Airport Express by calling 888-284-3826. You can also visit the Web site at www.airportexpress.com and print out a $2.00-off coupon.

The "L." Chicago's transit rail system is known as the "L" (after the elevated portions of track). While the "L" may be storied, it is not always convenient. I have found it somewhat difficult to navigate (both physically and mentally), and the stops are often blocks from where you want to go. However, it is by far the cheapest way to get downtown. All you'll need is a couple of bucks. You can buy "L" passes at the airport station. The "L" is part of the Chicago Transit Authority (CTA), and its passes are good on CTA buses.

Rental car. All of the major companies have desks at O'Hare. Rental car agencies are located on the lower level near the baggage claim areas of terminals 1, 2, and 3. Please look for signs and courtesy phones. If you're stuck in terminal 5, you can contact the rental agencies via the courtesy phones on the lower level. Many rental car agencies also offer courtesy buses to various automobile pickup and drop-off areas. The rental car buses can be crowded at times, and dragging your luggage on and off can be a bit of a hassle. When I fly to O'Hare with several in my company, I usually take the rental car bus to pick up the rental car while someone else gets my bags (and hers) from the baggage claim. I then circle back around and pick up everyone.

MIDWAY INTERNATIONAL AIRPORT (MDW)

Midway may be the smaller of Chicago's airports, but it's just as easy (and often cheaper) to get downtown from there. It is ten miles from the city core, and you'll have the option of taxi, shuttle, the "L," or car.

Taxi. Catch taxis at the lower-level curbside. Expect to pay $25.00–$30.00 to get downtown. For wheelchair accessible vehicles, please call United Dispatch at 800-281-4466.

Shuttle. As usual a shuttle is cheaper than a taxi for one person, but sharing a taxi with others in your group might make it the cheaper solution. Airport Express offers shuttle service to most places in the city. It will cost you about $19.00 to get from Midway to a downtown location. Just make sure you arrive between 6:00 AM and 11:30 PM. Does someone in your party use a wheelchair? Don't worry. Airport Express offers accessible vehicles. However, it is suggested that you arrange for them in advance. You can contact Airport Express at 800-654-7871 or via the Web site: www.airportexpress.com (where you can also print off a $2.00 coupon!).

The "L." If you've read the O'Hare section, you know I am not the biggest fan of Chicago's mass transit system. Nevertheless, I understand that some of you ladies don't feel that you've been to a city until you've gotten down and dirty with the locals on the trains. The "L" is the rail portion of the Chicago Transit Authority (CTA) system. You will need to walk through the parking garage to the Transit Center to catch an Orange Line train. It will take you about thirty minutes to get downtown.

Rental car. All the big guys have desks at Midway. Rental car agencies are located inside the terminal, lower level arrivals. Rental car pickup and drop-off points are located on level 2 of the parking garage.

AMTRAK

Afraid to fly? Hate to drive? Want to make getting there part of the fun? Then the train may be for you! Chicago is a hub in the Amtrak passenger rail systems, which means you can get there via rail from many parts of the country. A train can be a lot of fun for a group, but check out Amtrak.com for everything that is involved.

Getting Around

If your visit to Chicago keeps you focused on the Magnificent Mile of downtown, a car is not really necessary. Taxis are readily available as well as the Chicago CTA system. Visitor passes, which cost $5.00 per day, are good on all CTA buses and trains. You can call the Chicago Transit Authority at

888-YOUR-CTA (888-968-7282) or go to www.transitchicago.com for more information. You may also want to try the Chicago Trolley Company. You can buy an all-day pass for $25.00 or $22.50 online. They provide a hop-on/hop-off service that includes stops at the Sears Tower, the theater district, the Navy Pier, and many places in between. You can get more information at www.coachusa.com/chicagotrolley.

Attractions

There is plenty to do in Chicago. Here are just a *few* ideas:

SEARS TOWER

233 South Wacker Drive | 312-875-9447 | www.theskydeck.com |
Hours: May–September, 10:00 AM to 10:00 PM, last arrival 30 minutes prior to closing; October–April, 10:00 AM to 8:00 PM, last arrival 30 minutes prior to closing

I thought I would start with the obvious, and what is more obvious than one of the tallest buildings in the Western Hemisphere? Of course there is more to do in this tower than walk through the doors. You can pay $12.00 to ride some of the world's fastest elevators up 1,353 feet to the world-famous Skydeck. Trust me, on a clear day there is no better way to see Chicago (and Michigan, Indiana, and Wisconsin). The Skydeck is enclosed, so don't worry about rainy weather (though it will limit your view). This is a great first stop on your tour of the city. The exhibits in the Skydeck point out many of Chicago's attractions and can orient you to the urban landscape. The entire Sears Tower experience is handicapped accessible, and you can even buy discounted tickets for large groups.

THE FIELD MUSEUM

1400 South Lake Shore Drive | 312-922-9410 (information) | www.fieldmuseum.com |
Hours: daily, 9:00 AM to 5:00 PM

Ready for a trip to Africa? How about a visit to ancient Egypt? Do these things and more at Chicago's Field Museum of Natural History. An old gal named Sue is the museum's premier attraction. What makes Sue so special? Well, she is the largest and most complete *Tyranosaurus Rex* skeleton ever found. Also at the Field you can look at some of the best bling that nature has to offer. A visit to the Grainger Hall of Gems is a must for any lady with a taste for large, shiny rocks. On top of these things there are hundreds of exhibits of nature, science, and human culture. The Field Museum is a Chicago must-see. The museum is handicapped accessible and offers discounts for groups of fifteen or more.

NAVY PIER
600 East Grand Avenue | 312-595-7437 | www.navypier.com | Cost: *free!*

Navy Pier is Chicago's most visited tourist attraction, so there is no denying that it has some appeal. However, I just don't get it. If you're in the mood for a half-baked carnival with an interesting, if gimmicky, mix of shopping combined with throngs of unruly children and frazzled adults, then Navy Pier is for you! Many people have had a great time at the Pier, but I honestly think there are much better ways to spend time in this grand city.

FRANK LLOYD WRIGHT HOME AND STUDIO
951 Chicago Avenue | 708-848-1976 | www.wrightplus.org | Hours: Monday–Friday, 11:00 AM, 1:00 PM, 3:00 PM; Saturday– Sunday, 11:00 AM to 3:30 PM (tours every 20 minutes) | Cost: $12.00

Frank Lloyd Wright's legacy in American architecture is unmatched. Here we have a unique chance to peek at the first twenty years of Wright's illustrious career. The home and studio served as a laboratory for Wright and showcase many of the design signatures that punctuate his work around the world. The neighborhood also holds many Wright homes, and you can take guided and self-guided tours that feature these gems. It is important to arrive early for the guided tour of the home and studio. The tour is popular and often sells out. Groups of ten or more need to make reservations.

MUSEUM OF CONTEMPORARY ART
220 East Chicago Avenue | 312-280-2660 | www.mcachicago.org | Hours: Tuesday, 10:00 AM to 8:00 PM; Wednesday–Sunday, 10:00 AM to 5:00 PM | Cost: *free!*

The Museum of Contemporary Art (MCA) is your door into the strange world of modern art. I am not kidding, ladies, this place is a trip. MCA is constantly rotating parts of its collections and changing special exhibits. You never know what you're going to see on the wall . . . or floor . . . or ceiling. This place is truly remarkable. Depending on what's on display, the pieces here can reaffirm your love of art while inspiring debate on what art is. MCA offers free guided tours at different times during the day. If you are part of a group, MCA is happy to help you arrange your own special tour of the museum.

SHEDD AQUARIUM
1200 South Lake Shore Drive | 312-939-2438 | www.sheddaquarium.com | Hours: Memorial Day–Labor Day, daily, 9:00 AM to 6:00 PM, Thursday, until 10:00 PM; Labor Day–Memorial Day, weekdays, 9:00 AM to 5:00 PM, weekends, 9:00 AM to 6:00 PM | $8.00 Aquarium only; $27.50 Premium pass

No trip to Chicago would be complete without a visit to the world-famous John G. Shedd Aquarium. In this one location you can witness one of the most diverse collections of aquatic life outside the ocean. There are almost 22,000 animals from more than 1,500 species held in the Shedd's tanks. The Shedd has been around for some time, but the last couple of decades have seen two major additions. The Oceanarium, opened in 1991, is the world's largest indoor aquatic mammal habitat. The 2003 addition of the Wild Reef features examples of reef life from more than 25 different interconnected habitats. Like most of Chicago's attractions, the Shedd Aquarium is handicapped accessible and offers special deals to large groups.

Shopping

There is no better place to shop than Chicago's Magnificent Mile. More than 450 retail outlets surround this one-mile stretch of Michigan Avenue. Believe me when I say there is a little bit of everything. Let me list a few for you: Tiffany & Co.; Nordstrom; Saks; Cartier; Lord & Taylor; Armani; Chanel; and Hermes. There are a good number of more affordable choices, but there isn't room to list them all here. The Magnificent Mile is a pretty walk in its own right. It is lined by mature trees and well maintained. Some say it's one of the best places to see the seasons in Chicago.

If you're looking for someplace eclectic to shop, head to Wicker Park. It features amazing boutiques such as Pump (shoes) and Paper Doll (unique gifts). A fascinating antiques shop, Modern Times, is also in the neighborhood.

Entertainment

You will never be wanting for something to do in the Windy City. Chicago is home to renowned musicians, improv groups, and theater companies.

LYRIC OPERA OF CHICAGO

20 North Wacker Drive | Northwest corner of Madison and Wacker | www.lyric-opera.org | 312-332-2244

If you visit the city between September and March, do what you can to buy tickets for the Lyric Opera (getting in can be tough because many of their shows sell out). The Lyric is regarded as the number two house in American opera and has a sterling reputation around the world. Some of opera's biggest stars and brightest new arrivals can be seen on the Lyric stage. There is little that can compare to the experience of watching a grand opera unfold. Oh, and don't worry about the language barrier. All operas have English translations projected for the benefit of the audience. The Lyric also provides listening aids for those of us with worn-out ears.

STEPPENWOLF THEATRE COMPANY

1650 North Halsted Street | 312-335-1650 | www.steppenwolf.org

Steppenwolf is a world-famous theater company that has grown many renowned actors and actresses. Joan Allen, John Malkovich, Gary Sinese, Gary Cole, and Laurie Metcalf cut their teeth on Steppenwolf scenery. Often one of the bigger names will come back to join the rest of the ensemble for a production. Check the schedule to see what and who are playing. But even if you don't recognize the actors' names, a show at Steppenwolf is guaranteed to be a memorable performance.

CHICAGO SHAKESPEARE THEATER

800 East Grand Avenue (on Navy Pier) | 312-595-5600 | www.chicagoshakes.com

Chicago Shakespeare Theater (CST) has a fabulous new home on Navy Pier, and the company presents an impressive repertoire of classical theater. One highlight of shows at CST is the small performing venues that put you close to the performance. If you drive to the show, be sure to mention to the Navy Pier parking guard that you are there to see Shakespeare. The theater has dedicated parking that is available even when the garage is posted as "full." CST is completely accessible and even offers large-print programs and listening aids. Groups can be accommodated, and CST can help you arrange a special evening around the show.

SECOND CITY

1616 North Wells | 312-664-4032 | www.secondcity.com

John Belushi, Gilda Radner, Bill Murray, and Mike Myers. What do these comedians have in common? They all got their start at Chicago's Second City comedy troupe. Known for cutting-edge comedy and biting satire, Second City is a national cultural institution. The troupe pretty much invented modern comedic improv. There is no better way to end a long day of shopping and touristing than to sit down and laugh your pants off. Second City has a great dinner and show program for groups, and the theaters are accessible.

Eateries

LUTZ CAFÉ & PASTRY SHOP

2458 West Montrose Avenue | 773-478-7785 | www.lutzcafe.com | Dessert | $

Lutz Café & Pastry Shop has been a Chicago tradition since 1948. Pastries, tortes, marzipan, and more are available here. Pick up a box for your group, or dine in at the garden. When you stop by Lutz's, you are getting a true taste of the sweet side of Chicago. The Café also offers scones and tea during the afternoon.

SWEET MANDY B'S

1208 West Webster Avenue | 773-244-1174 |
www.centerstage.net/restaurants/sweet-mandy-bs.html | Dessert | $

I am afraid there is no place sweeter than Sweet Mandy B's. This place is a good old down-to-earth bake shop with more treats than can be named. There is usually a crowd here, but one bite of a Mandy B's Whoopie Pie is well worth any wait.

CAFÉ BA-BA-REEBA!

2024 North Halsted | 773-935-5000 | www.cafebabareeba.com | $–$$

Café Ba-Ba-Reeba! is the best place for tapas in town. Sit down and enjoy fine Spanish cuisine surrounded by lively Mediterranean decor and a laid-back atmosphere. This one-of-a-kind restaurant (except for the new sister restaurant in Las Vegas) has been serving Chicago for years.

JOE'S BE-BOP CAFÉ

At Navy Pier | 312-595-JAZZ (312-595-5299) | www.joesbebop.com | $–$$

Have you found yourself being overrun by school groups on Navy Pier? Then slip into Joe's Be-Bop Café. This fun joint will relieve your hunger and soothe your ears with the smooth sounds of jazz. Joe's also has great options for groups.

TASTE OF CHICAGO

Grant Park | www.tasteofchicago.us | $–$$

If you're in town around the Fourth of July holiday, then you have to take advantage of the annual Taste of Chicago Festival. This is your chance to sample more than seventy of Chicago's best establishments in one park. This ten-day event attracts more than 3.5 million people a year.

UNO CHICAGO GRILL

Various Locations | 1-866-600-8667 | www.unos.com | $–$$

Looking for the original Chicago deep-dish pizza? All you need to do is look around for your nearest Pizzeria Uno or Uno Chicago Grille. Members of your party not big pizza buffs? Don't worry. Uno has greatly broadened the menu over the years to include a wide variety of entrées and flavors. There is something for everyone.

Hotels

HOTEL ALLEGRO

171 West Randolph Street | 312-236-0123 | www.allegrochicago.com | Moderate

This sister to the Burnham is known for treating all of its guests like stars. While it is a little less expensive than some other luxury hotels, you will still get the full-service treatment. Allegro is located next to the Palace Theatre, which hosts Broadway-style shows (sometimes before they get to Broadway!). If you can't afford the Drake or Burnham but still want four-star treatment, book a room at Hotel Allegro.

HOTEL BURNHAM

1 West Washington | 312-782-1111 | www.burnhamhotel.com | Luxury

The boutique luxury Hotel Burnham is located inside a masterpiece of a building. The 110-year-old glass-and-steel Reliance Building was transformed into a hotel in 1999. Ever since then, Hotel Burnham (named after the building's architect) has been getting rave reviews. While the hotel naturally attracts architecture buffs, it also provides top-line services.

THE DRAKE

140 East Walton Place | 312-787-2200 | www.thedrakehotel.com | Luxury

If you want to find the jewel in Chicago's hotel crown, then this Hilton property is your place. The Drake has hosted countless celebrities and high-ranking government officials since it opened in 1920. In fact, Queen Elizabeth has spent a night or two here. The Drake experience is second to none in terms of luxury.

DENVER, COLORADO

Denver Metro Convention and Visitors Bureau
1555 California Street, Suite 300
Denver, CO 80202
303-892-1112
800-233-6837
www.denver.org

There is a reason they call Denver the Mile High City. I am not sure what it is, but I know there must be a reason. Just kidding. It has that name because it is way up in the mountains. There is a step on the capitol building that stands precisely one mile above sea level. Besides its height claim, Denver is a sports haven with plenty of culture and Western hospitality mixed in. This sprawling destination extends from the Rocky Mountain foothills and attracts both tourists and business travelers.

Getting There

DENVER INTERNATIONAL AIRPORT (DIA)

The people of Denver are very proud of their airport—and they should be. DIA is a modern, well-equipped, and spotlessly maintained facility. Flying in or out of DIA will be one of your more comfortable airport experiences.

Taxi. After you pick up your bags, head outside to the ground transportation pickup area. Go to Island 1. Here a cab dispatcher will help you get a taxi. A ride downtown will take between thirty-five and forty-five minutes and costs about $45.00.

Shuttle. Several shuttle companies offer rides from DIA into downtown Denver. (There are also shuttles in every other direction.) SuperShuttle operates here and charges $19.00 each way to downtown hotels. You may want to do some research and see if any of the other companies have specials. Denver's public transportation agency offers SkyRide, which will bus you directly into downtown for $8.00. However, once you get off the bus at the designated spot, you are on your own to reach your hotel.

Limo/sedan. Access Shuttle and Limousine offers private sedan service from DIA to downtown Denver for $55.00. You can take two more people with you for that rate in a four-door sedan. For four to seven passengers the fee is $75.00 (total, not per person).

Rental car. The rental car desks are conveniently located in the terminal. DIA has bucked the trend of moving car agencies off-site. However, once you check in, you will have to ride a shuttle to your vehicle.

Getting Around

Downtown Denver is a pedestrian-friendly area and very walkable. Should you get tired or end up carrying lots of packages, free shuttle buses travel up and down the Sixteenth Street Mall. They stop on every corner. If you plan to venture outside Denver or want to explore in the mountains, a rental car may be your best bet. Of course, there is always your friendly taxi service.

Attractions

Denver is known as the culture capital of the West. Several institutions help it back up this claim.

DENVER ART MUSEUM
100 West Fourteenth Avenue Parkway | 720-865-5000 |
www.denverartmuseum.org | Hours: daily, 10:00 AM to 5:00 PM; closed Monday |
Cost: $13.00; $10.00 for 65+

The Denver Art Museum has a couple of very impressive collections. First, its Native American collection of art and artifacts is one of the most complete in the world. This collection contains more than 18,000 objects and spans two millennia. It also has an unrivaled set of Western art. Artists in this collection include Frederic Remington, John Mix Stanley, George Catlin, and Charles Deas. Although not as exceptional as the Native American and Western holdings, several notable pieces of European and classical American art have space in the museum.

U.S. MINT

320 West Colfax Avenue | 303-405-4757 | www.usmint.gov | Hours: Monday–Friday, 8:00 AM to 3:30 PM | Cost: *free!*

The Denver Mint is one of only two places in the world where you can watch the production of U.S. coins. The mint has been around since 1863 but didn't start stamping coins until 1906. Before that, its work was with the gold that miners found in the hills. You won't get to stamp any coins yourself, but you will get an overhead view of the process. The gift shop offers nifty items. The U.S. Mint is the best free show in town, and reservations are recommended.

THE MOLLY BROWN HOUSE MUSEUM

1340 Pennsylvania Street | 303-832-4092 | www.mollybrown.org | Hours: vary by season | Cost: $6.50; $5.00 for 65+

Molly Brown was a Red Hatter long before there were red hats. Her unique style and matter-of-fact approach to life have been immortalized countless times on stage and screen. The house, just like its previous owner, has proven itself to be unsinkable. The grand estate was built by silver barons and was at one time the Colorado Governor's Mansion. It has also seen many years of decline and decay and was once threatened with demolition. Luckily a smart group of Denverites saw the historic significance of the house, bought it, and restored it to its Victorian splendor. You'll want to put a tour on your to-do list.

DENVER BOTANIC GARDENS

1005 York Street | 720-865-3500 | www.botanicgardens.org | Hours: vary by season | Cost: $13.00; $10.00 for 65+

You wouldn't think you'd find a thousand tropical plants in Denver, but you'd be wrong. The warm-weather plants are housed inside the signature Boettcher Memorial Tropical Conservatory. However, the bulk of the gardens are located outside, grouped in different categories. It doesn't matter whether you are a plant addict or just have a passing interest in greenery, the Denver Botanic Gardens are a top-notch attraction.

COLORADO STATE CAPITOL
200 East Colfax | 303-866-2604 | Cost: *free*!

The Colorado State Capitol is a sight to see both inside and out. The building is a smaller replica of the Capitol Building in Washington, D.C., but is just as impressive. There are free guided tours and a self-guided brochure tour. You will be much better served by booking a guided tour in advance. The guided tours are much more informative than the brochures and well worth the planning ahead. I warn you that even though everything at the Capitol is free, finding and paying for parking can be a pain.

Shopping

Indoors and outdoors Denver has great shopping. One place that you will want to stop is the massive upscale Cherry Creek Shopping Center. Here you will find a wide variety of stores such as Anthropologie, Tiffany & Co., Brooks Brothers, Neiman Marcus, and Nordstrom. For more local flare and a nice outdoor shopping experience, try Cherry Creek North. It has a varied selection of fashion boutiques, art galleries, and spas.

Entertainment

OPERA COLORADO
695 South Colorado Boulevard | 303-778-1500 | www.operacolorado.org | Show times and prices vary

Opera Colorado is the premier producer of grand opera in the Rocky Mountain region. The company often brings in internationally recognized superstars to headline its productions. You will want to check the Opera Colorado Web site to see if a show or special event is running during your stay.

THE DENVER CENTER FOR THE PERFORMING ARTS
1101 Thirteenth Street | 303-893-4000 | www.denvercenter.org

The Denver Center for the Performing Arts is the cultural focal point of the state of Colorado. A wide variety of performances takes place in this venue. The Denver Center Theatre Company is the largest professional repertory company in the state. The company has consistently presented exceptional productions and rules the Denver theatrical scene. The Denver Center also brings in major out-of-town productions, including the occasional pre-Broadway run.

BASEBALL

The Colorado Rockies, a major-league baseball team, play at Coors Field. The Denver weather makes catching a game a lot more comfortable than in some other cities, and the number of games on the schedule gives you plenty of opportunity to see the boys in action. Go to www.coloradorockies.com for more information.

BASKETBALL

The NBA's Denver Nuggets play at the Pepsi Center. It's a nice venue, and basketball is a quick-paced, exciting game to watch. For more information, go to www.nba.com/nuggets.

FOOTBALL

The Broncos are the NFL franchise in town. They play at Invesco Field at Mile High. To find out if they are playing while you are in town, go to www.denverbroncos.com.

SOCCER

Rounding out the big four is Denver's professional soccer team, the Colorado Rapids. They currently share Invesco Field with the Broncos but will be getting a state-of-the-art soccer-specific facility soon. Check the Web site: www.coloradorapids.com.

Eateries

BROTHER'S BBQ

568 Washington Street | 720-570-4227 | www.brothers-bbq.com | $

When I am in Denver and get a hankerin' for good old southern BBQ,

I head to Brother's. This place is the real deal. You can't fake good BBQ with a southern girl like me doing the tasting.

TAQUERIA PATZCUARO
2616 West Thirty-second Avenue | 303-455-4389 | $

If you want good Mexican food in Denver, there is only one place to go. Taqueria Patzcuaro serves up tacos, enchiladas, and fajitas better than anywhere else in town. The relaxed and fun atmosphere makes Taqueria Patzcuaro a great place for groups.

VESTA DIPPING GRILL
1822 Blake Street | 303-296-1970 | www.vestagrill.com | $$

Vesta is a cool, modern joint with a variety of interesting choices on the menu. Things are a little upscale here but still pretty relaxed. This is the place to take a group if you're looking for something nicer than the taco place but still not stuffy.

PALACE ARMS
321 Seventeenth Street (inside Brown Palace Hotel) | 303-297-3111 |
www.brownpalace.com/dining/palace_arms.cfm | $$$–$$$$

The Palace Arms elevates the notion of a hotel restaurant to a whole new level. The establishment offers an extensive menu of various styles. The steak is heavenly and the service top-notch.

Hotels

MAGNOLIA HOTEL DENVER
818 Seventeenth Street | 303-607-9000 | www.magnoliahoteldenver.com |
Moderate

The Magnolia is a nice boutique hotel at a nice price. Its central location makes it convenient to many attractions, and with its unique style it stands out among its competition.

HOTEL MONACO DENVER

1717 Champa Street at Seventeenth | 303-296-1717 | www.monaco-denver.com | Moderate/Luxury

The Hotel Monaco is a modern hotel in the classic style. The building is historic, but the features are state of the art. This is also considered one of Denver's most pet-friendly hotels!

THE BROWN PALACE HOTEL

321 Seventeenth Street | 303-297-3111 | www.brownpalace.com | Luxury

The Brown Palace has hosted presidents, royals, and celebrities throughout its 115-year history. The hotel radiates classical elegance. The staff do everything you would expect them to do and then some. Plus, you can always go downstairs for afternoon tea.

LAS VEGAS, NEVADA

Las Vegas Convention and Visitors Authority
3150 Paradise Road
Las Vegas, NV 89109
877-VISITLV (877-847-4858)
www.lvcva.com

Las Vegas has been called many things during its day, and some of those things were nicer than others. I don't have a problem with Vegas. In fact, I love the place. The mob influence is gone, and the sleaze isn't as pervasive as you might think. The city is full of lights, shows, shops, and the nicest casinos in the country. No matter what tribal gaming house you visit, none of them compare to the monsters on the Strip. Even if you don't gamble, you'll still find plenty to do in the place they call Sin City! No wonder they say, "What happens in Vegas, stays in Vegas!"

Las Vegas is an easy drive from some Southern California population centers, but the vast majority of people arrive by plane. However, if you're planning a long road-trip vacation, some winding around Arizona, New Mexico, and surrounding states on your way to Las Vegas can introduce you to wonderful scenery.

MCCARRAN INTERNATIONAL AIRPORT (LAS)

One thing that will most likely make McCarran different from your airport of departure: the 1,300 slot machines placed throughout the terminals. McCarran has been on the leading edge of airport technology for several decades. Its many firsts include electronic baggage tracking and multiple airline check-in kiosks. They are good at what they do at McCarran, but every year passenger volume increases and the airport is running out of room. Clark County has plans to have a relief airport up and running in 2017.

Taxi. Taxi cabs line up outside the baggage claim area. There are about a half-dozen companies that serve the airport. There is a $1.20 surcharge for all fares originating from the airport. It should cost you $10.00–$20.00 to get up to five people to most Strip hotels. Hotels located in the Fremont Street area may cost a few bucks over $20.00. You'll want to have cash on hand because very few Las Vegas cabbies take credit cards.

Shuttle. Several shuttle companies serve McCarran, and at least one of them operates twenty-four hours a day. Because of the multiple company competition and the relative closeness of the Strip to the airport, the shuttle rates are reasonable. The average is $5.00 to $6.00 for Strip hotels, and $7.00 for downtown hotels. In what is a rare occurrence, shuttle tickets for two people might actually be cheaper than a cab! Research one shuttle company at www.shuttlelasvegas.com.

Limo/sedan. Many of the same companies that offer shuttle service also hire out limos and sedans. The cars are almost always charged at an hourly rate instead of a flat destination rate. Prepare to pay $30.00–$50.00 per hour based on options and the company.

Rental car. McCarran Airport has a rental car center that is not connected to the terminal. You will need to catch the free twenty-four-hour shuttle to the off-site location. The shuttle runs every fifteen minutes out-side the baggage claim area at doors 10 and 11. All of the major rental car companies have desks at the rental car center. Las Vegas is one of those great cities where a rental car is definitely optional. Between public trans-portation and pedestrian walkways, you can get just about anywhere you want to go.

Getting Around

Las Vegas is flat, and many attractions are close together. Many people choose to walk to the various places. The city has been designed for walk-ing with raised walks and pedestrian paths, bridges, and people movers. Please note that the people movers usually move people *into* the casinos; you are on your own getting out. There may be a lot of casinos on the Strip, but there are only a few owners. Some neighboring and corporate-related casi-nos may have a direct connection of some sort. You can also use the public Las Vegas Monorail to go from one end of the Strip to the other. The per-ride pass is steep at $5.00, so if you plan on using the Monorail a lot, you should probably get a day pass or multipass.

Attractions

Las Vegas is crammed full of incredible, one-of-a-kind attractions. This city was built for tourists. Now how am I supposed to sum up all of that in a tiny little section? I'll do my best. I suggest the free attractions: Bellagio foun-tains, Treasure Island Pirate Ship Show, Mirage volcano, and more. Don't forget about nearby Hoover Dam.

FREMONT STREET EXPERIENCE
Fremont Street

So what would happen if you took what was once the most famous street in town, closed it to car traffic, and built a giant awning full of twinkling lights? You'd get the Fremont Street Experience, of course! Fremont Street was the original Vegas drag, and many famous "classic" casinos can be found there. Unfortunately as the giant resorts on the Strip became popular,

Fremont Street became neglected. A little over a decade ago casino owners decided to revive Fremont into a pedestrian mall with is own super light show. Millions of LED lights combine with state-of-the-art sound to create shows for the VivaVision canopy. Stroll along the revived Fremont Street, and get a feel for old-school Vegas while enjoying modern technology.

THE ATOMIC TESTING MUSEUM

755 East Flamingo Road | 702-794-5161 | www.atomictestingmuseum.org | Hours: Monday–Saturday, 9:00 AM to 5:00 PM; Sunday, 1:00 to 5:00 PM | Cost: $12.00; $9.00 for 65+

The Atomic Testing Museum is perhaps the most historically fascinating attraction in Vegas. During the days of aboveground nuclear testing, Las Vegas was a favorite spot to view the distant explosions (and feel them nine minutes later). As a result, the atomic bomb and Las Vegas have an inseparable relationship. The museum includes artifacts from the Atomic Age, a history of nuclear development, hundreds of pieces of equipment used during the testing process, and several multimedia experiences. A museum on this topic could be very dry and boring, but the design and presentation at the Atomic Testing Museum will keep even the most ADD of us interested.

STRATOSPHERE TOWER

2000 Las Vegas Boulevard South | 800-998-6937 | www.stratospherehotel.com | Cost: $10.95 tower admission; rides additional

The Stratosphere Tower may be a touch out of the way from some of the other attractions, but you will not regret the detour. First off, you shouldn't have any trouble finding the place. Just look for the tallest free-standing observation tower in the United States. After you purchase your ticket and ride the elevator up, you will be treated to the best view in Vegas. If you are an adventurous sort, go ahead and purchase ride tickets. The three thrill rides on top of the Stratosphere are worth the price of admission. There are also several good places to eat and shop attached to the Stratosphere. You can see a little farther during the day, but I still recommend the night view.

MADAME TUSSAUD'S LAS VEGAS

3355 Las Vegas Boulevard South (in the Venetian) | 702-862-7800 |
www.madametussaudslv.com | Hours and prices vary

Where else can you go and have your picture taken with your arm around Brad Pitt? How about performing with the Blue Man Group? Ever wanted to play with the hair of Captain Jack Sparrow or putt a few rounds with Tiger Woods? You can do all these things and more at Madame Tussaud's. I know that wax museums are a dime a dozen and the quality can be lacking, but Madame Tussaud's can be trusted for lifelike and touchable re-creations of your favorite (and least favorite) celebrities.

THE LIBERACE MUSEUM

1775 East Tropicana Avenue | 702-798-5595 | www.liberace.org | Hours: closed
Monday | Cost: $12.50; $8.50 for 65+

Would Las Vegas be the same place today if Mr. Showmanship had never taken the place by storm? Come one, come all and see the glitz, glamour, and shininess of all that was Liberace. From giant jewels to rare furs (before the fur taboo) to gilded pianos, they are all here in their gaudy grandness. Liberace was larger than life, and it is fitting that the museum dedicated to him has embraced the same persona. Nothing is toned down or tempered here. It's a couple of miles off the Strip so you might choose to take a cab. If you do take a cab, keep the receipt because the museum will give you $2.00 off admission.

MGM GRAND LION HABITAT

Inside the MGM Grand | 702-891-7777 | Hours: daily, 11:00 AM to 10:00 PM |
Cost: *free*!

This place might be best to visit after 9:00 PM when all the little kiddies are getting ready for bed (or at least they should be). Here you can get an up-close view (as close as you really would want anyway) of several wild cats. The lions take turns going on display; you never know which ones you are going to see. The MGM's trainers keep the lions active so that you may avoid the sleeping lion show that often happens at zoos.

GUGGENHEIM HERMITAGE MUSEUM

At the Venetian | 702-414-2440 | www.guggenheimlasvegas.org | Hours: vary | Cost: $19.50; $15.00 for seniors

The Guggenheim Hermitage is Las Vegas's best "traditional" museum. There are no wax figures, flashy outfits, or Geiger counters. The museum rotates works from its two partners: the Guggenheim in New York City and the Hermitage in Saint Petersburg, Russia. With two of the world's top museums supplying art, every exhibition features unique and priceless works of art from well-known masters. All lovers of art and even those with a passing appreciation need to make the time to visit the Guggenheim Hermitage.

Shopping

Shopping seems to have taken over as Las Vegas's second pastime—after gambling. Almost every new casino/resort development includes a shopping center with exclusive and high-end stores. You can find seriously satisfying shopping anywhere on the Strip. The most famous shops are at Caesars Palace, but there are plenty of other wonderful shopping opportunities. Just be careful because you'll probably end up spending all of that money you won on the slots.

Entertainment

I thought attractions were tough to write about, but I forgot there are twice as many entertainment options. There is no way to nail down what Las Vegas entertainment is. The traditional stage shows with flamingo dancers can still be found, but you also have superstar singers in custom-built theaters, world-famous magicians, and Broadway spectaculars. Here is just a taste of what you can do in Vegas:

BLUE MAN GROUP

At the Venetian | 800-258-3626 | www.blueman.com | Cost: $70.00–$120.00

The Blue Man Group may be from New York, but they have become synonymous with Las Vegas. An eccentric performing arts group unlike anything else, the men pull you into the performance with addictive beats on strange objects. The Blue Man show is interactive and enjoyable for people of all ages.

PHANTOM

At the Venetian | 702-414-9000 | www.phantomlasvegas.com | Cost: $55.00–$150.00

One of Las Vegas's newest spectacles, this revised edition of Andrew Lloyd Webber's *Phantom of the Opera* promises to amaze. The show has been Vegasized, which means the epic length has been trimmed down, and the sets, costumes, and effects have been ramped up. Some people may argue the artistic merit of such an adaptation, but they cannot deny the technical achievement of this new show.

PENN AND TELLER

At the Rio | 888-746-7784 | www.pennandteller.com | Cost: $75.00–$85.00

I have to admit that this is my favorite permanent show in Las Vegas. Penn and Teller use their trademark brand of straightforward humor and command of magic to teach you some of the industry's secrets. But don't worry; they don't spoil the magic. If anything, they enhance your enjoyment of the practice. Penn and Teller don't make you pay an arm and a leg for a good seat either.

DANNY GANS

At the Mirage | 800-963-9634 | www.dannygans.com | Cost: $100.00

Who the heck is Danny Gans? That's what I kept asking myself after a girlfriend raved to me about him. She told me he sold out a big theater at the Mirage every night, but somehow I had never heard of him. Well, I went to his show, and I know who he is now. Danny Gans is the man of a thousand voices. He does dead-on impressions of dozens of celebrities and has become one of the hottest tickets in town. His show has less glitz than other Vegas showcases, but the content is king and Gans is a funny man.

LANCE BURTON: MASTER MAGICIAN

At the Monte Carlo | 702-730-7160 | www.lanceburton.com | Cost: $66.00–$77.00

I first saw Lance Burton years ago when he played at the Hacienda Hotel and Casino. His show was great then, and it has gotten better. Since the departure of legends Siegfried and Roy, Lance Burton is the undisputed king of Las Vegas magic. Simply put, if you are going to a magic show in Vegas, this is the one to see.

Eateries

Once upon a time, Las Vegas was known as the home of super-cheap, super-large buffets. There are still some of them around, but the trend of late has been upscale eating at upscale prices. You can find, and pay for, some of the country's top restaurants in Las Vegas resorts. Of course, just like the rest of the town the Las Vegas culinary scene is in a constant state of renovation. In addition to the picks listed below, keep an ear to the ground for the latest hot spot.

CHOCOLATE SWAN
In Mandalay Bay | 702-632-9366 | www.chocolateswan.com | | Dessert | $–$$

Continuing the tradition of great food at Mandalay Bay, the Chocolate Swan brings you the best sweets in Vegas. The hand-crafted sweets are to die for and can make a nice evening out a great one.

BORDER GRILL
In Mandalay Bay | 702-632-7403 | www.bordergrill.com | $$–$$$

This is the place for Mexican food in Las Vegas. Stop looking; you won't find any better. The Border Grill is also a nice place to eat without having to mortgage your house, and the Mandalay Bay resort is a pleasant place to hang out.

LUXOR'S PHARAOH'S PHEAST BUFFET
In the Luxor | 702-262-4000 | $$–$$$

Pharaoh's Pheast Buffet is the best buffet value on the Strip. The selection is massive, and there is enough variety to satisfy the pickiest eaters among us. The whole place is decked out like an archaeological dig, and the lines can be very long.

PICASSO
In the Bellagio | 877-234-6358 | $$$

The name says it all. Here you dine in the presence of several of the master artist's works. Often labeled as the best restaurant in town, the Picasso features award-winning cuisine and an innovative design.

AUREOLE
In Mandalay Bay | 702-632-7777 | www.aureolelv.com | $$$–$$$$

Best known for its forty-foot wine tower and flying wine stewards, the Las Vegas Aureole captures the city's spirit beautifully. This high-ender has a delicious prix fixe menu and a wonderful sense of customer service. Reservations are required.

WYNN LAS VEGAS BUFFET
In the Wynn | 702-770-3463 | $$$–$$$$

This is the best buffet in town, but you pay for what you get. The Wynn Buffet is full of an amazing variety of scrumptious food. If you are a buffet addict, then you have to splurge and give this one a shot. Let me warn you: Be prepared to be disappointed at every other buffet for the rest of your life.

Hotels

There is no shortage of amazing places to stay in Las Vegas. Several of the largest hotels in the world are located just blocks from one another. It's hard to go wrong when you are staying at one of the big guys on the Strip. These places serve thousands of people nightly, and most run smoothly. There are better deals to be had downtown, but you pretty much get what you pay for.

HARRAH'S LAS VEGAS

3475 Las Vegas Blvd South | 702-369-5000 | www.harrahs.com | Moderate

Home of the Red Hat Society Musical "Hats," this luxurious hotel is at the heart of the strip! With seven restaurants, a luxurios spa and its new up-graded rooms Harrah's is your one-stop shop for fun and entertainment!

MANDALAY BAY

3950 Las Vegas Blvd South | 877-632-7800 | www.mandalaybay.com | Moderate

Located on the south end of the Strip, Mandalay Bay is almost across the street from McCarran International. Don't let that bother you, though. This is no airport. The Mandalay features several favorite places to eat and has spectacular views on the upper floors. If you're in the mood for something chic, you can check into the hotel at Mandalay Bay, which offers a modern, minimalist atmosphere.

NEW YORK, NEW YORK

3790 Las Vegas Blvd. South | 702-740-6969 | www.nynyhotelcasino.com | Moderate

The New York, New York is the king super-theme hotel. In some places it is almost as if they disassembled part of the city and reassembled it in Las Vegas. Its location on the Strip is prime, and the rates are great. It isn't really a resort-type place, but it typifies what many people think of when they think of Las Vegas.

BELLAGIO

3600 Las Vegas Blvd South | 702-693-7111 | www.bellagio.com | Luxury

The Bellagio ushered in a new era of super-super resorts. With a $1 bil-lion price tag you would expect this place to have everything. And it does. It is a spectacular facility that will leave you in awe. The rooms are large and comfortable, and the amenities are plentiful.

FOUR SEASONS HOTEL LAS VEGAS

3960 Las Vegas Blvd South | Las Vegas, NV 89119 | 702-632-5000 |
www.fourseasons.com | Luxury

The Four Seasons is on the top five floors of Mandalay Bay, but other
than that, they are completely separate facilities. Separate entrances, separate staff, separate check, and separate class. Mandalay is a nice place, but
the Four Seasons takes luxury to a whole new level. This is the best of the
best in Las Vegas hotels.

THE MIRAGE

3400 Las Vegas Blvd South | 702-791-7111 | www.mirage.com | Luxury

The Mirage was the first of the resort-style hotels that have sprung up and
down the Strip. Despite being the matriarch, the Mirage still has plenty to
give. The interior is amazing with its giant aquariums and rain forest. Its location on the Strip keeps you close to other superhotels and attractions.

THE VENETIAN

3355 Las Vegas Blvd, South | 877-883-6423 | www.venetian.com | Luxury

I saved the best for last. The Venetian is my favorite Las Vegas hotel. In
some ways it's a cross between New York, New York and the Bellagio. Let
me explain. Like the New York, New York, the Venetian is heavily themed
and highly detailed. On the Bellagio side, it is a paragon of luxury and
exactly what a super-resort should be. If it's in your budget, I highly recommend a room at the Venetian (the rooms are *really* big!).

LOS ANGELES, CALIFORNIA

Los Angeles Visitors and Convention Center
333 South Hope Street, 18th floor
Los Angeles, CA 90071
213-624-7300
800-228-2452
www.lacvb.com

You will find almost too much to do in LA. It is one of the most entertaining cities in the world. From the glamour of Beverly Hills to the sights of Venice Beach and Malibu, neighborhoods feel like a mini-theme park. You have Disney, Universal Studios, museums, the Walk of Fame, and more. The weather surrounding the City of Angels is simply wonderful. Summer can be hot, but not too hot, and the rest of the year the weather stays very pleasant. Whether you drive down Sunset Boulevard or you shop on Rodeo Drive, you're in for quite an adventure in Southern California.

Getting There

LOS ANGELES INTERNATIONAL AIRPORT (LAX)

Los Angeles International is one of the iconic airports of the world. It is seen in countless movies and television shows. LA works hard to keep its modern city image, and this effort shows at LAX.

Taxi. A taxi is an easy catch. Just walk outside and follow the signs. Because LA is so spread out, fares can vary greatly based on your hotel's location. You will be given a list of fares before you depart the airport, so you will have an idea about how much your ride will cost.

Shuttle. You have two shuttle company choices. Prime Time Shuttle and SuperShuttle offer service to surrounding areas. Your fare is based on your destination. You can get quotes and make reservations at www.primetimeshuttle.com and www.supershuttle.com.

Rental car. More than forty rental car companies serve the airport, but you will want to sign up with one of the majors because they are allowed to run shuttles. If you are comfortable driving in a big city, you will want to rent a car. LA is spread out, and there might be a sight or two not convenient to the Metro. GPS would be a good thing to have.

Metro. Free shuttle buses run between LAX and the nearest Metro Rail station. Take the "G" shuttle. If you have any questions, just ask the driver.

JOHN WAYNE AIRPORT (SNA)

John Wayne Airport is a good bit smaller than LAX and therefore somewhat easier to maneuver. Moreover, it's always fun to say, "I flew into John Wayne."

Taxi. Taxis are plentiful at SNA, but your fare will depend on where you are going. If you are worried about the cost, ask someone at your hotel when you make your reservation. He should be able to give you an estimate.

Shuttle. More than a dozen shuttle companies serve SNA. Some go everywhere while others have dedicated zones. Do some research, depending on where you are going. I always ask at my hotel for suggestions. SuperShuttle provides service here.

Rental car. This might be SNA's top advantage over LAX. The rental cars are walk-out, which means no shuttle! You should find your favorite rental company here.

Getting Around

Getting around LA can be a chore. The city is spread out, and nothing is close to anything else. LA has a nice Metro Rail system, but it doesn't go everywhere, as the systems do in New York or D.C. If you don't rent a car, you are most likely going to spend some time in a taxi. If you're not sure about the distance to your destination, ask your driver for an estimate. That's a lot better than being surprised by a huge fare.

Attractions

Whatever you want to do, chances are, you can do it in LA.

UNIVERSAL STUDIOS–HOLLYWOOD

100 Universal City Plaza | 800-864-8377 | www.universalstudioshollywood.com | Hours and prices vary by season

People have said that Universal Studios is a grown-up Disneyland. You can take the legendary backlot tour and see sets and soundstages. The park also has several state-of-the-art rides based on various movies. There are plenty of photo ops to be had here. Actors dressed as famous movie characters roam the lot, and movie props and set pieces are scattered throughout the park.

J. PAUL GETTY CENTER
1200 Getty Center Drive, Suite 100 | 310-440-7300 | www.getty.edu | Cost: free admission; $8.00 for parking

The Getty is one of the great museums of the world, and it's free! The center has an impressive display of sculptures, antiquities, and paintings spanning centuries of the human experience. The Getty is a must-see in LA. You take a tram from parking to the building.

HOLLYWOOD WALK OF FAME
Hollywood Boulevard at Vine Street | 323-469-8311 | www.hollywoodchamber.net/icons

I don't know why seeing your favorite stars' names in the sidewalk is so exciting, but it is. The Walk of Fame is a great free attraction. Finding the names of stars can be a challenge, though. I recommend that you visit the Web site and look up your famed one's location before you begin your journey.

HOLLYWOOD FOREVER CEMETERY
6000 Santa Monica Boulevard | 323-469-1181 | www.hollywoodforever.com | Cost: *free!*

Where do Mel Blanc, Cecil B. DeMille, Douglas Fairbanks Jr., Peter Lorre, Jayne Mansfield, Fay Wray, and Rudolph Valentino hang out? Hollywood Forever Cemetery is the final resting place for more stars than anywhere else. The former Hollywood Memorial Park has been rescued from years of neglect and restored to its former glory. Beyond the famous graves, this place has many interesting headstones and a nice view.

Shopping

You've got plenty of options for shopping in LA, but I prefer to stick to the clusters of high-quality shops. There is no need to venture to Beverly Hills, but you can if you want. Maybe your budget can afford the famed Rodeo Drive. The sixteen-square-block area is known as Beverly Hills' Golden Triangle. Universal City Walk has a decent selection of unique stores, but nothing terribly spectacular. I spend most of my time at the Hollywood and Highland Center. It's in the middle of everything and includes Louis Vuitton, Swarovski, and Celebrities. Third Street Promenade in Santa Monica offers trendy chain stores and boutiques.

Entertainment

Los Angeles is the entertainment capital of the world. There is bound to be something to do.

UNIVERSAL CITY WALK

Universal Center Drive | 818-622-4455 | www.citywalkhollywood.com

The City Walk entertainment district is adjacent to Universal Studios (plan a day at the studios and an evening on the Walk!). Everything you need for a good time is on the City Walk: food, fun, and shopping. Best of all, there is no admission fee!

THE GROUNDLINGS

7307 Melrose Avenue | 323-934-4747 | www.groundlings.com | Show times and prices vary

The Groundlings is California's top improv comedy troupe. Members provide nightly laughs and never do the same show twice. Many former Groundlings have been seen on nationally televised sketch shows and sitcoms.

CENTER THEATRE GROUP

213-628-2772 | www.centertheatregroup.com

LA isn't known for its theater, but it has at least one world-class company. The Center Theatre Group is a legendary troupe that runs three major houses. The group produces a wide variety of new and classic works and a mixture of musicals and straight plays.

Eateries

COMPARTE'S CHOCOLATIER

912 South Barrington Avenue | 310-826-3380 | www.compartes.com | Dessert | $

Very few places in the world have better chocolate than Comparte's. I am serious; this place is to die for. Go there!

PHILIPPE THE ORIGINAL

1001 North Alameda Street | 213-628-3781 | www.philippes.com | $

Philippe's is the place to go when you want quick, good, and cheap eats. The sandwiches at this classic deli-style eatery are second to none.

CA'BREA RESTAURANT

346 South La Brea | 323-938-2863 | www.cabrearestaurant.com | $$

Ca'Brea Restaurant features great Italian food at an even better price. The chef-owner is world-renowned, and his expertise comes across in the dishes served at his restaurant.

WATER GRILL

544 South Grand | 213-891-0900 | www.watergrill.com | $$$

The service might not always be up to par, but the meal is something not to pass up. The Water Grill has the best seafood in town.

HOLLYWOOD CELEBRITY HOTEL

1775 Orchid Avenue | 323-850-6464 | www.hotelcelebrity.com | Moderate

The Hollywood Celebrity is a cute Art Deco hotel right in the center of the action. The rooms are unique, and you don't feel that you are staying in just any other hotel. Stay at the Hollywood, and you'll feel that you are in Hollywood.

MAGIC CASTLE HOTEL

7025 Franklin Avenue | 323-851-0800 | www.magiccastlehotel.com | Moderate

The Magic Castle Hotel is one-of-a-kind. The rooms are large, and the service exemplary. By having a room here, you also have access to the exclusive Magic Castle Club, a favorite spot of many celebrities.

SOFITEL LOS ANGELES

8555 Beverly Boulevard | 310-278-5444 | www.sofitel.com | Luxury

The Sofitel rests between downtown LA and Beverly Hills. It brings a new standard of European luxury to the Hollywood area. The rooms are spectacular, and the service is exceptional.

LOUISVILLE, KENTUCKY

Louisville Visitor and Convention Bureau
One Riverfront Plaza
401 West Main Street, Suite 2300
Louisville, KY 40202
800-626-5646
www.gotolouisville.com

No matter whether you pronounce it "Loo-uh-vul" or "Looey-ville," you'll be in for a fun surprise! A major river, three interstates, and the Kentucky Derby have made Louisville a city like no other in Kentucky. This place is more than just horses, though; it's also culture, baseball bats, and boxing legends. A tip: Don't leave Louisville until you've purchased some Happy Balls from Old Louisville Candy Factory (the airport gift shop should have them).

Getting There

LOUISVILLE INTERNATIONAL AIRPORT (SDF)

Louisville International Airport (www.flylouisville.com) is nice, but it's nothing to write home about. The biggest issue may be the long walks to and from some gates. If you have mobility issues, be sure to request a wheelchair.

Taxi. Taxis will be available in the arrivals area. A cab to downtown costs $18.00–$20.00.

Shuttle. Louisville doesn't have a general shuttle service, but many hotels offer their own. Check ahead with your hotel, and ask if they have one and if it costs anything to ride.

Rental car. This is your best option in Louisville. Public transportation is complicated and time-consuming. Plus, taxi service can be limited. All of the big boys have desks here. If you reserve in advance, you shouldn't have trouble getting a car. Don't forget the GPS!

Getting Around

Louisville's Transit Authority of River City (TARC) provides city bus service for the Louisville area. The fare is $1.50. There is also a downtown trolley that provides service in the downtown Louisville area for $0.50 a ride. TARC customer service is 502-585-1234 or www.ridetarc.org. Taxis are also available. However, if you really want to be mobile in Louisville, I recommend renting a car.

Attractions

The styles and subjects of Louisville's major attractions are more diverse than you'll find in most places. Many cities have an underlying theme that runs throughout, but not Louisville.

CHURCHILL DOWNS

700 Central Avenue | 502-636-4400 | www.churchilldowns.com | Cost: $2.00 for the track; $10.00 for the track tour and museum

Louisville's top attraction also happens to be the most famous racetrack in the world. Churchill Downs has hosted the fabled Kentucky Derby for more than one hundred thirty years. Horse racing enthusiasts from around the world flock to the city just to spend time at this legendary facility. Even if horse racing is not your thing, I strongly encourage you to visit the museum. I thought I would prefer the action of a race, but the stories told at the museum are as compelling as anything you'll see on the track.

LOUISVILLE SLUGGER MUSEUM

800 West Main Street | 877-7-SLUGGER 877-775-8443 | www.sluggermuseum.org | Hours: vary by season | Cost: $9.00; $8.00 for 65+

I know a baseball bat museum isn't on the top of many "must visit" lists, but this place is definitely worth the price and time. The admission price gets you a tour of the factory, access to the museum (which has interesting artifacts), and a miniature souvenir bat. You can even have a bat personalized with your or your favorite sports fan's name. Place the order before you tour, and it will be ready by the time you leave. Be sure to pack your free souvenir bat in your checked luggage. TSA will not let you carry it in the cabin. If you purchase a larger bat, you'll probably want to ship it home.

MUHAMMAD ALI CENTER

144 North Sixth Street | 502-584-9254 | www.alicenter.org | Hours: Monday–Saturday, 9:30 AM to 5:00 PM; Sunday, 12:00 to 5:00 PM | Cost: $9.00; $8.00 for 65+

The Muhammad Ali Center rounds out Louisville's trifecta of attractions with surprising universal appeal. The center is a powerhouse of multimedia exhibits and interactive opportunities for education and growth. You don't have to be a boxing addict to enjoy and respect the life of Ali.

BELLE OF LOUISVILLE AND SPIRIT OF JEFFERSON

401 West River Road | 502-574-2992 | www.belleoflouisville.org |
Departure times and fares vary

The *Belle of Louisville* is the oldest steam-powered paddlewheel boat on the Mississippi. You can do an excursion only or bundle a meal with your trip. This boat is a lot of fun, and there is even a special Red Hat cruise! You can also sail on the younger *Spirit of Jefferson*, but I prefer the *Belle* and her calliope.

Shopping

Louisville isn't a shopping mecca, but there are still plenty of shops to keep you busy. Several malls in the area offer the standard retailers: Chico's, Dillard's, Gap, and J. C. Penney. For antiques, art galleries, and unique boutiques, try the Bardstown Road and Frankfort Avenue areas. If you have a car, you have a couple of choices for outlet centers, including Edinburgh Premium Outlets and Factory Stores of America about forty miles away.

MALL ST. MATTHEWS

5000 Shelbyville Road | www.mallstmatthews.com

This mall serves the affluent east side of the Louisville metro area. There are thirty stores, including Ann Taylor Loft, Aveda, bebe, Pottery Barn, and my favorite, J. Jill.

OXMOOR CENTER

7900 Shelbyville Road | www.oxmoorcenter.com

Sears, Macy's, Dick's Sporting Goods, Ann Taylor, and more can be found here.

JEFFERSON MALL

4801 Outer Loop | Louisville, KY 40219 | www.shopjefferson-mall.com

Shop at Old Navy, Dakota Watch Company, American Eagle, and more.

FOURTH STREET LIVE
Downtown | www.4thstlive.com

Fourth Street Live is an entertainment district of sorts that always has something happening. The city permits patrons to carry alcoholic beverages from venue to venue, which creates an open and fun street party atmosphere. You don't have to make any particular plans to head down to Fourth Street and have some fun!

DERBY DINNER PLAYHOUSE
525 Marriott Drive | Clarksville, IN | 812-288-8281 | www.derbydinner.com | Hours: daily, 6:00 PM

The Derby is this region's only professional dinner theater, and I mean professional. Even though some may consider dinner theater a lesser art form, the shows at the Derby are topnotch. You get your food from a buffet line, but it will be better than most meals you serve yourself. I really enjoy the Derby; it's at the top of my dinner theater list.

ACTORS THEATRE OF LOUISVILLE
316 West Main Street | 502-584-1205 | www.actorstheatre.org | Show times and prices vary

The Actors Theatre is one of the best theater companies in the country. Known for compelling and engrossing performances, the company's shows can sometimes be edgy and may be uncomfortable for the audience. However, they are always high-quality, memorable presentations.

GHOSTS OF OLD LOUISVILLE TOUR
218 West Oak Street | 502-637-2922 | www.ghostsofoldlouisville.com | Hours: Friday, 7:30 PM | Cost: $25.00 (private group tours can be arranged)

Venture into the night on the streets of Old Louisville if you dare! Many older cities have ghost tours, but this is one of the best. You spend part of your time on a minibus where you will witness "ghosts" walking in the night. You may also have a close encounter with one of Louisville's famous "permanent residents." The Ghosts of Old Louisville Tour is ghastly fun.

Eateries

HOMEMADE ICE CREAM & PIE KITCHEN
2525 Bardstown Road | 502-459-8184 | Dessert | $

How can you not love a place called the Homemade Ice Cream & Pie Kitchen? Ask anyone where to get a dessert fix, and she will point you in this direction. There are too many varieties of pastries, pies, and sweets to name here.

GENNY'S DINER
2223 Frankfort Avenue | 502-893-0923 | $

Genny's has the best burger and fries in all of Kentucky. This place is just your basic diner, but the food is bar none. No need to worry about feeling out of place here; the laid-back, relaxed atmosphere welcomes everyone.

JARFI'S BISTRO
501 West Main Street | 502-589-5060 | www.jarfis.com | $$

The locals eat at Jarfi's, so you know it must be good. The quality of food for the price is unmatched anywhere in the city. Jarfi's dishes are fun, yet refined, with a presentation that is as pleasing as the food itself. I can honestly say I had one of the best meals ever at Jarfi's. It is a true delight to experience.

LYNN'S PARADISE CAFÉ
984 Barret Avenue | 502-583-3447 | www.lynnsparadisecafe.com | $$

Whatever you do, when you go to Louisville, go to Lynn's Paradise Café. The pancakes are the best anywhere around. The quirky joint makes breakfast a blast and dinner a delight. From odd things on the wall to the fun-loving staff, you won't want to miss out on any of the Lynn's experience.

THE OAKROOM

500 Fourth Street | 502-585-3200 | www.seelbachhilton.com/hoteldining_
theoakroom.html | $$$

You can search all of Kentucky, but you won't find another five-diamond restaurant. The Oakroom is the king of Kentucky eateries. The chef takes great care to include local ingredients and recipes. Visit the Oakroom and experience true Bluegrass luxury.

Hotels

HOLIDAY INN LOUISVILLE–NORTH

505 Marriott Drive | 812-283-4411 | Moderate (Bargain)

The Holiday Inn–North is conveniently located near the airport, downtown, Churchill Downs, and other attractions. Derby Dinner Playhouse (see "Entertainment") and a water park are located nearby. The number one reason to stay here: a *free* airport shuttle!

GALT HOUSE HOTEL & SUITES

Fourth Street at the River | 140 North Fourth Street | 502-589-5200 | www.galthouse.com | Moderate

The Galt House is the only place downtown to stay on the Ohio River. The river views are wonderful. The double-revolving restaurant is neat.

THE BROWN HOTEL

335 West Broadway | 502-583-1234 | www.brownhotel.com | Luxury

The Brown is a hotel from another era—but in a good way. The lobby is grand, and the rooms remarkable. If you ever wanted to stay in one of the luxurious gems of yesteryear, then book a night at the Brown.

MIAMI, FLORIDA

Greater Miami Convention and Visitors Bureau
701 Brickell Avenue, Suite 2700
Miami, FL 33131
800-933-8448
www.gmvcb.com

Until now, I've never actually gotten to enjoy Miami from a tourist standpoint. Every time I was there I was wearing a suit, panty hose, and heels, and it was *hot!* Sure, it gets hot in Miami, especially during the summer, but there is much more to do in this coastal city besides work! The Miami area has its own culture, architecture, and cuisine. It is one place I have never been able to master navigating, so I strongly suggest that if you rent a car, spring for the GPS route finder. If you're sans wheels, plan on spending lots of time in a cab. There are some places in Miami in which it is better *not* to be lost.

Getting There

Unless you're within driving distance or plan on coming by boat, your best bet for getting to Miami is Miami International Airport. Amtrak also travels to Miami, but it is the end of the line and can be a long trip.

MIAMI INTERNATIONAL AIRPORT (MIA)

The unique transportation needs of this tip of the USA can make getting around complicated. That is why I recommend trying to navigate the Miami–Dade County public transportation system. To get from the airport to your hotel, you should plan on renting a car, taking a shuttle, or getting a cab.

Taxi. You'll be able to get a cab at the arrivals area just outside the baggage claim area. Rides from the airport are charged a flat rate based on the one to which you travel or a metered rate if your destination is outside an outlined zone. Your hotel should be able to tell you the approximate fare. Ask when you make your reservation. Most cab companies have handicapped accessible vehicles. You can request one from the staff person manning the taxi line.

Shuttle. MIA is served exclusively by SuperShuttle. Fares are per person and vary based on your destination. Fees to most destinations range from $15.00 to $25.00. You can make reservations ahead of time by calling 305-871-2000. Be sure to mention mobility concerns when making your reservation.

Rental car. The major rental companies and some locals have desks in the terminal. These are on level 1 in the baggage claim area. You will take a shuttle to the off-site pickup lot. Do not forget to ask for GPS! The GPS system will give you satellite-guided directions and will even make corrections for wrong turns.

AMTRAK
Miami is the last stop on the Silver Service and Palmetto lines. These run up the East Coast. If you do not live in that area of the country, you will have to travel to catch the train. The train station is in the middle of Miami proper, and you will need a cab to reach your hotel.

Getting Around

Renting a car is optional in Miami thanks to the Metrorail elevated rail system that serves downtown Miami and the Metromover that makes a 4.4-mile loop around downtown Miami and the Brickell and Omni business districts. The Metromover is free, and the Metrorail is an economical $1.50 per ride. You can find more information about getting around Miami at www.go.miamidade.gov.

Attractions

Since my work had occupied me on previous visits to Miami, I initially drew a blank when I tried to think of really interesting and fun things to do there. That blank was *very* short-lived. This area is full of unique experiences.

HOLOCAUST MEMORIAL
Meridian Avenue | 305-538-1663 | www.holocaustmmb.org | Hours: daily, 9:00 AM to 9:00 PM | Cost: free

There is no other monument in the world that better captures the human emotion surrounding the Holocaust. The memorial provides stark visuals and encourages introspection. The forty-two-foot centerpiece sculpture is a haunting masterpiece. Do not cheat yourself by making this a drive-by attraction. Stop and take the time to explore the memorial as it was designed. You will leave changed. The memorial is accessible to those with limited mobility.

MUSEUM OF CONTEMPORARY ART

770 Northeast 125th Street | 305-893-6211 | www.mocanomi.org | Hours: Tuesday–Saturday, 11:00 AM to 5:00 PM; Sunday, noon to 5:00 PM | Cost: $5.00 for adult; $3.00 for student or senior

Housed in a facility that is itself a work of art, the Miami Museum of Contemporary Art showcases the best contemporary artists and works. Here you will find creative pieces and emerging art superstars. The Museum of Contemporary Art is famous for its history of spotting the "next hot thing." Cutting-edge art isn't for everyone, but we can all appreciate the work and imagination that go into major pieces. Who knows? The artist of that piece you just saw could be the next Picasso. And to think, "you knew him when." The Miami Museum of Contemporary Art has been designed so that patrons with disabilities can enjoy its exhibits.

BASS MUSEUM OF ART

2121 Park Avenue | 305-673-7530 | www.bassmuseum.org | Hours: Tuesday–Saturday, 10:00 AM to 5:00 PM; Sunday, 11:00 AM to 5:00 PM | Cost: $12.00 for adult; $10.00 for senior; $6.00 for student

The Bass Museum is the premier visual arts center of the Miami area. The collection focuses on European classics but contains a wide range of styles and eras. This city-owned institution also sponsors acclaimed touring exhibitions. On its grounds, the Bass Museum boasts an intriguing selection of modern sculpture. But the true gems are inside. Be sure to view the Rubens masterpiece *The Holy Family*. The facility is completely accessible, and if you've been before but not recently, still take the time to visit. The museum recently completed an expansion that doubled its size.

GOLD COAST RAILROAD MUSEUM

12450 Southwest 152nd Street | 305-253-0063 | www.goldcoast-railroad.org | Hours: Monday–Friday, 10:00 AM to 4:00 PM; Saturday–Sunday, 11:00 AM to 4:00 PM | Cost: $5.00

Who does not love trains? The Gold Coast Railroad Museum is an all too often overlooked Miami destination. Anyone who has even the slightest fondness for the rails will be in heaven here. The collection contains more than forty pieces of historic railroad equipment. They include everything from giant steam engines to the only twentieth-century rail car built exclusively for the use of the U.S. president. The museum also has an extensive model train collection on display. The facility is handicapped accessible.

MIAMI SEAQUARIUM

4400 Rickenbacker Causeway | 305-361-5705 | www.miamiseaquarium.com | Hours: daily, 9:30 AM to 6:00 PM (ticket booth closes at 4:30) | Cost: $31.95 includes all shows; $189.00 for the dolphin experience

The Miami Seaquarium isn't the biggest or newest aquarium out there, but it is still impressive. Here you can see dolphins, a killer whale, and manatees. There is also a 235,000 gallon coral reef aquarium. If you are willing to spend more money, you can sign up for the two-hour dolphin program. You'll learn all about the sea mammal and get up close and personal with one. There are minimal health requirements so visit the Web site or give them a call if you have any questions.

Shopping

Shopping is a favorite pastime in Miami, and there are plenty of options for you. I've narrowed it down to two spots where you can get just about anything. If you prefer super high-scale and luxury shops, then head to the Bal Harbour Shops. This is one of the highest-rated malls in the country. For those of you who want a more "Miami" experience, visit the Lincoln Road Mall. Lincoln Road is a seven-block pedestrian mall with more than four hundred shops, restaurants, and boutiques. A true Miami original, it offers a full range of merchandise, people, and experiences. If shopping is not your game but you enjoy people watching, Lincoln Road is a good place for that.

Entertainment

Miami is famous for its nightlife, and there is plenty to do. Contrary to popular belief, it isn't all about parties. Miami has a very strong theater scene and a well-respected fine arts community. In fact, the proliferation of professional theaters in Miami has made it difficult for me to pick just a couple of examples. There is no excuse for hanging out in your hotel room at night.

TEATRO AVANTE
744 Southwest Eighth Street | 305-445-8877 | www.teatroavante.com | Show times and prices vary

Teatro Avante is a one-of-a-kind Miami institution that should not be missed. The theater company produces both contemporary and classical Spanish language productions. Those of us who don't speak Spanish can take advantage of the English supertitles used for each performance. The company has a strong Cuban influence and is as close to watching theater in Havana as you can get without violating an embargo. The theater is handicapped accessible.

ACTORS' PLAYHOUSE AT THE MIRACLE THEATRE
280 Miracle Mile | 305-444-9293 | www.actorsplayhouse.org | Show times and prices vary

Actors' Playhouse is located in the historic Miracle Theatre, an amazing specimen of the Art Deco architecture for which this region is known. Actors' Playhouse is a premier regional theater company and employs more Equity actors (meaning, they belong to the professional acting union) than any other South Florida company. The Playhouse features a wide variety of mainstream productions and sometimes has more than one show playing at once. Take a chance and visit the beautiful Miracle Theatre. You will not be disappointed. The historic Miracle Theatre is completely handicapped accessible.

GABLE STAGE AT THE BILTMORE

1200 Anastasia Avenue | 305-446-1116 | www.gablestage.org | Show times and prices vary

When the Florida Shakespeare Theatre's home was destroyed in Hurricane Andrew, the members of the troupe had to find a new place to present their acclaimed productions. Fast forward a couple of years and they moved into the legendary Biltmore complex and changed the name to Gable Stage. They still perform Shakespeare and the classics on which the company was founded, but the focus has shifted to modern, often provocative, productions. This is an edgy theater experience, but one well worth the price of admission. Check the Web site for any additional Shakespeare Festival performances. The Gable Stage theater and the Biltmore complex are handicapped accessible.

FLORIDA GRAND OPERA

1300 Biscayne Boulevard (Carnival Center) | 201 Southwest Fifth Avenue,
Ft. Lauderdale (Broward Center) | 305-854-1643 | www.fgo.org | Show times vary |
Cost: starting at $10.00

Florida Grand Opera is the country's sixth oldest company and has a distinct history in American opera history. After sixty-six years Florida Grand Opera maintains the level of quality for which it has always been famous. The company regularly presents established opera stars and showcases the newest talent. I highly recommend that everyone have at least one epic opera experience in her life, and Florida Grand Opera is a great place for that. Seasoned opera patrons will find that Florida Grand Opera holds its own with the other major American companies. The Florida Grand Opera performs in two different halls. Each of them is handicapped accessible.

Eateries

SPIGA

1228 Collins Avenue | 305-534-0079 | www.spigarestaurant.com | $$

You are going to thank me for this recommendation. Spiga is one of Miami Beach's best kept secrets. In fact, I wouldn't know about it had I not stumbled in by accident. This humble little restaurant has the best Italian food in town. I cannot stress this enough: You haven't been to Miami until you have had a meal at Spiga.

CAPTAIN'S TAVERN
9621 South Dixie Highway | 305-666-5979 | $$–$$$

It would be irresponsible of me to send you all the way to Miami and not give you the name of a good seafood place. Here is the name of the best. Miami's location on the ocean promises that the fish will be fresh, but that is only half the battle. For fresh fish perfectly prepared, head to the Tavern.

THE FORGE
432 Forty-first Street | Miami Beach | 305-538-8533 | $$$

You get Continental cuisine surrounded by historic artifacts at the Forge. The food is very good and relatively reasonably priced. History buffs will be fascinated by all of the artifacts decorating the restaurant. The Forge is a favorite of Miami locals having a night on the town.

Hotels

ALBION HOTEL
1650 James Avenue | Miami Beach | 305-913-1000 | www.rubellhotels.com | Moderate

This is my kind of hotel. Its great location and laid-back atmosphere make it a pleasant escape from the hustle and bustle of the city. Modern designer hotels can be pretentious, but you never get that feeling at the Albion. If you want to be near the beach but not the beach crowd, book your room here. The prices are one of the best values in the Miami hotel market.

BAY HARBOR INN & SUITES

9660 East Bay Harbor Drive | Bay Harbor Islands | 305-868-4141 |
www.bayharborinn.com | Moderate

Bay Harbor Inn is out of the way but not too far. This small hotel has a homey feel that makes for a very pleasant stay. The Bay Harbor is just blocks away from some of the best shopping in town. It also serves as a training ground for students at the local hospitality college. Come and meet the future leaders of the hotel industry!

HOTEL IMPALA

1228 Collins Avenue | Miami Beach | 305-673-2021 |
www.hotelimpalamiamibeach.com | Moderate/Luxury

The Hotel Impala has a distinctive European flair. It is also a famous rest stop for many Hollywood celebrities. The Hotel Impala provides an oasis of luxury and has a reputation of treating each guest like the *only* guest. You will spend the day on the beach and the night in the Mediterranean.

BILTMORE HOTEL

1200 Anastasia Avenue | 305-445-1926 | www.biltmorehotel.com | Luxury

As far as legendary goes you cannot do much better than the historic Biltmore Hotel. Built in 1926, the hotel has had its up and downs, but today it is at the height of its splendor. The Biltmore is great for golfers; it has its own eighteen-hole course. The Biltmore can be a pricey place to stay, but tours are free, whether you have a room or not. They depart several times a day, and you can call the hotel for more information.

THE NATIONAL HOTEL

1677 Collins Avenue | Miami Beach | 305-532-2311 | www.nationalhotel.com | Luxury

The National is famous around the world for its 205-foot-long swimming pool. In fact, you might even witness a film being shot there during your stay. A 1997 renovation brought this 1930s era gem back to life. Go ahead, relax and enjoy your time in an Art Deco masterpiece.

MINNEAPOLIS/ST. PAUL/BLOOMINGTON, MINNESOTA

Bloomington Visitors and Convention Center
7900 International Drive, Suite 990
Minneapolis, MN 55425
952-858-8500
800-346-4289
www.bloomingtonmn.org

Minneapolis, Minnesota, may not be the first place that comes to mind when you think of great travel destinations, but for the Red Hat Society, where shopping is the official sport, Minneapolis (or actually Bloomington) absolutely earns a place on the list. On the surface Minneapolis may not seem to have as much to offer as some similarly sized metros, but it holds its own weight in cultural institutions. The area is also known worldwide for its shopping opportunities. You may not want to spend a full week here, but for a few days out of town or a long weekend with the girls, consider Minneapolis/Bloomington/St. Paul. Economically, if you exclude the shopping, it can be a good bet. The hotels are fairly priced, and you don't have to rent a car unless you really want one. If you check around, you will find that most of the hotels offer a continental breakfast and free shuttles to the airport and Mall of America. The Bloomington Tourism Bureau (www.bloomington.org) can be a wealth of information about the area.

Getting There

MINNEAPOLIS–ST. PAUL INTERNATIONAL AIRPORT (MSP)

Minneapolis–St. Paul International Airport is a modern facility that serves the Tri-City area. Many hotels have shuttles from MSP, and there is a light rail system into downtown Minneapolis. The airport has two major terminals. They are not labeled 1 and 2 or A and B. Instead they are named after people: the Lindbergh Terminal and the Humphrey Terminal.

Taxi. Taxi service is available at both passenger terminals. In the Lindbergh Terminal, you'll need to head up to the tram level taxi stand. From Humphrey Terminal, you'll need to head down to the ground transportation center.

Shuttle. Many area hotels have free airport shuttles, especially the ones in the Mall of America area. This is something to consider when choosing your place to stay. SuperShuttle fills in the gaps for the hotels that don't provide shuttles for their customers. Taking the SuperShuttle will cost $20.00 each way. For more information go to www.supershuttle.com.

Rental car. Public transportation and hotel shuttles should get you just about everywhere you want to go. But you can still rent a car if you feel so inclined. All the big boys have desks in the Hub Building. You'll need to catch the airport tram to get there.

Getting Around

Make sure that your hotel is near (or offers a shuttle to) one of the light rail stations. The light rail runs from downtown Minneapolis to the Mall of America with several stops, including the airport, in between. It is safe, easy to use, and maybe even fun. If you plan on going lots of places via the Metro train, then pick up a $6.00 day pass.

Attractions

THE MALL OF AMERICA
60 East Broadway | Bloomington | 952-883-8800 | www.mallofamerica.com

So why do we have a mall in the attractions section? Well, this isn't a regular mall. It's a place for everything. You could visit the area for a week and spend your entire time exploring this shopping center on steroids!

The Park at MOA. The Mall of America has its very own theme park! There are roller coasters and other thrill rides. Thirty attractions are spread over seven acres. You may be inside the mall, but the Park at MOA works hard to feel like a traditional place of amusement.

A.C.E.S. flight simulation. Who says flying is for boys? At A.C.E.S. you can dogfight with your Queen Mother in a faithfully replicated fighter jet cockpit! These simulators are the closest thing to flying an F-18 you can get without signing up for the U.S. Navy. If the F-18 is a little fast for you, try the P-51 Mustang simulator.

Underwater Adventures Aquarium. Take a break from shopping and visit the world's largest underwater aquarium! This place is famous for its sharks, but there are 4,500 different creatures overall. Get a belly view of one of those sharks in the three-hundred-foot-long curved tunnel. It's like scuba diving without getting wet!

MINNESOTA ZOO

13000 Zoo Boulevard | Apple Valley, MN 55124 | 952-431-9200 | www.mnzoo.com | Hours: daily, except Thanksgiving Day and Christmas Day | Cost: zoo only, $12.00 for ages 13–64; $8.25 for 65+; | zoo/IMAX combo, $19.00 for ages 13–64; $14.25 for 65+

A visit to the Minnesota Zoo can provide a respite or at least a distraction from the magnetic pull of the Mall of America. It is easily accessible and can factor right into that low-cost/no-cost transportation mind-set. Take your hotel's free shuttle to the Mall of America, then catch the MVTA bus line #440. It runs from the Mall of America to the Apple Valley station and stops at the zoo on the way. It's only about a ten- to twelve-minute trip. The bus does not run on Sunday, so factor that into your planning. If you are driving your own vehicle, there is a $5.00 parking charge.

The zoo monorail allows you to get an overview of the zoo while enjoying the narrative of a resident naturalist guide. You can see the Bactrian camels and Siberian tigers from the monorail. It will give you a bird's-eye view and help you plan the route you would like to take for the rest of your time in the zoo. A monorail ticket costs $3.50 per person.

If you happen to be in the Minneapolis/St. Paul/Bloomington area during the summer months, check out Subway Music in the Zoo. The Music in the Zoo Concert series is in its fifteenth season and plays host to great artists such as Bruce Hornsby, Bela Fleck & the Flecktones,

> ### Good to Know
>
> The Bloomington, Minnesota, tourism Web site (www.bloomingtonmn.org) has a discount package called the Big Ticket. It's $57.00 for adults and $44.00 for children ages three to twelve. It is a three-day bundled attraction pass that saves you about 30 percent on five top attractions in the Minneapolis/ St. Paul/Bloomington area. You might want to check it out online.

and others. The concerts are held at the Weesner Amphitheater on the zoo grounds. The concert series schedule is found at the zoo Web site. Many shows sell out, so you may want to buy tickets in advance.

MINNEAPOLIS INSTITUTE OF ARTS

2400 Third Avenue South | 612-870-3131 | www.artsmia.org | Hours: daily, except Monday, 10:00 AM to 5:00 PM; Sunday, opens 11:00 AM | Cost: *free*!

After the mall has separated you from most of your money, you will want to visit the Minneapolis Institute of Arts. Not only is this world-class museum a welcome change of pace, it is absolutely free! The museum features thousands of pieces that span the breadth of human history. This is a comprehensive museum with works of various eras and styles. There are plenty of well-known artists and pieces to be seen here.

THE FREDERICK R. WEISMAN ART MUSEUM

University of Minnesota campus | 333 East River Road | 612-625-9494 | www.weisman.umn.edu | Hours: Tuesday, Wednesday, Friday, 10:00 AM to 5:00 PM; Thursday, 10:00 AM to 8:00 PM; Saturday–Sunday, 11:00 AM to 5:00 PM | Cost: *free*!

Once you set foot on the campus you shouldn't have trouble figuring out which building is the Weisman. The structure itself is a work of art designed by legendary architect Frank Gehry. The Weisman focuses on contemporary and modern art. As a result it has some really, shall I say "interesting," pieces. Oh, and it is free.

Shopping

The first thing you'll need to do is to visit one of the guest services booths or Mall of America gift stores and purchase a $9.95 coupon book. This baby will save you many times its cost! The mall is anchored by four huge department stores: Nordstrom, Sears, Bloomingdale's, and Macy's. In between the anchors are miles of specialty shops. You might want to get a mall map and plan your trip before starting on your journey. There is a whole lot of ground to cover from one end to another.

Here are a few of my favorite shops:

A Simpler Time (third floor). A Simpler Time started right here in the Mall of America with the goal of giving shoppers "an island of nostalgic tranquility" among the crowds and sea of Gaps and Hollisters. Weather vanes, wood signs, clocks, and pedal cars are only a few of the interesting items you will find here.

The Afternoon (second floor). The Afternoon carries a variety of jewelry, pottery, frames, cards, and other unique items. The name originated from its early beginnings as an art gallery when it opened only limited hours in the afternoon. Check it out at www.theafternoon.com.

Bow Wow Meow (third floor). Bow Wow Meow is a specialty boutique that features all sorts of gifts and surprises for our furry friends at home. The gourmet assortment of treats for dogs and cats is intriguing, even if you are not a pet owner.

European Gifts (first floor). If the closest you are ever going to get to shopping in Europe is the Mall of America, experience European Gifts. From beer steins to Hummels, nutcrackers to clocks, you can browse through the store and experience that European flair without ever crossing the pond.

Lake Wobegon USA (third floor). Lake Wobegon is a regional gift store, which you don't see in many parts of the country. It offers a large selection of Minnesota-related books and souvenirs. As you may have guessed, it specializes in Garrison Keillor and *A Prairie Home Companion* merchandise.

Explore Minnesota Store (first floor, near the north entrance). The Explore Minnesota Store is a wealth of information about Minnesota. There are free maps and literature as well as trained travel counselors to answer your questions. Check it out. You may find a destination to add to your list of places to visit.

Entertainment

Let's see, we have one world-class shopping center and two world-class museums. Would it be too much to add world-class theater?

THE GUTHRIE THEATER
818 South Second Street | 612-377-2224 | www.guthrietheater.org |

The people of Minneapolis love live theater, and this place is the reason why. The Guthrie is known around the world as the premier resident house of the United States. The shows produced here are consistently on par with (or above!) anything you will see on Broadway. An evening at the Guthrie is a must-do for anyone visiting the area.

MINNEAPOLIS MUSICAL THEATRE
824 Hennepin Avenue | 952-544-1372 | www.aboutmmt.org

If the show at the Guthrie doesn't seem up your alley, check out Minneapolis Musical Theatre. The shows here are all musicals (duh!) and are usually done very well. Sometimes there is no better way to end a trip than with a little song and dance.

ORPHEUM, STATE, AND PANTAGES THEATRES
Hennepin Theatre District | 910 Hennepin Avenue | Minneapolis | 612-373-5600 | www.hennepintheatredistrict.org

The three historic theaters are now under single ownership and bring some of the hottest shows to town. Each building is a historic landmark, and the interiors have been preserved. Concerts, touring shows, and other acts take advantage of these grand houses.

MYSTIC LAKE CASINO
2400 Mystic Lake Boulevard | Prior Lake | 952-445-9000

The Mystic Lake Casino is just twenty-five miles from downtown Minneapolis and Mall of America. Like most things in the Tri-City area, if you can get to the Mall of America, you can get to the casino. Mystic Lake provides a shuttle bus to and from the Mall of America. It is conveniently timed to coincide with the bingo sessions. Call the Mystic Bus information hotline at 952-496-7235 for more information. Mystic Lake Casino and Hotel is home to standard casino games including nickel slots, blackjack, bingo, and more. It is also host to a pretty amazing entertainment lineup. Great artists such as Tony Bennett grace the New Mystic Showroom stage as well as multiple comedy shows including NBC's *Last Comic Standing*. Check out the www.mysticklake.com Web site to see who will be playing while you are in the area.

Sign up for a Club Mystic card as soon as you enter the casino. You will earn reward credits with every game that you play. You only need six hundred credits to receive Classic Card status. Once you reach Classic Card status, you will qualify for the Mystic Free 55+ Club Breakfast & Bingo Session. It happens every Tuesday morning and is free for members who have a Classic, Gold, or Platinum Club Card. If you don't have a club card, you can get one by purchasing a breakfast ticket that includes a bingo package for $14.00. These sessions are early, 8:00 AM and 9:45 AM. The Mystic Lake Casino Hotel is an alcohol-free facility.

HUMPHREY METRODOME
34 Kirby Puckett Place | Minneapolis

Minneapolis has two high-level professional sports teams. Both call the legendary Humphrey Metrodome home.

MINNESOTA TWINS
Take me out to the ball game! Really! I am all about those peanuts and Cracker Jacks. There is something to be said for the sport of baseball. Of course, it will never replace the official Red Hat sport of shopping, but it sure can be a fun way to spend an afternoon. The Minnesota Twins actually have an official 55+ fan club called the Golden Sluggers Club. You can join for only $29.00, and you get all sorts of neat trinkets like an official Twins cap, a Minnesota Twins fleece blanket, 15 percent off at the Twins Pro Shops, and other interesting stuff. The Twins also have a group outing plan. All groups of twenty-five or more receive great discounts on seats, discounts on concessions, and the group's name displayed on the Metrodome scoreboard during the game! You can make group arrangements online by going to www.minnesota.twins.mlb.com, then tickets and then group events, or call 612-375-7454, or write Minnesota Twins, Metrodome, 34 Kirby Puckett Place, Minneapolis, MN 55415. Minnesota Twins tickets are

priced from $10.00 to $108.00, depending on the seat selection and the opposing team.

MINNESOTA VIKINGS

What can I say about the meanest, toughest, fastest, roughest guys in America wearing purple? Well, it is just a sight to behold! You gotta love 'em. Single tickets are available for the games and usually go on sale in mid-summer through Ticketmaster.com. Ticket prices start at $75.00 each and go all the way up to $620.00. Check the schedule and experience the world of the National Football League in purple! Group sales for the Vikings start with forty or more people. There are a few other packages available, but all seem rather pricey. You can check out the Web site at www.vikings.com or call 612-338-4537.

Eateries

A BAKER'S WIFE PASTRY SHOP

4200 Twenty-eighth Avenue South | 612-729-6898 | Dessert | $

Whenever I crave something sweet in Minneapolis, I head over to A Baker's Wife Pastry Shop. Can you guess what it sells? Sweet, sweet pastries.

HELL'S KITCHEN

89 South Tenth Street | 612-332-4700 | www.hellskitcheninc.com | $$

This quirky little place has the best food for the price in town. The menu is varied but can best be described as American. It serves breakfast and lunch during the week but is famous for the weekend brunch. Reservations are recommended for the weekend.

GOODFELLOWS

40 South Seventh Street | 612-332-4800 | $$$

Goodfellows is the place to go when you want great food plus great service and don't mind paying. The prices are high, but the meal is worth every penny. Go ahead. Treat yourself.

EATING AT THE MALL

Hungry while you are shopping? Well, there is no need to leave the Mall of America. The mall has several restaurants with a wide variety of cuisine.

Bubba Gump Shrimp Co. The Mall of America may not be next to an ocean, but it still delivers fresh seafood at Bubba Gump. Don't worry. There are a couple of less fishy choices for the landlubbers out there. Since it is a shrimp shop, you may not think of Bubba Gump Shrimp Co. as a place for great dessert, but the Chocolate Cookie Sundae is pretty tasty!

Famous Dave's BBQ. Visit Dave's, and get ready for some of the best BBQ this side of the Mason-Dixon Line.

Johnny Rockets. Johnny Rockets blasts you back into the 1950s with the cool retro atmosphere and delicious food.

Twin City Grill. Twin City Grill offers the standard fare in a comfortable sit-down-and-relax setting.

Hotels

BLOOMINGTON HYATT (FORMERLY AMERISUITES)

7800 International Drive | Bloomington | 952-854-0700 | Moderate

I am a big fan of suite-type hotels, and this one is certainly worth noting. Recently renovated, it combines the convenience of an in-room kitchenette with microwave and refrigerator, free high-speed Internet, and a complimentary continental breakfast with a free shuttle to the largest shopping mall in America!

CROWNE PLAZA–BLOOMINGTON

5401 Green Valley Drive | Bloomington | 952-831-8000 | www.cpmsp.com | Moderate

The Crowne Plaza is close the mall and the airport. It has easy access to downtown and a free airport shuttle.

HILTON MINNEAPOLIS/ST. PAUL AIRPORT MALL OF AMERICA

3800 American Boulevard East | Bloomington | 952-854-2100 | www.hilton.com | Moderate

This Hilton is the official hotel of the Mall of America. Naturally it has mall access. It also provides a free shuttle to the airport.

MYSTIC LAKE CASINO HOTEL

2400 Mystic Lake Boulevard | Prior Lake | 952-445-9000 | 800-262-7799 | Moderate

Mystic Lake Casino Hotel is a full-service hotel with standard hotel rooms and suites. It is connected to the casino for your "convenience." You can check out the layout of the rooms at www.mysticlake.com/hotel. The Web site offers a wealth of information and very often great specials that include dining and gift shop discounts. Add the on-site spa and the Meadows at Mystic Lake world-class golf course, and you may find that Mystic Lake is a vacation all its own.

NASHVILLE, TENNESSEE

Nashville Convention and Visitors Bureau
One Nashville Place
150 Fourth Avenue North, Suite G-250
Nashville, TN 37219
615-259-4730
800-657-6910; fax: 615-259-4126
nashcvb@visitmusiccity.com

Thinking about taking a trip to Nashville? Well, let me tell you, there is a lot more to this city than country music (but there is plenty of that)! Nashville is truly a big city with a small town feel. There is plenty to do, and the people are still friendly and even the Chinese restaurants serve sweet tea. One of several jewels in the Nashville crown is the largest (and getting larger) hotel in America outside Las Vegas. The Gaylord Opryland Hotel and Resort (not to be confused with the defunct Opryland theme park) is something you have to see to believe. If you are ready for some honky-tonk line dancing, sprinkled with a little history and a dash of high culture, then put on your boots and head to Nashville.

You essentially have two options to get to Music City: wheels or wings. Nashville boasts an international airport and is a convergence point for Interstates 24, 65, and 40. If you are the road trip sort, the drive to Nashville passes through some really pretty country. Many major cities have direct flights to Nashville, and very few places are more than one connection away.

NASHVILLE INTERNATIONAL AIRPORT (BNA)

For better or for worse Nashville follows the grand southern tradition of mediocre public transportation. Once you arrive at the airport you will have three choices to get into town: taxi, hotel shuttle, or rental car. There is a city-wide bus line, but you'd probably have better luck getting around town by navigating a maze blindfolded.

Taxi. You can grab a cab outside the baggage claim area. Just follow the signs. There is a $22.00 flat rate to go downtown or to the Opryland Resort. Several local cab companies offer handicap-accessible vehicles, but request that you call ahead and ask for one. One of the friendly people at the airport information desk should be able to help you with this.

Shuttle. Many hotels offer complimentary hotel-to-airport shuttles. Be sure to check when you make your reservation. There are also general shuttle services. If you are heading to a downtown, West End, or Music Row hotel, you can hop the Gray Line Airport Express (615-883-5555; www.graylinenashville.com). The service is available 5:00 AM to 11:00 PM, departs every fifteen to twenty minutes from the airport, and costs $12.00 one way and $18.00 round-trip. No reservation is required. For those of you staying in Cool Springs, Brentwood, or the Opryland area, you will need to use ShuttleMax (615-361-6184; www.shuttlemax.net). The service is a little more expensive, but the company seems very proud of the first-class shuttle experience. ShuttleMax requests that you make reservations in advance but will accept walk-ons when space is available. The cost is $22.00 one-way and $36.00 round-trip.

Rental car. Most major agencies have desks here, and the cars are located in the parking garage attached to the terminal.

Getting Around

Nashville city bus service (MTA) is one option for navigating around town. MTA recently added hourly trips to and from the Nashville International Airport and downtown Music City for just $1.25 each way. You can call the MTA customer center at 615-862-5950 or go to www.nashvillemta.org for more information. Parking can be tough to find in downtown Nashville, and the bus service is certainly an alternative to that. However, I have to admit that Nashville is one of those places I always rent a car.

Attractions

COUNTRY MUSIC HALL OF FAME AND MUSEUM
222 Fifth Avenue South | 615-416-2001 | www.countrymusichalloffame.com

I am sure there are a certain number of you who are inclined to skip this entry. *Don't.* I have only recently become a fan of country music, but the Hall of Fame and Museum is a place I am happy to visit again and again. Here you will find more than a history of country music; you will find the history of *American* music. Anyone with an interest in music, culture, or history will find plenty to keep her interested. The museum is full of interactive, high-tech exhibits and has a contemporary design. For all you Elvis fans don't miss a chance to take a look inside his golden Cadillac. The museum has rotating exhibits that feature noncountry artists such as Ray Charles. If you come to Nashville, you must make this a stop.

RYMAN AUDITORIUM
116 Fifth Avenue North | 615-458-8700 | www.ryman.com

Even though this Nashville landmark no longer houses the Grand Ole Opry, it is still known as the "Mother Church of Country Music." Built in 1892 as the Union Gospel Tabernacle, it has hosted hundreds of famous people, including noncountry celebrities such as Ethel Barrymore, Helen Keller, Bela Lugosi, and Eleanor Roosevelt. Today the Ryman is a highly regarded concert hall for modern pop acts, and many current country stars feel drawn to play here. You can visit the museum and wander the auditorium every day from 9:00 AM to 4:00 PM. Hours are sometimes adjusted to accommodate shows, and if you want something to do one evening, check the Ryman schedule; one of your favorite artists might be playing.

FRIST CENTER FOR THE VISUAL ARTS
919 Broadway | 615-244-3340 | www.fristcenter.org

This first-class venue hosts important visiting arts exhibitions from around the world. From ancient Egyptian artifacts to pop art icons you never know what you're going to see at the Frist (unless you check the Web site). If you're a fan of Art Deco architecture, then you definitely want to visit the Frist. The center is located in the old main Nashville post office, which is a piece of art itself. The Frist also offers occasional reduced and free admission nights. You can call or check online for specific dates. This isn't a must-go, but I encourage you to check the schedule and see if there is an exhibition that interests you.

BELLE MEADE PLANTATION
5025 Harding Road | 615-356-0105 | www.bellemeadeplantation.com

Belle Meade Plantation holds a couple of unique places in history. It was home to five generations of the Harding-Jackson family. During that time, it grew from 250 acres to more than 5,000. It saw a Civil War skirmish in its front yard: bullet holes can still be seen on the columns of the ornate main house. The plantation also became one of the premier thoroughbred horse farms in the nation. Some modern-day Kentucky Derby winners can trace their lineage back to the original Belle Meade Plantation. Today the plantation is a 36-acre park including the main house and several outbuildings. The first floor of the antebellum mansion is handicapped accessible However, the second floor and other historic structures are not.

THE HERMITAGE
4580 Rachel's Lane | 615-889-2941 | www.thehermitage.com

The Hermitage was the home of President Andrew Jackson, and a mansion he built for his wife, Rachel, is the centerpiece. The mansion has been restored to appear as it did when Jackson lived there and contains many original pieces of furniture bought by the Jackson family. The mansion tour is guided by historical interpreters in period garb. You can also wander the grounds and visit President Jackson's tomb and see the remains of slave quarters. With the self-guided "Beyond the Mansion" tour you can get a broad understanding of life on the estate. The people at the Hermitage have made every effort to make these historic sites accessible to all.

THE PARTHENON
Centennial Park | West End Avenue and Twenty-fifth Avenue | 615-862-8431

The centerpiece of the Tennessee Centennial Exposition of 1897, this is the full-size replica of the Athens Partheneon. Although the original structure was planned to be temporary, the city opted to reconstruct a permanent Parthenon in 1931. A forty-two-foot statue of Athena Parthenos, the goddess of wisdom, waits inside (she must have been a Red Hatter!).

Shopping

Nashville is not known as a shopping mecca, but you can still spend a lot of time in the stores. Go to Green Hills Mall in the middle of the city if you want upscale shops like Tiffany & Co., Godiva, and Benetton. You can have dinner at the Cheesecake Factory while you're there. There is also a quaint shopping district called Hillsboro Village, filled with eclectic shops and restaurants, near this area of the city. If you are staying in the Opryland area, you can head over to the massive Opry Mills Mall. If you can't find what you are looking for there, then you probably can't buy it.

Entertainment

At night Nashville comes alive with a variety of entertainment options.

THE HONKY-TONKS
Lower Broadway

If you want the quintessential Nashville experience, then hail a cab and ask the driver to take you to Lower Broad. Here you will find the clubs for which Nashville is famous. Places like Tootsie's Orchid Lounge, Legends Corner, and the Stage feature up-and-comers on the country stage and occasional surprise jams from established stars. I know country music isn't for everyone, but don't worry. Just stroll up Second Avenue to B. B. King's Blues Club or another club for a variety of music styles.

GRAND OLE OPRY
2804 Opryland Drive | 615-889-6611 | www.opry.com

There is no other show out there like the Grand Ole Opry. Every Friday and Saturday night country music stars from past and present (nowadays more past than present) gather to entertain 4,400 members of the theater audience and thousands more via the live broadcast. The Opry House is located on the campus of the Opryland Resort, so it's easy getting there if you are staying at the resort. If you are in a downtown hotel, ask someone at the front desk how long it will take you to get there. The Opry is some distance from downtown, and there is constant road construction on the way. The Opry isn't for everyone, but if you grew up with country music or the Opry radio broadcast, you'll have a great time.

LIVE THEATER
Various

For those of you in the mood for a show, Nashville has a variety of theater options. You can catch Broadway shows on tour at the Tennessee Performing Arts Center (www.tpac.org). The acclaimed regional theater company, Tennessee Repertory, offers local productions that rival those in bigger cities (www.tnrep.org). For dinner and a show try Chaffin's Barn Dinner Theatre where the stage descends from the ceiling (www.dinnertheatre.com).

NASHVILLE SYMPHONY
One Symphony Place | 615-687-6500 | www.nashvillesymphony.org

Nashville's vast music heritage is echoed by its highly respected symphony orchestra. The Nashville Symphony calls the $120 million Schermerhorn

Symphony Center home. The Schermerhorn is said to be one of the most remarkable facilities of its kind in the United States. The Symphony plays a varied repertoire and has concerts throughout the year. Even if there is not a concert during your stay, the Schermerhorn itself is worth a look.

BLUEBIRD CAFÉ
4104 Hillsboro Road | 615-383-1461 | www.bluebirdcafe.com

The Bluebird might be called a café, but people don't flock here for the food. Countless hit songwriters have gotten their start performing in the round at the Bluebird. Garth Brooks was a regular here before he made it big. The Bluebird is all about the music. When the music starts, everything else comes to a halt. Feel like talking during a performance? They might just ask you to take your talking outside. The Bluebird is small and on some nights can fill up quickly. I recommend grabbing dinner somewhere else before the show and arriving a little early. Be sure to know where you are going. The café is located in a nondescript strip mall and is easy to overlook.

Eateries

ARNOLD'S COUNTRY KITCHEN
605 Eighth Avenue South | 615-256-4455 | $

Pull up to a table at Arnold's and you'll feel like a local. This place is famous for its meat-and-three deal. Arnold's is open only during the week for lunch, but it is well worth adjusting your schedule. If anyone ever asks you, "Are you from Nashville?" just say, "Of course I am. I ate at Arnold's." By the way, this is not a place for people with dietary restrictions.

CAFÉ COCO
210 Louise Avenue | 615-321-2626 | www.cafecoco.net | $

Now, if you are ready to walk a little bit on the wild side, try Café Coco. It has been touted by some as one of the best dessert places in Nashville, however the ambiance may be a little too "alternative" for some. Open twenty-four hours a day, Café Coco serves more than dessert, but it is a great place to grab coffee and something sweet. The dessert selection rivals anything else you'll find in town, and the hip atmosphere enhances the experience.

MONELL'S

1235 Sixth Avenue North | 615-248-4747 | www.monellsdining.citysearch.com | $$–$$$

A true Nashville original, Monell's brings a whole new meaning to family-style dining. Get ready to sit at a table with strangers, pass the peas, and swap stories. A dinner at Monell's is almost like a family reunion, except you're not always sure who is related to whom. While it's not for the shy, Monell's will give you a memorable evening. This place is great for groups; just call ahead.

NEW ORLEANS MANOR

1400 Murfreesboro Road | 615-367-2777 | www.neworleansmanor.us | $$–$$$

Sandwiched between the airport and an office park, this Nashville land-mark seems out of place. The restaurant is located in an old plantation house and offers a seafood feast. An impressive buffet with crab, prime rib, and a lot more stands ready for looting. If you leave here hungry, it's your own fault. The manor is only open for dinner Tuesday through Saturday. It does accept reservations.

CHAPPY'S ON CHURCH

1721 Church Street | 615-322-9932 | www.chappys.com | $$$

Chappy's was originally located in Long Beach, Mississippi, but when that restaurant was destroyed by Hurricane Katrina, Chef John Chapman made the decision to relocate to Nashville. Everyone in town is glad he did. The menu boasts New Orleans–style seafood and Creole dishes. There is tamer fare for those of you with weaker stomachs. Chef Chappy himself often comes out to visit with his customers. For groups there are private rooms available.

DOWNTOWN NASHVILLE HILTON

121 Fourth Avenue South | 615-620-1000 | www.nashvillehilton.com | Moderate/Luxury

For those people planning to spend a lot of time in downtown Nashville, the Hilton is for you. A well-appointed modern hotel, the Hilton is within walking distance of many Nashville attractions and landmarks.

GAYLORD OPRYLAND

2800 Opryland Drive | 615-889-1000 | www.gaylordhotels.com/gaylordopryland | Moderate/Luxury

The massive atrium of this destination resort contains a forty-four-foot waterfall and a river you can tour on flatboats. Shopping, restaurants, amusement—it's all here. The hotel shares a campus with the Grand Ole Opry House and is within walking distance of Opry Mills Mall. However, if you want to visit downtown attractions, you'll need to find transportation.

More Hotel Choices Soon

There are currently more than a half-dozen hotels of all types under construction in the Nashville area. If none of the above meets your needs, you will be able to find something that does. Be advised that if you visit in June, the yearly CMA Festival quickly fills most of the rooms in the city.

LOEWS VANDERBILT HOTEL

2100 West End Avenue | 615-320-1700 | www.loewshotels.com/en/hotels/vanderbilt-hotel/overview.aspx | Luxury

Loews Vanderbilt is a hotel to the stars. As Nashville's premier luxury lodging, the Loews attracts many of the rich and famous who visit the city. It features its own art gallery and is across the street from the beautiful Vanderbilt University campus. Loews Vanderbilt, like all hotels in this luxury chain, is pet friendly and even has room service items for your furry little friend.

NEW ORLEANS, LOUISIANA

New Orleans Convention and Visitors Bureau
2020 St. Charles Avenue
New Orleans, LA 70130
800-672-6124
www.neworleanscvb.com

Travelers have lots of questions surrounding the condition of New Orleans these days. Are the streets still flooded? Is there anything left to do? Is it safe? Considering the media attention the city gets, no one is surprised by the inquiries. Let's go ahead and get them out of the way. *Are the streets still flooded?* No. The floodwaters have been pumped out of the city for quite some time. *Is there anything left to do?* Yes! The French Quarter and other major tourist areas received little hurricane damage and were untouched by flood waters. Most of the high-water flooding (over the roofs of houses) took place in residential areas. There is just as much to do now as there was pre-Katrina. This place is hopping! *Is it safe?* The short answer here is yes. Unless you plan on trekking dark streets alone at night to purchase illegal substances, you should be safe. The tourist areas in the French Quarter are crowded, well lit, and well patrolled. Visiting New Orleans is like visiting any large city; just use common sense. I lived the early years of my life in New Orleans, and it will always have a piece of my heart. Don't let wild rumors and unfounded fears keep you from visiting this fabulous city.

Getting There

The preferred method to travel to New Orleans is airplane. However, you also have the option of car or Amtrak. Many cruises depart from the city, so you could add a couple of "in the city" days to your boat trip.

LOUIS ARMSTRONG NEW ORLEANS INTERNATIONAL AIRPORT (MSY)

Flights to and from New Orleans have been picking up at a steady pace. The airport has also gone through some upgrading, though it is not quite state of the art. MSY is actually small enough not to be overwhelming to the inexperienced traveler. Follow the signs and you'll have your bags and be in a cab in no time.

Taxi. Let me say something about the taxis in New Orleans. They come in all shapes, sizes, colors, and smells. There appears to be no standard. Some have lighted taxi signs, but others do not. Sometimes you can't tell a vehicle is a taxi until you're standing next to it and see the decals. The fare for one or two people from the airport to most hotels is $28.00. There is an additional fee of $12.00 per extra person. If you are traveling as a couple or small group, a taxi is your best value.

Shuttle. One shuttle service in New Orleans serves the major tourist areas. The one-way trip to your hotel will cost $13.00 per person. This will save you money over a cab if you are traveling alone. You can get all the information you need and make reservations online at www.airportshuttleneworleans.com.

Rental car. Driving around New Orleans can be a touch confusing, and parking downtown can be expensive. If you insist on renting a car, you can visit the majors at the counters on the lower level.

Getting Around

New Orleans is notoriously flat, and therefore a very easy city to walk. Almost every major tourist attraction is located in the same walkable radius. The walk might be a mile or more in some cases, but the flat terrain makes it no worse than a couple of laps around the mall. Just be careful during the summer months. July and August are sweltering, and it is easy to overextend yourself. At night you should be safe walking in the French Quarter. If your hotel is outside the Quarter, ask the desk staff the preferred route to take. Otherwise use the same common sense you would use in any city at night.

Attractions

The biggest attraction in New Orleans is the city itself. The "Naw'lins" attitude of friendliness, live and let live, and lagniappe is truly a pleasure to experience. There is just something about this place.

THE FRENCH QUARTER
www.frenchquarter.com

People come to New Orleans to visit the French Quarter. In fact many of the other attractions, restaurants, hotels, and entertainment we'll review can be found here. The preservation laws that have been on the books here since the 1920s have kept almost all of the eighteenth-century structures intact. Just think, most of the French Quarter buildings standing today were built while New Orleans was part of Spain!

There are dozens of shops, galleries, knickknack shops, and unexplainable stores to browse in the Quarter. You will find a variety of dining options like nowhere else: everything from Cajun to Italian at prices from hole-in-the-wall to four-star. The best way to experience the French Quarter is to take an afternoon and explore. Don't be afraid to visit the shops on the side streets where you will discover many of the best deals and interesting objects.

JACKSON SQUARE

This park is in the center of the French Quarter. It is home to a famous statue, a grand view of Saint Louis Cathedral, and various artisans and tarot readers. There are also musicians and buskers, who will keep you entertained for a tip. Take a stroll here. It's a beautiful place and you never know what talent you may encounter.

AUDUBON AQUARIUM OF THE AMERICAS
1 Canal Street | 504-581-4629 | www.auduboninstitute.org | Hours: 10:00 AM to 5:00 PM; closed Monday | Cost: $17.00; $13.00 for 65+

This superaquarium lost almost all of its ten thousand aquatic specimens in the Hurricane Katrina aftermath (because of power failure, not wind or flooding). However, the world-renowned institution is back in operation and better than ever. There is no indication on the inside or outside of the building that anything happened. The exhibits are full and fascinating. Besides the thousands of fish, the aquarium is known for its penguins, otters, and white alligator (all Katrina survivors). The penguins are cute, but I love watching the otters play. In the Amazon section there is an anaconda large enough to swallow Queen Sue Ellen's shoe collection!

NATIONAL WORLD WAR II MUSEUM

945 Magazine Street | 504-527-6012 | www.nationalww2museum.org | Hours: 9:00 AM to 5:00 PM; closed Monday | Cost: $14.00; $8.00 for 65+

This museum was originally designed to focus on the D-Day invasion, but it is being expanded to encompass the whole war. However, for now D-Day is the main subject. The exhibits and illustrations are truly impressive and have a way of putting different aspects of the war into perspective. The memorabilia and artifacts take you back in time. This museum will prove interesting to those who did and those who didn't live through this historic era. The museum's plans for the future are impressive, and there may be much more to see by the time you visit.

HARRAH'S NEW ORLEANS

8 Canal Street | 504-533-6000

We all know that casinos outside Las Vegas can be a crap shoot. How-ever, this one is a good bet. There are 115,000 square feet of gaming space, a large buffet, and cocktails. It is clean and well maintained. There are table games and many slot varieties. The casino is located between several down-town hotels and the French Quarter.

WALKING TOURS

Many companies offer walking tours of various curiosities in New Orleans. Most try to fill a niche. You can tour with a parapsychologist, guides dressed as vampires, or other specialized guides. New Orleans Magic Walking Tours are my favorites because they are known to give you the straight dope. (Call 504-588-9693 for more information.) You won't have to figure out what is true and what your guide is exaggerating (or making up!) for effect. But if you want a ghoulish tour, by all means take one. Almost every tour company offers a couple of basic tours (sometimes in combos).

French Quarter tour. This tour is a good introduction to the various locations in the French Quarter.

Haunted New Orleans/ghost tour. You will most likely meet some-where in the French Quarter. Your guide will then take you to haunted sites in the area. You probably won't see a ghost, but most guides have at least one "close encounter" story to share. These nighttime tours are usually full of interesting history and stories.

Cemetery tours. After the French Quarter, New Orleans is probably best known for its cemeteries. Something about all of the above-ground vaults oozes intriguing creepiness.

HURRICANE KATRINA TOUR
504-569-1401 | www.graylineneworleans.com | Cost: $35.00

Most of the city you see as a tourist looks as if the Hurricane Katrina disaster never happened. However, it did happen, and much of the city still bears the scars. The Katrina tour is an educational experience. You will tour some of the hardest-hit areas where rescuer symbols and roof cut-outs still mark many homes. In many areas you will see where one house has been restored next to a house without windows and with four-foot-tall weeds in the yard. The organizers don't want the tour to be a spectacle; they hope when you see the real impact of what they consider to be a man-made disaster, you will become passionate about making sure it never happens again. I highly recommend this tour.

Shopping

Some of the New Orleans shopping scene has yet to recover from Katrina, but there is still plenty to buy. I would avoid the Riverwalk. Many stores that I used to like there have closed. Otherwise, the French Market in the French Quarter is a great area. For traditional upscale mall shopping, you'll want to head to the Shops at Canal Place. But I've found everything I could possibly want in the French Quarter.

Entertainment

New Orleans is famous for keeping her guests entertained until the wee hours of the morning. Music is king here, and you'll find some of the best the country has to offer.

BOURBON STREET

Bourbon Street is known around the world as the party capital of America. Even if you are not the hard-partying sort, you might want to stroll down Bourbon one evening. It is completely safe, parts are closed to traffic, and you'll see interesting characters. The people-watching here is almost as good as the music in the clubs. How much fun you have on Bourbon Street depends on what you like to do. The street is crowded with people, even in the off-season, so you need to be mobile. Many people on Bourbon Street are going to be tourists too, so don't feel insulted if someone tells you that he doesn't know how to get to St. Louis Street. There will be plenty of uniformed police, and they are always happy to help. If you plan on barhopping, take a cab back to the hotel. Don't try to navigate the French Quarter's side streets. Just be smart, listen, look for music/atmosphere you like, and enjoy yourself!

PRESERVATION HALL

726 St. Peter Street | 504-522-2841 | www.preservationhall.com | Cost: $8.00 cover

Preservation Hall is *the* place for jazz in the city for jazz. The building is two hundred years old, and it has been a jazz hall since the 1920s. This place is crowded and popular, but it is not wild. Early in the evening families can often be spotted. If you are looking for a little bit of true New Orleans downhome jazz, then you need to go to Preservation Hall.

LE PETIT THEATRE DU VIEUX CARRE

616 St. Peter Street | 504-522-2081 | www.lepetittheatre.com

This nonprofessional community theater is worth a mention because it is the oldest such organization in the country. Founded in 1916, Le Petit Theatre du Vieux Carre has been producing shows for almost all of those years in the same location!

SOUTHERN REPERTORY THEATRE

365 Canal Street | 504-522-6545 | www.southernrep.com

The Southern Repertory Theatre is a well-regarded professional house. The company focuses on contemporary works, including occasional debuts by A-list playwrights. Most of the time you won't recognize the name of the show playing here, but don't let that deter you. Be sure to read about it before you go. Who knows? You might just discover a new favorite play!

PRO SPORTS

The Superdome and New Orleans Arena have been repaired and returned to service. If you want to go to a good game, check on whether the NFL's Saints or the NBA's Hornets are in town. The people of New Orleans take their sports seriously and consider the complete return of their teams a keystone moment in the city's recovery. Don't try to walk to a game from your hotel. The distance and neighborhoods are not a good combination. After the game, take a cab to Bourbon Street to celebrate the victory or drown the sorrows of defeat.

Eateries

I was worried that Katrina had washed away the unique New Orleans culinary community. I am relieved to report that I was worried over nothing. Many restaurants have come back, and the new ones fit in perfectly with the scene. If anything, the fare is a little more diverse now (and I thought that would have been impossible). You know you are in New Orleans when you can get gumbo to go in a Styrofoam bowl, walk to the other end of the block, and be seated for four-star service.

ANGELO BROCATO ICE CREAM & CONFECTIONERY

214 North Carrollton Avenue | 504-486-1465 | www.angelobrocatoicecream.com | Dessert | $

The Brocato family business suffered major damage during Katrina, but the main store is back up and running. I couldn't be happier. They have the sweetest ice cream in town. All of the ice cream and gelato is made daily on-site and served to hundreds of hungry customers. Ice cream isn't the only option here, though; you can choose from a scrumptious selection of pastries and other desserts.

CAFÉ DU MONDE

800 Decatur Street | 800-772-2927 | www.cafedumonde.com | Dessert | $–$$

The Café du Monde has been serving the citizens of New Orleans since 1862. It is open twenty-four hours, seven days a week. It closes only for Christmas and the occasional hurricane. The coffee here is classic and can be ordered black or au lait (half coffee/half hot milk). The reason everyone comes here is the beignets. Beignets are square fritters covered with sugar. They are the simplest, sweetest mess you will ever eat. Besides juice and other drinks, beignets are the only item served here, so plan this as a before- or after-meal trip (or late night snack!).

CAFÉ ADELAIDE

300 Poydras Street (inside the Loews Hotel) | 504-595-3305 | www.cafeadelaide.com | $$–$$$

Chef Danny Trace has turned this place into a must-stop on a New Orleans culinary tour. Featuring what they call a boosted New Orleans bistro cuisine, Café Adelaide takes traditional dishes to the next level. Even the off-hours bar menu is exceptional. The restaurant is not huge, and the atmosphere is great for a relaxing meal. After dinner you can move over to the adjacent Swizzle Stick Lounge for a nice cocktail and live music.

CAFE GIOVANNI

117 Decatur Street | 504-529-2154 | www.cafegiovanni.com | $$$–$$$$

I love, love, love this place. Three nights a week the evening meal includes performances by local opera singers. And they aren't your average "singing waiters" either. They are truly talented and have pleasant voices. Even with the singing it is still easy to carry on a conversation. But don't come for the singers; come for the food. Renowned Chef Duke prepares dishes that melt in your mouth. May I recommend that you forget the menu? I always order the Chef's Tasting Menu and let Chef Duke feed me what he sees fit. I have not been disappointed. He doesn't go crazy with the dishes, but you'll probably try something for the first time and you might even fall in love with it! You should make reservations. Groups can be accommodated.

FRENCH QUARTER DIVES

As you explore the French Quarter, you will notice many restaurants. Some of them look like giant tourist traps, and some look like barely more than taco carts. Let me encourage you to explore the less traveled food stops. You will be surprised by the variety and general quality of the food. New Orleanians are very serious about what they put into their mouths. Ask the hotel staff where *they* would eat, not where they're supposed to tell you to eat.

Hotels

BIENVILLE HOUSE

320 Decatur Street | 504-529-2345 | www.bienvillehouse.com | Moderate

Bienville House is a historic French Quarter property that is convenient to Bourbon Street, the aquarium, and the Shops at Canal Street. This place is a great value when you consider the price, location, and cleanliness. The staff is friendly, and a continental breakfast is included with your stay.

HOTEL ROYAL

1006 Royal Street | 504-524-3900 | www.melrosegroup.com | Moderate/Luxury

The Hotel Royal is full of French Quarter charm. Located in a historic nineteenth-century home, the Royal is no cookie-cutter chain product. The location keeps you close to much of the French Quarter action so you'll save on taxi fares. The building is pretty, and you'll probably end up taking pictures in front of it. How often can you say that about your hotel?

LOEWS NEW ORLEANS HOTEL

300 Poydras Street | 504-595-3300 | www.loewshotels.com | Luxury

Planning on bringing your furry best friend? Then the Loews is the place to stay. Like all the hotels in the small chain, the New Orleans hotel is very pet friendly. Yet you don't need to have a four-legged pal to enjoy the luxury of this hotel. The rooms are spacious, the views beautiful (the lowest room floor is the elventh floor), and the service top-notch. The hotel is located just blocks (a very easy walk) from the French Quarter and across the street from Harrah's, several river attractions, and the convention center.

NEW YORK, NEW YORK

New York City's Official Visitor Information Center
810 Seventh Avenue, between Fifty-second & Fifty-third Streets
212-484-1222
www.nycvisit.com

I love New York. I have to say, it has me under its spell. There is so much to do and see! Broadway, restaurants, museums, shops, parks, and more! You'll never find the time to do everything that you want to do. New York is truly the ultimate destination. New York for business or pleasure, it just can't be beat. When I am here on business, I stay close to the office where I am to work. That typically puts me either in the financial district or on the east side around Forty-eighth and Lexington. The east side is just a block away from Fifth Avenue and the greatest shopping experience you can imagine. When I say shopping, I mean hard-core, real-deal shopping! Chanel, Gucci, and Cartier are right there at Fifth and Madison. If shopping is more of a sideline and not the primary motivation of your New York experience, do whatever you can to stay around Seventh and Broadway. The theater district, the Jumbotron with the advertisements, the crowds, and the New York feeling of the city that never sleeps are right there. No wonder New York City was the number one requested city to be included in *The Red Hat Society Travel Guide*.

Getting There

With two airports (three if you count Newark) and Amtrak service, getting to New York is not difficult at all. Once you get there, you have multiple ways of maneuvering around the city. New York is one of those places where having a car is not only optional, but it can be a great liability. Early in my travels to New York I rented a car, thinking I would need one. I drove it out of the Avis lot and into the hotel parking garage. It sat there at a rate of $35.00 per day (who knew the hotel charged more per square inch for parking than for the room itself) until I drove it out of the lot and back to the airport.

JOHN F. KENNEDY INTERNATIONAL AIRPORT (JFK)

Taxi. Every one of the nearly dozen terminals at JFK has taxi stands outside the arrivals area. Get in the taxi stand line, and wait your turn. Drivers may approach you and offer to take you to Manhattan for a "great rate." *Ignore them*. These guys are not licensed, and you run great risk by riding with them. There is a flat fee of $45.00 for any destination in Manhattan.

Shuttle. Several van services serve the airport. Also, if you find yourself at the wrong airport, there is a shuttle that goes to LaGuardia. The Manhattan SuperShuttle will take you to most hotels on the island for $19.00 per person. Find more information at www.supershuttle.com or 800-BLUE-VAN (800-258-3826).

Limo/sedan. A couple of companies can pick you up at JFK. Make all the arrangements well beforehand with the company. One of your local limo companies might be able to help you make these reservations.

Rental car. Several major rental companies have a desk here. You will have to catch a shuttle outside your terminal that will take you to the rental car center. I don't know why you're renting a car, but I guess I can't stop you.

Subway. You can reach New York's fabulous subway system via the JFK AirTrain. It picks up at every terminal. A connection to the closest subway station will cost $5.00; you will need to purchase a MetroCard for that. See more about the subway below.

LAGUARDIA AIRPORT (LGA)

Taxi. You can catch a taxi outside the arrivals area of the terminal. Get in the taxi stand line, and wait your turn. Drivers may approach you and offer to take you to Manhattan for a "great rate." *Ignore them*. These guys are not licensed, and you are at risk to ride with them. A cab ride into Manhattan costs $31.00–$36.00.

Shuttle. Different shuttles are available, including one to JFK. However, the most comprehensive Manhattan service is SuperShuttle (www.supershuttle.com or 800-BLUE-VAN [800-258-3826]). It will take you to your hotel on the big island for $16.00 per person.

Rental car. You can choose from the major rental car companies at LGA. You'll need to grab a shuttle from the terminal to get to your car—if you are renting a car, that is. I don't really see why you would, but if you so desire, there will be one for you.

Subway. There is no direct subway connection to LaGuardia. You can reach it by taking a bus, but at that point it becomes more trouble than it is worth. The rate for cabs and shuttles into Manhattan is typically reasonable enough that you might as well take one of them.

Getting Around

BIG APPLE GREETER

Want to be shown around New York by someone who really knows his stuff and not have to pay a fee? Big Apple greeters are enthusiastic people who want to introduce visitors to the New York City they know. They also are available to teach you how to use the subway or buses. They are organized by a nonprofit organization and do not expect tips. However, request your tour a month in advance. It will happen between 9:00 AM and 3:00 PM and last two to four hours. The tour request is available online at www.bigapplegreeter.org, but if you want to talk to someone before you fill out your form, you can call 212-669-8159.

SUBWAY

Learning how to use the subway is perhaps one of New York City's most intimidating tasks. It is also the least expensive and most efficient way of navigating NYC. If you take a Big Apple tour, you will get a personal lesson about the subway. The first thing to do is to find a subway map. If you have trouble reading it, ask the concierge at your hotel which train you should take to get started. You will need a MetroCard to use the subway. You can buy it from a MetroCard vending machine, station booth, or neighborhood store. If you plan on riding the subway more than once a day, you should get a Fun Pass, and if you think you will use it more than three days, you should get a seven-day Fun Pass ($24.00). A one-day Fun Pass costs $7.00, but you can't get it at a station booth. You have to use a vending machine or buy it from a neighborhood store. Some machines take cash, and some take credit or debit cards. The subway system is big, and sometimes even pros take the wrong train. If you are nervous, just ask one of the many MTA people (they wear orange smocks) for help. Many New Yorkers are friendly and may be willing to help you as well. When in doubt, ask.

BATTERY PARK

The damaged sculpture from the World Trade Center Plaza is on display in the northwest corner of the park. Along with the ball is an eternal flame in memory of the victims of 9/11. You will also see many vendors and performers in the park, some good, some not so good. Walk around and check them out before you decide to give money to any of them. You may see guys carrying big garbage bags or briefcases (but they will not be dressed in business suits). These guys are vendors, but of a different type. They often sell purses, watches, and sunglasses with brand names like Prada, Kate Spade, Gucci, and Oakley. They will say "purses" or "sunglasses" under their breath. Now, I don't think these guys have permits or a clear return policy, so purchase at your own risk. A little hint, though: never pay full price.

STATUE OF LIBERTY

www.nps.gov/stli | Hours: daily, 9:30 AM to 5:30 PM | Cost: ferry to island, $11.50; $9.50 for 62+

You can take a cab or the subway to Lady Liberty. Both ways you end up in Battery Park. As soon as you get to the park, buy your tickets to the Statue. Liberty Island closes, but the monuments at Battery Park do not. There is a good chance you will wait in line to get on the boat. Security—much like airport security—is set up before you load the boat, so be prepared for that. Tickets for the island ferry are available at the ticket booths in the park. If you would like to go into the pedestal of the statue (not into the Statue, because that is no longer allowed), you can purchase tickets online at www.statuereservations.com or call 866-STATUE4 at least twenty-four hours in advance. After you have had your fill of Lady Liberty, hop back on the ferry to . . .

ELLIS ISLAND

Ellis Island was the gateway to America for many immigrants. Maybe some of your family members passed through there. When you get off the boat, head to the big red building. That is the visitor center. It has three stories, and on each story of the building there is information about the history behind Ellis Island. You can see a collection of artifacts and limited engagements of live theater. Ellis Island includes the American Immigrant Wall of Honor; this memorial lists more than 700,000 names. Pick up a brochure and explore all that Ellis Island has to offer. Its rich history is too often overlooked.

CENTRAL PARK

Central Park is 843 acres large on the island of Manhattan. It serves as the backyard for all those in the city who do not have backyards. It is also beautiful and offers many attractions, with something for everyone.

Central Park Carousel. The current carousel, built in 1951, takes you on a three-and-a-half-minute ride. It costs $1.25 a ride and is open, weather permitting, daily, April through November, from 10:00 AM to 6:00 PM. Then from November to April it is open only on weekends from 10:00 AM to 4:30 PM.

Conservatory Garden. If you love flowers, you have to check out the Conservatory Garden at Fifth Avenue and 105th Street. It is open daily from 8:00 AM until sundown. From April to November you can take a free tour on Saturdays at 11:00 AM. A blooming schedule is available online at www.centralpark.com.

Conservatory Water. More than one movie has shown remote control boats being steered on the Conservatory Water. During some times of the year, you can rent a sailboat from the Central Park Sailboat Concession. It is located on the east side of Central Park between Seventy-second and Seventy-fifth Streets.

Dairy. The Dairy, which originally provided families traveling through the city with fresh milk, now serves as the official visitor center. If you want information about specific events in the park when you are there, go here to find out. You will also find Central Park souvenirs here. It is open from 10:00 AM to 5:00 PM, Tuesday through Sunday. It is located in the middle of the park at 65th Street.

Mall. Seen in many movies, the mall is a picturesque walkway through trees. It is a wide walkway, where people sit and socialize, read, or do anything they please. Walk all the way through the mall, and you see sculptures of famous literary authors. The mall is located midway through the park between Sixty-sixth and Seventy-second Streets.

Obelisk. The Obelisk, originally erected in ancient Egypt, was transplanted to Central Park in 1881. You can see it on East Side Drive at Eighty-first Street.

Shakespeare Garden. Another beautiful garden, it is located on the west side between Seventy-ninth and Eightieth Streets.

Swedish Cottage. The Marionette Theater that is entertaining to people of all ages is located on the west side of the park at Seventy-ninth Street. Tickets are $5.00 for children and $6.00 for adults. Reservations are required, so call first, 212-988-9093.

Victorian Gardens/Wollman Rink. During the winter, you will find the Wollman Rink on the east side between Sixty-second and Sixty-third Streets. During the summer, you will find a mini amusement park called Victorian Gardens. For additional information and the cost of admission, call 212-439-6900.

MUSEUMS

I could write an entire book on the museums of the Big Apple. New York City offers a wide variety of culture repositories, such as Alice Austen House Museum, American Craft Museum, American Folk Art Museum, American Museum of Natural History, American Museum of the Moving Image, Artists Space, Bronx Museum of the Arts, Children's Museum of the Arts, Children's Museum of Manhattan, International Center of Photography, Solomon R. Guggenheim Museum, Hayden Planetarium, Jewish Museum, Intrepid Sea-Air-Space Museum, National Museum of the American Indian, Metropolitan Museum of Art, Museum of Television and Radio, New York Transit Museum, New York City Police Museum, New York City Fire Museum, and Theodore Roosevelt's Birthplace, just to name a few. Since I'm not writing an entire book on the museums of the Big Apple, I'll have to focus on two of my favorites: the American Museum of Natural History and the Museum of Modern Art.

AMERICAN MUSEUM OF NATURAL HISTORY

Central Park West at Seventy-ninth Street | 212-769-5100 | Hours: daily, 10:00 AM to 5:45 PM | Cost: $10.00; $7.50 for 65+

The American Museum of Natural History consists of four floors and a lower level of more than 500,000 objects. It includes artifacts, replicas, and an amazing collection of dinosaur fossils, one of the biggest collections in the world. The first thing you need to do when you enter the museum is to buy your ticket. If you pay with cash, you'll wait in line for your ticket. However, if you use a credit or debit card, you may purchase your ticket at some automated booths. There you can get your map and ask when the next free tour begins. Museum volunteers will show you several exhibits and provide you with a wealth of information during the tour. If you are hungry and have time before your tour starts, then head down to the lower level and grab a bite at the cafeteria-style museum Food Court. Or you may choose a cafe on the first or fourth floor. The cafes are open only on Saturday and Sunday unless otherwise posted. The museum is a big place. Get there early, and plan to spend several hours.

MUSEUM OF MODERN ART

Fifty-third Street, between Fifth and Sixth Avenues | 212-708-9685 | www.moma.org | Hours: Saturday–Thursday, 10:30 AM to 5:30 PM; Friday, 10:30 AM to 8:00 PM | Cost: $20.00; $16.00 for 65+

The Museum of Modern Art contains a vast collection of art. With many different styles and collections of art, the museum will prove a joy for art gurus and novices alike. The museum's collection includes Picassos, Warhols, Van Goghs, and Monets. If you are hungry, you can stop by Cafe 2 for cafeteria-style dining. Another full-service cafe is located on Terrace 5. A chic restaurant named the Modern is located on the first floor at its own entrance. If you would like to coordinate a personal tour, call 212-708-9685 to find out about rates and availability.

TIMES SQUARE

Perhaps the most recognizable location in New York City, Times Square is full of people, shops, restaurants, and more. The New York City Visitor Center is located near Times Square, and a police department branch is located right in the middle of it. There is a lot to take in here, and you'll want to make at least one visit after dark. It's the only way to get the full effect.

CHINATOWN

In Chinatown, a lot of people are packed in a small space. It is located right off Canal Street. Here you will find fresh fish, knickknacks, bric-a-brac, and other goods. Dozens of souvenirs and trinkets are for sale. This is the best place to buy cheap but interesting gifts for friends. Right around the corner is Little Italy; if you want real Italian food, this is the place to go.

EMPIRE STATE BUILDING
Fifth Avenue between Thirty-third and Thirty-fourth Streets | Cost: $18.00; $16.00 for 65+

You can get one of the highest views in NYC from the Empire State Building. It has 103 floors and 1,860 steps, and it is 1,440 feet tall. There is a security check, and no bottles are allowed past the check. You can choose from two observatories: one on the 86th floor, and one on the 102nd floor, which costs an additional $15.00.

ROCKEFELLER CENTER
600 Fifth Avenue | New York, NY 10111 | Hours: daily, 8:00 AM to midnight | Cost: $17.50 for adult; $16.00 for senior; $11.25 for child

Created by John D. Rockefeller, the Rockefeller Center is said to have one of the best views in New York City. Located in mid-Manhattan, the center offers a view from 70 stories high that stretches for miles on every side. You can purchase tickets in advance by calling 877-NYC-ROCK. If you purchase tickets by phone, you must do it a minimum of three hours in advance. Tours for Rockefeller Center are available, except on Thanksgiving Day and Christmas Day. The tours last an hour, and start every two hours after 11:00 AM until 5:00 PM, except on Sunday when tours end at 3:00 PM. Tours cost $10.00 for children and seniors and $12.00 for adults. Art and observation tours are available for a different cost from regular tours.

NEW YORK CITY'S OFFICIAL VISITOR CENTERS
New York City's Official Visitor Centers are the best places to get information about New York and what is going on while you are there. They offer free coupons and brochures for places around the city. Times vary depending on location, and holiday hours vary. You can call the visitor center for information at 212-484-1222. Please note, not all services are available at

all locations so one quick call may save some frustration. Check the informative Web site at www.nycvisit.com.

NEW YORK CITY'S OFFICIAL VISITOR INFORMATION CENTER
810 Seventh Avenue, between 52nd & 53rd Streets | 212-484-1222 |
Hours: Monday to Friday 8:30 AM to 6 PM; Saturday & Sunday 9 AM to 5 PM

You can purchase MetroCards and CityPasses (front-of-the-line access to New York City's top attractions and museums) as well as tickets for Gray Line New York Sightseeing double-decker tours (a stop for the tours is directly in front of the Midtown Visitor Center).

NYC HERITAGE TOURISM CENTER
Southern tip of City Hall Park on the Broadway sidewalk at Park Row |
Hours: Monday–Friday 9:00 AM–6:00 PM; Saturday and Sunday, 10:00 AM–5:00 PM.
Open seven days a week.

Interactive displays, brochures on history-themed tours and attractions and knowledgeable staffers to help visitors find out about the people, places and events of historical importance in New York City.

CHINATOWN
The Official Visitor Information Kiosk for Chinatown is located at the triangle where Canal, Walker and Baxter Streets meet | Hours: Monday–Sunday: 10 AM–6 PM; Saturday: 10:00 AM–7:00 PM.

The kiosk has a red and gold dragon and neon pagoda roof and there's an eight-foot-tall translucent map of the area on its western wall.

HARLEM
Harlem Visitor Information Center (In the lobby of the Apollo Theater) | 253 West 125th Street (between Frederick Douglass and Adam Clayton Powell Jr. Boulevards) | Hours: Monday–Friday 10:00 AM–6:00 PM

FINANCIAL DISTRICT

Federal Hall Information Center at the Federal Hall National Memorial | 26 Wall Street | Hours: Monday–Friday 9:00 AM–5:00 PM, except for federal holidays

Shopping

Many people come to New York City for one primary reason: to shop. Every retailer, wholesaler, and designer worth a penny has a presence in the city. You can usually find several shops in a cluster. If shopping is your focus for your visit, the area of Fifth and Madison will dazzle you. Chanel, Gucci, and Cartier are lined up for your indulgence. Times Square holds a few flagship stores and some unique shops. If you don't mind questionable authenticity but love a great deal, an afternoon in Chinatown will suit you well.

Entertainment

BROADWAY

There is something "on Broadway" for everyone (but many shows are not actually on the street called Broadway). Musicals, comedies, dramas—you can find it all here. Except for rare occasions, tickets are available online, but if you want to get the best deal on tickets, visit the TKTS booths in Times Square or South Street Seaport. Every day Broadway shows turn in unsold tickets or house seats. At the TKTS booths you can scoop up these tickets for half price. They sell only same-day tickets, and not every show is always available. But I have never been disappointed with a visit to a TKTS booth. The Times Square booth line gets long early. I always head to the South Street Seaport location where I can often walk right up to the ticket window.

THE METROPOLITAN OPERA

Lincoln Center | 212-362-6000 | www.metoperafamily.org/metopera

The Met is the grande dame of Western Hemisphere opera companies. There is no greater house to be played on this side of the world. The operas are of a scale that is rarely rivaled, and the talent is the best of the best. No lover of music, theater, or art should skip the Met. The schedule may not fit with yours, but if it does, take the time and spend the money. You can also contact the company for tours to the Metropolitan Opera House.

Eateries

MAX BRENNER: CHOCOLATE BY THE BALD MAN

841 Broadway (between Thirteenth and Fourteenth Streets) | 212-388-0030 | www.maxbrenner.com | $$

In keeping with our motto of eating dessert first, I must say that Max Brenner: Chocolate by the Bald Man in Union Square is one great place to do it. For those who love chocolate, it is an absolute no-brainer. For those of you who aren't die-hard chocolate fans, it will work for you too. Chocolate is certainly the focus, but the menu includes sandwiches and salads should you absolutely feel the necessity to eat "real food" before diving into your dessert. The sandwiches and salads are good and large enough to share. The cafe takes reservations Monday through Thursday for parties of fifteen or more, but other than that, you are on your own. We arrived with a party of six at 7:00 PM on a Saturday, and it took us about one hour to be seated. There is a small gift shop that will be a diversion while you wait. If they offer samples of the cocoa-covered caramelized pecans, do not pass them up!

PATRICK CONWAY'S

40 East Forty-third Street | 212-286-1873 | www.patrickconways.com | $$

If you can't get to Ireland to dine in an Irish pub, at least go to one in New York City. One of my favorites is Patrick Conway's. If you have never experienced the atmosphere of an Irish pub, Pat Conway's is a great place to do it. The dark wood bar and beamed ceiling create a comfortable atmosphere. The warm greeting from the waitstaff (all of whom seem to be supporting that delightful Irish accent) will have you dreaming of the Old Country. I've heard rave reviews about the Black Jack Burger but my favorite is the Shepherd's Pie.

JEKYLL AND HYDE CLUB

Fifty-seventh Street and Sixth Avenue, just below Central Park | 212-541-9505 | www.jekyllandhydeclub.com | $$–$$$

If you want a unique dining experience, head over to the Jekyll and Hyde Club. The club employs professional actors who don't break character while they walk around and talk to diners. There are also animatronic musical acts. The Jekyll and Hyde Club accepts only American Express and, of course, cold, hard cash.

Hotels

THE BEDFORD HOTEL

118 E. 40th Street | 800-221-6881 | www.bedfordhotel.com | Moderate

The Bedford Hotel is a charming hotel very close to Grand Central Station, Park Avenue, and shopping. Recently redone, it has a varitey of room sizes, all with small kitchettes containing a mini refrigerator and some with microwaves. The rooms are large by NYC standards and the staff is exceptional. It has a large European clientele and you meet the most facinating people in the lobby.

BROADWAY INN

264 West Forty-sixth Street | 800-826-630 | www.broadwayinn.com | Moderate

If you're coming to New York City for the theater experience (why wouldn't you be?), consider the Broadway Inn. This little charmer right in the middle of the action has great staff and free breakfast. The deals are good here. If you can get a room, take it.

THE EXCELSIOR HOTEL

45 West Eighty-first Street | 212-362-9200 | www.excelsiorhotelny.com | Luxury

The Excelsior Hotel has recently been restored to glory. This West End property brings you Old World elegance without emptying your bank account. The rooms are a good size and well appointed. The staff is top-notch, and the hotel is rated four stars for service.

ORLANDO, FLORIDA

Orlando Visitor and Convention Bureau
6700 Forum Drive
Orlando, FL 32821
407-363-5800
800-972-3304
www.orlandoinfo.com

Orlando has to be the hardest city I have written about. There is just too much to do here: Walt Disney World, SeaWorld, Universal Studios, and more! An unfortunate side effect of all these things to do is the millions of other people who cram themselves into the Orlando area every year. The best piece of advice I can give is to avoid all school holidays and most of the summer. You can look anywhere online for all the information you need about the superparks, so I am going to tell you about some things to see that are not on every list. I hope you don't mind, but if you do, feel free to spend a day with the mouse.

Getting There

Plane, train, or automobile—all three will help you get to the Orlando area. When considering your mode of travel, you should think about convenience, price, atmosphere, and personal preference. In other words, I can't and I won't make that decision for you!

ORLANDO INTERNATIONAL AIRPORT (MCO)

Since Orlando is one of the top tourist destinations in the world, it is no surprise that just about everybody flies in to MCO. Once you get there you'll have your choice of taxi, hotel shuttle, private shuttle, or limo. You can also grab a rental car, which might fit in better with your plans.

Taxi. MCO has two entrances, side A and side B. You can hail a cab on either side as long as you head down to the ground transportation level (level 1). Unfortunately there are no government-mandated flat fees, so you will pay meter rates. These rates can vary greatly, depending upon your destination in the Orlando area. Don't be afraid to ask the driver for an approximation of the fare. You can get to downtown Orlando for $35.00, but it's going to cost you $60.00 to go to Walt Disney World. If you have special transport needs, you might want to make a reservation ahead of time. You can do so at www.mearstransportation.com.

Shuttle. Many airport area hotels offer complimentary shuttles, but for most other hotels you have to pay a third-party shuttle service. The good news is that unless you are traveling in a group of four or five, the shuttle is usually a better deal than a taxi. The better news is that the shuttle company that serves MCO has an amazingly detailed Web site at www.mearstransportation.com, or you can call 407-423-5566.

Limo/sedan. Dozens of limo services serve the airport. And as much as I would like to try them all, I just don't have the energy. That's why I recommend Mears Transportation. I know I've mentioned the company already, but it is really the only comprehensive transport service at the airport. Visit the all-purpose Web site at www.mearstransportation.com or dial the sedan service at 407-423-5566.

Rental car. Alamo, Avis, Budget, Dollar, National, and some company called L & M offer in-terminal service on level 1. For Enterprise, Hertz, Thrifty, and a half-dozen local companies, you'll need to hitch a ride on their courtesy shuttles.

AMTRAK

There is limited Amtrak service coming in from New York and Miami. If riding the rails is your thing and the train stops close by, you should consider hopping aboard. All the details can be found at www.amtrak.com.

Getting Around

Getting around Orlando and choosing the best way to do it depend on the area where you are staying. The greater Orlando area, including downtown Disney, is served by taxis and the city's Lynx bus system. The bus stops are marked with a distinctive Lynx catpaw print. The standard one-way fare for Lynx is $1.50. Single-day passes cost $3.50.

If you are focused primarily on the downtown Orlando area, the Lymmo service may suit your needs. It serves twenty-one stops in the downtown area, and it is free.

For more information on Lynx or Lymmo, contact customer service at 407-841-5959 or www.golynx.com.

Another way to get around Orlando is the I-Ride Trolley. It serves primarily the International Drive Resort area. This includes SeaWorld, Universal Studios, Prime Outlets Shopping, Orlando Premium Outlets, and countless restaurants and hotels. I-Ride Trolley single fare is $1.00, and unlimited ride day passes start at $3.00. You can call 407-354-5656 for more information or go to www.iridetrolley.com.

Attractions

I promised to focus on some of Orlando's lesser-known (but no less entertaining) attractions. However, I am not so thick as to assume that no one will want to visit the big guys. So for your convenience, dear reader, I provide basic information on them.

WALT DISNEY WORLD/DISNEY ATTRACTIONS

407-939-6244 | www.waltdisneyworld.com | Hours: vary by season | Cost: many ticket packages are available for Disney attractions. One-day park passes start at $40.00

UNIVERSAL STUDIOS/ISLANDS OF ADVENTURE

407-363-8000 | www.universalorlando.com | Hours: vary by season | Cost: Universal offers several options to visit its parks and attractions. One-day, one-park passes start at $60.00

SEAWORLD

800-4-ADVENTURE | www.seaworld.com | A special site for mature markets is www.seniors4adventure.com/seaworld/fla/index.html | Hours: vary by season | Cost: different ticket options available; one-day, one-park passes start at $65.00; Group discounts available

Now that we have that out of the way, let's see what else Central Florida has to offer.

HARRY P. LEU GARDENS

1920 North Forest Avenue | 407-246-2620 | www.leugardens.org | Hours: daily, 9:00 AM to 5:00 PM; closed Christmas Day | Cost: $5.00 for adult

In 1936 Harry P. Leu bought a house and some land and started what would turn out to be one of the country's great gardens. More than two thousand plants from around the world make up this remarkable collection of flora. For those of you with an interest in local history, the 1888 Leu house is open for tours. Give them three weeks' notice and the staff of the gardens will be happy to put together a special tour for your group. A self-guided group tour is also available. At $5.00 per person this is the best deal in Orlando!

KENNEDY SPACE CENTER VISITOR CENTER

45 minutes east of Orlando on State Road 405 | 321-449-4444 | www.kennedyspacecenter.com | Hours: daily, 9:00 AM to —varying closing times; closed Christmas Day | Cost: $38.00 for adult, includes basic tour, IMAX, Hall of Fame, and all attractions and exhibits

Many of us have at least one or more events from the space program etched into our memories. Be it the moon landing or the *Challenger* explosion, events that originated here have had an unquestionable impact on the world. Now you can get up close and personal with NASA in a way that would have been unthinkable during the great space race. Included with your admission is a hop-on/hop-off bus tour that will take you to several storied sites on the campus. You can also enjoy an eye-popping adventure at one of the back-to-back IMAX theaters. Those of you with a sense of adventure might want to try the center's new shuttle launch simulation. Check at the admission desk for the time of the "Meet an Astronaut" talk. They have one every day, and it's your chance to chat with someone who has been in space! The center is completely handicapped accessible.

ORLANDO MUSEUM OF ART

2416 North Mills Avenue | 407-896-4231 | www.omart.org | Hours: Tuesday–Friday, 10:00 AM to 4:00 PM; Saturday–Sunday, noon to 4:00 pm; closed Mondays & major holidays | Cost: $8.00 for adult; $7.00 for 65+

The Orlando Museum of Art has a long history of bringing some of the finest traveling exhibits in the world to town. The museum also has an impressive collection that it rotates in and out of its galleries. The collection consists mainly of a wide variety of American art, but there are many interesting African pieces. I suggest that you plan to devote at least two hours to properly take in the exhibits. Before you leave for Orlando, you might want to check the museum's Web site to see what traveling exhibit will be featured during your stay. The museum and its galleries are completely handicapped accessible.

DISCOVERY COVE
6000 Discovery Cove Way | 407-370-1280 | www.discoverycove.com | Hours: daily, 9:00 AM to 5:30 PM; check-in begins at 8:00 AM | Cost: $279.00 with dolphin experience; $179.00 without dolphin experience

This all-inclusive island of adventure is a theme park like no other. I almost hesitate to call it a theme park. The park keeps crowds manageable by limiting daily admission to one thousand. As a result, you need to purchase your passes in advance, sometimes months in advance. Your ticket includes a continental breakfast and a sumptuous lunch. You will also swim with dolphins, wade with stingrays, feed tropical birds, and have a number of other once-in-a-lifetime interactions. Your ticket also includes a seven-day pass to SeaWorld Orlando or Busch Gardens in Tampa Bay. There are other, more expensive, packages that allow for greater animal interaction with even fewer guests. Discovery Cove works hard to make as many of its experiences open to those with limited mobility as possible. But many of the park's attractions involve wading and swimming.

Shopping

There is a wide variety of shopping experiences in Orlando. For the outlet junkies out there you will enjoy the 110 shops at Orlando Premium Outlets. Downtown Disney offers its own selection of unique shops and boutiques. If you're seeking a more laid-back shopping binge, head to the Pointe Orlando outdoor mall.

Entertainment

You might be worn out after a day of theme parks and shopping, but you won't want to miss the Orlando nightlife. From dinner theater to dance clubs, Orlando has a little bit of everything.

PIRATE'S DINNER ADVENTURE

6400 Carrier Drive | 800-866-2469 | www.piratesdinneradventure.com | Show times vary by season | Cost: $55.95 for adult; group rates available

You may choose from several themed dinner shows in town, but this one is by far the most exciting. Combining acting, singing, acrobatics, sword fighting, and special effects, the Pirate's show is a true spectacle. The cast and crew of 150 make up one of the largest dinner theater staffs in the area. Be sure to practice your "Arrgh!" because this is a very interactive dinner theater show. The theater is completely accessible.

CIRQUE DU SOLEIL

1478 East Buena Vista Drive (downtown Disney) | 407-939-7600 | www.cirquedusoleil.com | Hours: Tuesday–Saturday, shows at 6:00 and 9:00 PM | Cost: $63.00–$112.00

Located in the downtown Disney complex, Cirque du Soleil's *La Nouba* is an unforgettable experience. The show delivers the seemingly impossible aerobatics for which the group is known, along with a rich visual design. See acts like the flying trapeze, aerial cradle, and the silk aerial ballet as you watch the battle between the Cirques and the Urbains. It's an expensive show, but you will not be disappointed.

ORLANDO SHAKESPEARE THEATER

812 East Rollins Street | 407-447-1700 | www.orlandoshakes.org | Show times and dates vary | Cost: $10.00–$35.00

From humble beginnings in 1989 to a 50,000-square-foot complex and a year-round schedule, the Orlando Shakespeare Theater (OST) proves that there is life in the classics yet. Check the schedule, and if there is a show during your visit, be sure to grab tickets. Often putting classic shows in modern settings, OST can bring new life even to plays you have seen many times before.

THEATRE DOWNTOWN

2113 North Orange Avenue | 407-841-0083 | www.theatredowntown.net |
Show times and dates vary | Cost: $18.00 for adult; $15.00 for student or senior

For those of you in the mood for theater a little edgier than Shakespeare, I present Theatre Downtown. One of Orlando's top professional venues, Theatre Downtown prides itself on presenting theater for the thinking person. While the company often mixes classics and new works into the schedule, be prepared for an experience different from your average local theater. Consistent in creativity and quality, a Theatre Downtown show is always a treat.

Eateries

CHARLIE'S GOURMET PASTRIES

3213 Curry Ford Road | 407-898-9561 | www.charliesgourmetpastries.com |
Dessert | $

This local mainstay has been pumping out the sweetest treats in Orlando since 1971. Ask the locals and they'll say Charlie's is *the* place for dessert. The selection of well-priced pastries, cookies, cheesecakes, and breads will satisfy even the pickiest sweet tooth.

JIMMY BUFFETT'S MARGARITAVILLE

6000 Universal Boulevard (City Walk) | 407-224-2155 |
www.margaritavilleorlando.com | $$

This one is for all the Parrot Heads out there! Of course you don't *have* to be a Jimmy Buffett fan to enjoy Margaritaville, but it helps. Famous for its eponymous drink and the Cheeseburger in Paradise, Margaritaville also offers seafood and traditional land-based fare. Check out the renowned desserts!

LE COQ AU VIN

4800 South Orange Avenue | 407-851-6980 | lecoqauvinrestaurant.com | $$

Considering it is one of the area's most renowned restaurants, Le Coq Au Vin is reasonably priced. Fans of French cooking will be in heaven here. You may also bring your own favorite wine (the restaurant has a fine selection also). It alls sounds fancy but feel free to wear comfortable clothes appropriate for dining.

EMERIL'S ORLANDO

6000 Universal Boulevard, Suite 702 (City Walk) | 407-224-2424 | www.emerils.com/restaurants/orlando_emerils | $$–$$$

Bam! Are you ready for some kicking Creole cuisine from the legendary Emeril? The high-energy atmosphere of all of Emeril's restaurants is complemented by the Orlando location in Universal City Walk. The restaurant is open for lunch and dinner; every Emeril fan should stop by for a bite.

Hotels

CELEBRATION HOTEL

700 Bloom Street | 407-566-6000 | www.celebrationhotel.com | Moderate

Located in the Disney-created town of Celebration, this hotel sometimes seems far away from the hustle and bustle of Orlando. It is a good choice for those leery of staying in a park-affiliated megaresort. The 115 rooms are decorated in a turn-of-the-century style but contain all of the modern amenities. Don't plan on walking to Orlando attractions; take the hotel's Disney World shuttle.

PARK PLAZA HOTEL

307 Park Avenue South | 407-647-1072 | www.parkplazahotel.com | Moderate

The Park Plaza is for those who really want to get away from the theme park crowd. Kids are welcome here, just none under five. A quiet and classy joint since 1922, the Park Plaza is truly unique for this area. Fine dining and cultural establishments are within walking distance. Getting to the bigger attractions will require some travel.

GAYLORD PALMS RESORT

6000 West Osceola Parkway | 407-586-0000 | www.gaylordpalms.com | Moderate/Luxury

Gaylord Resorts are famous for their giant atriums, and the Gaylord Palms is no exception. More than four acres of glass cover the atrium that recreates several Florida landmarks such as the Everglades. You'll also have your choice of several on-site restaurants and activities. The Gaylord Palms is convenient to Walt Disney World, but you might have to do some traveling to other attractions.

PEABODY HOTEL

9801 International Drive | 407-352-4000 | www.peabodyorlando.com | Luxury

The Peabody Orlando brings all the luxury of its Memphis namesake to central Florida. Spoil yourself at this four-star landmark hotel with state-of-the-art amenities and a renowned on-site spa. The hotel is also in the middle of Orlando action on International Drive. Be sure to catch the marching of the Peabody ducks every morning and evening.

PHILADELPHIA, PENNSYLVANIA

Philadelphia Convention and Visitors Bureau
1700 Market Street, Suite 3000
Philadelphia, PA 19103
215-636-3300
www.philadelphiausa.travel

Philadelphia positively oozes history, culture, and fun. As the second largest city on the East Coast and the birthplace of American democracy, Philadelphia has held a key position in American history. Here you will find the storied Liberty Bell and the historic Independence Hall. There is plenty of new Philadelphia to explore too. Other attractions include the slightly more modern Philadelphia Museum of Art and the contemporary Adventure Aquarium. Despite its large population, Philadelphia is a very manageable city to visit. Don't let big city fears keep you from visiting this American gem.

Getting There

As a population center on the crowded eastern American seaboard, there is plenty of easy access to Philadelphia. Other East Coasters may have an easy drive into the city. People a little farther out may be able to catch a high speed train and zoom into downtown in no time. Of course for those of us farther away, there is the airport.

PHILADELPHIA INTERNATIONAL AIRPORT (PHL)

Philadelphia International Airport has almost as complex and interesting a history as the city that it serves. The airport was dedicated in the 1920s by Charles Lindbergh on a goodwill tour after his famous trans-Atlantic flight. It later overtook the emergency shipbuilding yards of World War I and was shut down for security reasons for several years during World War II. Ever since PHL reopened to commercial air traffic in 1945, it has been undergoing almost constant renovation and expansion.

Taxi. You can catch a cab in zone 5 of what is called the Commercial Transportation Roadway. I know it sounds complicated but just follow the signs. The average cab in town will limit you to three passengers, though some will accommodate four. There is a flat rate of $25.00 between the airport and central Philadelphia. If you are going someplace other than the center of the city, there is a $10.00 minimum for all rides originating at the airport.

Shuttle. Several shuttle companies serve the airport, and the rates vary. The shuttle that will serve you also depends on where you need to go in town. Since PHL is so close to downtown and also has a high-speed rail link, I recommend taking a taxi or a train into downtown. More information on shuttles can be obtained by calling the Philadelphia International Ground Transportation Department at 215-937-6958.

Rental car. Philadelphia International Airport is well served by major rental car companies. To pick up your car, you will need to catch a rental car shuttle in zone 2. Ask the counter agent for directions if you are driving into town.

High speed train. The High Speed R1 SEPTA train will take you to several convenient center city stops for just $5.50. Even if you have to take a cab from or transfer trains at one of the stops, this could be your cheapest option. Check with your hotel for tips on how to use SEPTA to reach your hotel from the airport.

Getting Around

Philadelphia has a comprehensive passenger rail system through its SEPTA service. There are both regional trains and local lines. The system navigation isn't as streamlined as many places, but if you can master the system, you can get just about anywhere inexpensively. Don't be reluctant to ask hotel staff or SEPTA employees for assistance and route planning.

Attractions

By far Philadelphia's top attractions are ones related to the early history of the United States. Though it lost out in the bid for being the nation's capital (to a nonexistent Washington, D.C.) and was eventually surpassed by New York City in population, many historians believe that Philadelphia has had more impact on American history than any other city. However, Philadelphia doesn't just live in the past; plenty of modern attractions and activities supplement the historical side of things.

INDEPENDENCE NATIONAL HISTORICAL PARK
Chestnut Street between Fifth and Sixth Streets | 215-965-2305 | www.nps.gov/inde | Cost: *free*! (for the most part)

Philadelphia has the distinction of being home to some of the most important historic sites in North America. Fortunately most of these sites are pretty close together and are part of the National Park Service. Here is a sample of what you can do:

INDEPENDENCE HALL
I do not know why people get so excited about this old building. I mean, it is not like anything important ever happened here. Oh, okay. Maybe a couple of minor things such as the signing of the Declaration of Independence and the Constitution and the meeting of the Second Continental Congress.

This is the most popular tour in Philadelphia, and tickets go quickly during the peak season of March to December. The timed-tickets are free if you do a same-day pickup, or you can pay a nominal fee to reserve your spot in line online at www.recreation.gov.

THE LIBERTY BELL

The Liberty Bell is the most famous bell in the world. There is good reason for this. The Liberty Bell has a colorful history that includes ringing for important events in the early years of the United States, being hidden in a manure wagon to escape the British, being recast more often than a daytime soap opera, becoming a key symbol in the antislavery movement, and being rumored to be purchased by Taco Bell. The bell now resides in the new Liberty Bell Center and can be visited without charge or ticket. You will have to go through airport-style security, and lines can form during peak times.

CONGRESS HALL

Congress Hall may be Independence Hall's nerdy little brother, but it, too, has been home to several events of historic note. Congress Hall served as the U.S. Capitol for ten years, beginning in 1790. The hall also hosted presidential inaugurations for John Adams and George Washington. Let's see, what else? Oh, it served as the birthplace for several states, the U.S. Mint, and the United States Navy. Congress Hall is never as crowded as Independence Hall but in many ways is just as historically significant.

THE SECOND BANK OF THE UNITED STATES

In the end the Second Bank of the United States didn't fare much better than the First (also in Philadelphia). Both died. However, the Second Bank left the city with a remarkable example of Greek Revival architecture. If you want to see what those people you learned about in Independence Hall looked like, the Second Bank building is the place. The building now houses a large gallery of portraits of several people of influence in early America.

FRANKLIN COURT

This somewhat odd attraction is located on the site of Benjamin Franklin's home (a structure long lost). Franklin Court contains a steel "ghost" frame of that house. It is a really interesting way to present something that has vanished into the mists of history. Below the court, you will find a museum about Benjamin Franklin and his life. The museum includes a film presentation, Franklin artifacts, and an eighteenth-century printer's office.

CHRIST CHURCH
Christ Church traces its roots to 1695. The church is informally known as "the nation's church" because many early American leaders worshiped in its pews. The congregation offers hourly tours of its building for no charge, though it asks for donations. The building, a couple of blocks from Independence Park, is not nearly as popular as the burial ground across the street from the park. It will cost you a couple of dollars to tour the historic burial ground, the final resting place for Benjamin Franklin and four other signers of the Declaration of Independence. For more information go to www.oldchristchurch.org.

NATIONAL CONSTITUTION CENTER
The National Constitution Center may be the most modern site (2003) in the park, but it is dedicated to history. The center is a remarkable interactive museum that traces the history of the Constitution and its effects through the history of the United States. Exhibits include live action multimedia performances, Supreme Court reenactments, and life-sized bronze castings of the Founding Fathers. The NCC is the best way to wrap your head around all of the historical information and experience you get from the park's other sites.

MUTTER MUSEUM
19 South Twenty-second Street | 215-563-3737 | www.collphyphil.org/mutter.asp | Hours: Daily, 10:00 AM to 5:00 PM | Cost: $12.00; $8.00 for 65+

The Mutter is a historic house of medical oddities. The collection first went on display in 1858 and has grown to more than twenty thousand objects. Included in the collection are the famous Soap Lady, a plaster cast of the conjoined twins Chang and Ang, two thousand objects extracted from people's throats, and scores of brains, tumors, and other bodily objects floating in jars. The museum even has a presidential angle; it displays the cancer growth of President Grover Cleveland. Don't worry. It's not all as gross and off-putting as it sounds. The historical setting and display are a fascinating look into the history of the science of medicine.

ELFRETH'S ALLEY
215-574-0560 | www.elfrethsalley.org | Cost: $5.00

You are probably wondering why I would send you to a random alley in town. Well, I assure you this is no random alley. Elfreth's Alley is the oldest continually occupied residential area in the United States. The Alley was opened in 1702, and the current thirty-two structures were built between 1728 and 1836. The only house regularly opened to the public houses the Elfreth's Alley Museum. There are several guided tours every day.

PHILADELPHIA MUSEUM OF ART
Benjamin Franklin Parkway at Twenty-sixth Street | 215-763-8100 | www.philamuseum.org

After you have finished taking in all of the history that Philadelphia has to offer, the museum is next on the must-see list. The Philadelphia Museum of Art is in the top five of major museums in the United States. It doesn't focus on one style or age of art; instead it presents what is almost a history of mankind in artistic objects. The museum is famous around the world for its top-notch special exhibitions, some of which have been visited by hundreds of thousands of viewers. The impressive museum building is also the location of the famed "Rocky Steps," from their iconic use in the *Rocky* films.

Shopping

Philadelphia is world class in every way, and that includes shopping. Many of you will be in a historic mood and have a craving for antiques. The perfect place to stop is Antique Row, three blocks of antique and curio shops. For a more modern experience, go just out of town to the Plaza and the Crown at King of Prussia. This complex is the largest shopping center on the East Coast. A uniquely Philadelphia place to visit is Reading Terminal Market, which is packed with local vendors.

Entertainment
_____

Philadelphia is known around the world as a city of culture, and it takes this label very seriously. It has several renowned theater companies, at least two major opera stages, a handful of touring houses, and spectacular instrumental organizations.

PHILADELPHIA THEATRE COMPANY

480 South Broad Street | 215-985-0420 | www.phillytheatreco.com | Show times and dates vary

This storied theater company has just moved into a wonderful new performance space. The Philadelphia Theatre Company regularly produces world premieres and has sent several shows off to Broadway. Big-name actors also enjoy performing here.

PRINCE MUSIC THEATER

1412 Chestnut Street | 215-972-1000 | www.princemusictheater.org | Show times and dates vary

The Prince Music Theater, named after Broadway producer and director Hal Prince, is Philadelphia's top source for professionally produced theatrical musicals. The productions here are consistently good and occasionally amazing.

INTERACT THEATRE COMPANY

2030 Sansom Street | 215-568-8077 | www.interacttheatre.org | Show times and dates vary

The InterAct Theatre is the place to go if you're looking for something new and edgy that will make you think. The InterAct is known as Philadelphia's socially conscious theater. The shows can range from slapstick satire to very dark drama, but all have something important to say.

ARDEN THEATRE COMPANY

40 North Second Street | 215-922-1122 | www.ardentheatre.org | Show times and dates vary

The Arden Theatre Company is yet another top theater company that calls Philadelphia home. The company presents a combination of world premieres and previously performed plays. Being able to choose from the Philadelphia Theatre Company, InterAct, and the Arden, you should be able to find at least one interesting show during your visit.

OPERA COMPANY OF PHILADELPHIA

1420 Locust Street | 215-893-3600 | www.operaphilly.org

Show times and dates vary

The Opera Company of Philadelphia is a top-tier producer of grand opera. The company usually produces five shows a year, so you will need to check the schedule before you hit town. Each production is large and impressive, and presents world-class talent.

THE PHILADELPHIA ORCHESTRA

260 South Broad Street | 215-893-1900 | www.philorch.org | Show times and dates vary

The Philadelphia Orchestra is regarded as one of the top organizations of its kind in the world. No music lover should visit the city without planning an evening here. The orchestra has maintained a level of performance seldom experienced anywhere else.

CURTIS INSTITUTE OF MUSIC

1726 Locust Street | 215-893-5252 | www.curtis.edu | Performance times and dates vary

The Curtis Institute of Music is famous for turning out top musicians by the dozen. Now is your chance to hear some of them before they hit it big and start charging an arm and a leg. The Curtis often has free showcases and recitals; the institute also maintains its own Opera Theatre. Check the Curtis site to see what is happening during your stay.

Eateries

The food scene in Philadelphia is diverse. This city has been attracting immigrants from around the world for centuries. With these immigrants came a unique blend of tastes and preferences.

MARÖN CHOCOLATES AND SCOOP DE VILLE
1734 Chestnut Street | 215-988-9992 | Dessert | $

This place is a Philadelphia legend. The shop opened in the 1850s and has been satisfying Philly's sweet tooth ever since. You can stick with the classic Marön Chocolate concoctions or visit the Scoop de Ville to try the gourmet ice cream.

PINK ROSE PASTRY SHOP
630 South Fourth Street | 215-592-0565 | Dessert | $

Pink Rose Pastry Shop is an amazing dessert place. Don't take my word for it—locals and tourists alike crowd into this place. It has all the sweet baked goods you can imagine, and maybe some that you can't.

PAT'S KING OF STEAKS
Ninth at Wharton and Passyunk | 215-468-1546 | www.patskingofsteaks.com | $–$$

Pat's King of Steaks is the home of the legendary Philly cheese steaks. How could you come to Philadelphia and not get one of them? The joint is open twenty-four hours, so it will fit anywhere in your schedule.

PHILADELPHIA FISH & COMPANY
207 Chestnut Street | 215-625-8605 | $$

Seafood lovers *have* to try this place. The fresh raw materials combined with the expertise of the chef create seafood delights that are hard to match. So if you think things that swim taste good, then Philadelphia Fish & Company is for you.

RISTORANTE PANORAMA
14 North Front Street | 215-922-7800 | $$

Ristorante Panorama is the best Italian food value in town. It serves handmade pasta and other classic Italian dishes. Wine lovers will also enjoy choosing from more than two hundred types of vino.

JAKE'S RESTAURANT
4365 Main Street | 215-483-0444 | www.jakesrestaurant.com | $$–$$$

Jake's is pretty well known around the area as a good, reasonably priced place to eat. Don't let the name fool you; it is no diner or dive. Jake's is comfortable and well appointed. A wide variety of both water-based and land-based food is served.

OVERTURES
609-611 East Passyunk Avenue | 215-627-3455 | $$$

Overtures is styled in the French tradition of restaurants. However, the chef is known to be a little creative with the classic dishes. This location is small and cozy and perfect for a relaxed dinner before or after a show.

Hotels

You will find new hotels and old hotels and old hotels made new. There are super-upper-class hotels and dive hotels. There are hotels next to every attraction you plan to visit and hotels that aren't near anything at all. Here are a few of my sister Red Hatters' favorites. They are clean, unique, and well located.

ALEXANDER INN

Twelfth and Spruce Streets | 215-923-3535 | www.alexanderinn.com | Moderate

The Alexander is a wonderful independent boutique that could probably raise its rates, yet refuses to do so. The staff work hard to make sure that you will enjoy your stay and spread the word. The hotel's location is convenient to many attractions and restaurants. Guests are treated to a free breakfast buffet.

ANTIQUE ROW BED & BREAKFAST

341 South Twelfth Street | 215-592-7802 | www.antiquerowbnb.com | Moderate

The Antique Row Bed & Breakfast is located in a charming little row house in a charming little neighborhood. Naturally it is located close to Antique Row where you can "curio shop" to your heart's delight. The rooms are well appointed and unique, and the neighborhood, which has several good restaurants, is a nice place for a walk.

PENN'S VIEW HOTEL

Front and Market Streets | 215-922-7600 | www.pennsviewhotel.com | Moderate

Penn's View Hotel works hard to capture the look and feel of old school Philadelphia. The small size of the hotel means the staff can give guests a little extra attention. The hotel is also located in the Market Street area of Old Philadelphia. There is plenty to do and enjoy within walking distance.

LOEWS PHILADELPHIA HOTEL

1200 Market Street | 215-627-1200 | www.loewshotels.com | Luxury

The Loews Philadelphia is one of the small chain's most remarkable locations. The hotel is housed in Philadelphia's first skyscraper. The hotel is known for its views and the legendary Loews hospitality, which extends to your pets.

SAN ANTONIO, TEXAS

San Antonio Visitors Information Bureau
317 Alamo Plaza
San Antonio, TX 78205
800-447-3372
www.sanantoniocvb.com

"Remember the Alamo!" Come to San Antonio and you will. You'll also remember SeaWorld, the Paseo Del Rio, great art, and nice people. There is more to Fiesta City than you think. Many people are pleasantly surprised by San Antonio when they venture off the beaten path into various tree-shaded corners. The city is also a great place to practice your Spanish if you're not quite ready for immersion in Mexico.

Getting There

San Antonio may be out in the Wild West, but it is plenty easy to get to. The city is surrounded by major interstates, and an international airport serves the city. The good folks at Amtrak even pull into a station there.

SAN ANTONIO INTERNATIONAL AIRPORT (SAT)

San Antonio International Airport is a small international airport. Its stature, however, makes it a little easier to get in and out of than its larger cousins. With service from sixteen airlines, you shouldn't have trouble finding a flight here, whether you're coming from Mexico or Montana.

Taxi. Both terminals have taxi stands outside their respective baggage claim areas. Taxis charge a minimum of $8.00 for any ride from the airport. A ride downtown costs $18.00–$20.00.

Shuttle. Only one shuttle serves the airport so that eliminates the opportunity to shop for the best deal. SATRANS offers one-way passage to downtown for $14.00. You can purchase a round-trip ticket for $24.00. You can purchase tickets curbside; reservations are not necessary. Be sure to visit www.saairportshuttle.com, and print out a $2.00 off coupon.

Limo/sedan. Several companies offer car service to and from the airport. You can find a complete list here: www.sanantonio.gov/aviation/limos.asp.

Rental car. The major rental car companies have desks in the terminals. They will give you instructions on picking up your car.

AMTRAK

The steam engines of yesteryear may be long gone, but the passenger train is still hip in San Antonio. San Antonio is the terminus of two major Amtrak routes, one that begins in Chicago and the other that originates in Los Angeles.

Getting Around

San Antonio's downtown streetcar service provides transportation to many downtown locations, the Alamo, the Spanish Governor's Palace, the King William Historic District, and downtown shopping. The fare is only $1.00. If your primary focus is the downtown area, renting a car may be optional for you.

A VIA bus route makes stops at places such as the San Antonio Museum of Art, the Japanese Tea Garden, and San Antonio Botanical Garden, just to name a few. Schedules are seasonal, but more information is available at VIA's Downtown Information Center, 260 East Houston, 210-362-2020.

Attractions

The Alamo and SeaWorld have little in common except both are San Antonio natives. You may not find the sheer number of attractions here that are in some cities, but the quality is consistent.

THE ALAMO

300 Alamo Plaza | 210-255-1391 | www.thealamo.org | Hours: Monday–Saturday, 9:00 AM to 5:30 PM (hours extended during summer); Sunday, 10:00 AM to 5:30 PM | Cost: *free!*

"Remember the . . ." Oh, wait. I have already used that one. More than three hundred years old, the Alamo is one of the most recognized historic sites in America. An epic thirty-eight-day siege took place between a small number of Texans and the Mexican Army led by Santa Anna. The Texans eventually lost, but their legacy has lived on. Visit this landmark and enjoy the museums of Texas history on its grounds. Some gardens out back are worth a stroll. The Alamo is a popular attraction that is also educational. Be prepared to encounter other visitors from various cultures.

PASEO DEL RIO (THE RIVER WALK)
210-227-4262 | www.thesanantonioriverwalk.com | Cost: *free!* (attractions may require admission fee)

Second only to the Alamo, the River Walk is one of San Antonio's most famous attractions. The walk is a collection of interesting shops, restaurants, and hotels that run along the San Antonio River. The River Walk covers a lot more ground than you might expect, and some parts are more exciting than others. Still, the development continues making sure there is something to see on every block. Maps and guides may be helpful, but sometimes it's easy just to follow the crowd. If you want a hotel in the middle of the action, check into one of the several located on the River Walk. If you are a fan of old theaters, visit the spectacular Aztec on the River. A side note: every January the city drains (yes, *drains!*) the river for cleaning and maintenance.

SEAWORLD
10500 SeaWorld Drive | 800-700-7786 | www.seaworld.com | Hours: vary; open March–December | Cost: tickets start at $44.09, not including special online discounts

SeaWorld rounds out the big three of San Antonio attractions. This park is the largest of its kind in the world. There's plenty to see and do here, and it is easy to spend an entire day inside the complex. The animal exhibits are presented in interesting and educational ways, and there are some thrill rides to keep your adrenaline pumping. SeaWorld also offers evening programs in the summer that are well worth hanging around for. Whenever planning a trip to SeaWorld, check online for deals or packages. Sometimes you can save a bundle!

SAN ANTONIO MUSEUM OF ART

200 West Jones Avenue | 210-978-8100 | www.samuseum.org | Hours: vary; closed Monday | Cost: $8.00; $7.00 for 65+

The San Antonio Museum of Art is one of the most underappreciated institutions of its type in the country. Despite its impressive and unique collection, it seems to miss a spot on many people's lists of things to do. Well, I will not let you make that same mistake. The museum is housed in the historic old Lone Star brewery. The castlelike buildings are themselves an interesting treat. The museum's collection is not limited to any particular region or era, but it holds the nation's largest collection of Latin American art. The museum is not the oldest, prettiest, or largest in the world, but at the price it is an incredible value.

Shopping

The people of San Antonio are more than happy to help you unload some cash in exchange for goods. The city isn't a shopping mecca, but it has a few good spots. For something local, artsy, and unique to the area head over to Artisans Alley. A more traditional shopping experience is the spectacular North Star Mall where you will find all of your favorite national chains. Outlet shopping can be found just a bit out of town at the Prime Outlets in San Marcos.

Entertainment

THE SPURS

www.nba.com/spurs

The San Antonio Spurs are one of the NBA's hottest teams. They play fast-paced professional basketball at the massive AT&T Center. During the season you can purchase tickets for as little as $10.00 in the nose-bleed section, and they go up from there to more than $200.00. You would be well advised to purchase your tickets well in advance of your visit.

MAJESTIC THEATRE

224 East Houston Street | 210-226-3333 | www.majesticempire.com |
Show times, dates, and prices vary

The Majestic Theatre is an amazing specimen of the theatrical houses of
yesteryear. The Majestic now hosts the national tours of several Broadway
spectaculars a year. Along with its sister theater, the Empire, the Majestic
hosts famous comedians, singers, and concerts. Check the schedule corre-
sponding to the dates of your visit.

ARNESON RIVER THEATRE

South Alamo at Nueva | 210-207-8610 | www.lavillita.com/arneson | Show times,
dates, and prices vary

You never know what kind of show will be playing at the Arneson.
Sometimes it's a clogging extravaganza; sometimes it's a strained piece of
classical theater. But you should go because it is something to do and it is a
unique facility. The Arneson is built on the River Walk with the audience
on one side of the river and the stage on the other! This outdoor experience
is a truly rare treat.

Eateries

CENTRAL MARKET

4821 Broadway Street | 210-368-8600 | Dessert | $

The best place for dessert in San Antonio is a grocery store (yes, a grocery store) with a wonderful bakery. The great thing about Central Market
is that you can get your sweets and other essentials. How convenient is
that!

GUENTHER HOUSE

205 East Guenther Street | 210-227-1061 | www.guentherhouse.com | $

Guenther House is located on the former estate of the family that founded
Pioneer Flour Company. The menu is simple, but everything is good. Take
some time to visit the rest of the house after your meal.

ÁCENAR

146 East Houston Street | 210-222-2362 | www.acenar.com | $$–$$$

Mexican food is not hard to find in San Antonio, but this place serves it with a flair. Colorful rooms and flamboyant dishes are highlights of Ácenar. This River Walk eatery should be on your must-munch list.

Hotels

MENGER HOTEL

204 Alamo Plaza | 210-223-4361 | mengerhotel.com | Moderate

The Menger is a spectacular historic hotel. Built in 1859, the hotel has gone through many refinements, but has not lost its charm. When you sleep here, you are in the presence of history. Teddy Roosevelt, U.S. Grant, and many others have stayed at the Menger. The hotel is even rumored to be haunted!

SAN DIEGO, CALIFORNIA

San Diego Convention and Visitors Bureau
2215 India Street
San Diego, CA 92101
www.sandiego.org

The San Diego Zoo is world famous, but there is a lot more to this Southern California town than its collection of exotic fauna. San Diego is a coastal city and a cultural crossroads. Both distinctions give it a unique flavor in food and fun. Living up to its reputation of being home to some of the finest weather in the United States, San Diego's balmy climate is certainly inviting! Beware, just because you are in Southern California doesn't mean it's all shorts and bikinis. My daughter Emily and I were scrambling to buy fleece and sweatshirts when we were there in May.

Getting There

SAN DIEGO INTERNATIONAL AIRPORT (SAN)

Taxi. Several taxi companies serve the airport. Your fare will depend on where you are going. There are no flat-rate specials.

Shuttle. A few shuttle companies serve SAN. Shopping around may get you a better rate, but all of these guys are usually within a few bucks of each other. To get to your shuttle, you will have to walk to the Transportation Plaza. You will see directions posted throughout the airport.

Limo/sedan. You can have a limo pick you up from any of the licensed limousine companies. But confirm that the company has a license to operate at the airport when making your reservation.

Rental car. All of the national companies and a few locals offer airport service. You will have to take a shuttle from the Transportation Plaza to pick up your vehicle. Just follow the signs.

Getting Around

San Diego is served by both city bus routes and fifty miles of light rail trolley service. The trolley lines circle downtown San Diego and connect Old Town, East County, Mission Valley Qualcomm Stadium, Petco Park, and the border of Mexico. Trolley fares are $1.00 each way, or you can get a one-day tripper for $5.00. Bus fares are $1.00 to $4.00, depending on your route. For more information you can call the Regional Transit Information Service at 619-233-3004 or go to www.sdmts.com. The last few times I went to San Diego, I did not rent a car; instead I enjoyed the public transportation options.

Attractions

Variety is the spice of life in San Diego. You will find a wide range of things to do. Some will challenge your mind, some a lot of fun, and others just relaxing.

SAN DIEGO ZOO

Park Boulevard and Zoo Place | 619-231-1515 | www.sandiegozoo.org | Hours: vary by season | Cost: $33.00

If you go to only one zoo in your lifetime, make sure this is the place. Not only is the zoo one of San Diego's premier attractions, but it is the best-known zoo in the world. Four thousand animals reside here. With innovative displays and acres of natural habitat, there's enough sightseeing to last you for hours upon hours. It is one of the few places you can see a giant panda outside Asia.

SEAWORLD SAN DIEGO

500 SeaWorld Drive | 800-25-SHAMU | www.seaworldsandiego.com | Hours: vary by season | Cost: $57.00

SeaWorld is like a zoo but with a lot more water. You come here to see and play with the exotic residents of our oceans. The world's most famous killer whale, Shamu, performs every day in front of excited crowds. The park has several specials for visitors over age fifty, so call or check out the Web site before you go.

MARITIME MUSEUM OF SAN DIEGO

1492 North Harbor Drive | 619-234-9153 | www.sdmaritime.org | Hours: daily, 9:00 AM to 8:00 PM | Cost: $12.00

The Maritime Museum of San Diego is a must-see for anyone who has ever had even a passing interest in sailing. Your admission gets you access to several historic ships including the oldest active vessel in the world and a decommissioned Soviet submarine. Adventure sail packages will take you out on the water in one of the historic vessels.

SAN DIEGO MUSEUM OF ART

1450 El Prado | 619-232-7931 | www.sdmart.org | Hours: daily, 10:00 AM to 6:00 PM; closed Monday | Cost: $10.00; $8.00 for 65+

The Museum of Art is San Diego's premier cultural attraction. The museum boasts an impressive collection that includes European masters, important American works, and an extensive selection of Asian art. In addition to a significant permanent collection, the San Diego Museum of Art brings in world-class traveling exhibitions.

OLD TOWN TROLLEY TOUR
619-298-8687 | www.oldtowntrolley.com | Cost: $30.00 at the gate; $27.00 online

An Old Town Trolley Tour is a great way to get an overview of San Diego. On the two-hour narrated sightseeing tour, you will make ten stops at some of the most interesting sites in San Diego. You can stay on for the whole tour, noting those attractions you want to visit at your leisure, or you can hop on and hop off as the mood strikes you, enjoying lunch on Coronado or strolling through Seaport Village.

Shopping

You will find plenty of stuff to buy during your visit to San Diego. I always stop at the Fashion Valley Shopping Center. This great outdoor shopping mall has a Neiman Marcus, Gucci, Saks, Lacoste, Louis Vuitton, and more. I also try to visit the Gaslamp Quarter with its quirky and chic local shops.

Entertainment

San Diego works hard to promote its arts community. You can find out what is going on at www.sandiegoartandsol.com.

NATIONAL COMEDY THEATRE
3717 India Street | 619-295-4999 | www.nationalcomedy.com | Hours: Friday and Saturday, times vary | Cost: $15.00

The name says it all. This is the place to go when you want an evening of good, clean fun. The National Comedy Theatre is an improv troupe that never produces the same show twice. Better yet, *you* get to help write it.

LA JOLLA PLAYHOUSE

2910 La Jolla Village Drive | 858-550-1010 | www.lajollaplayhouse.org | Show dates and prices vary

La Jolla Playhouse is one of the top theatrical producing companies in the world. The La Jolla was founded by a group that included Gregory Peck and has been led by inspiring, innovative personalities ever since. A show at La Jolla will not disappoint.

MYSTERY CAFE DINNER THEATRE

121 Broad Street | 619-544-1600 | www.mysterycafe.net | Show times and prices vary

Sometime you just want to sit back, chew some food, and have some fun. That's what the Mystery Cafe Dinner Theatre is all about. You'll have a great time at the interactive show as the action takes place all around you. Who knows? You might just become a part of the drama!

THE OLD GLOBE

1363 Old Globe Way | 619-23-GLOBE | www.theoldglobe.org | Show times and prices vary

The Old Globe is a Tony Award–winning house that produces works year-round. The Old Globe is also California's oldest professional theater. There are three stages that showcase a wide variety of works. Some shows even make it to old Broadway!

SAN DIEGO OPERA

1200 Third Avenue, 18th floor | San Diego, CA 92101-4112 | www.sdopera.com

If your trip to San Diego occurs between January and May, check out the San Diego Opera. It is highly acclaimed throughout America and the world. The programs vary from the classics to new works. With internationally renowned conductors and the world's finest vocal artists, you will not be disappointed.

HODAD'S
5010 Newport Avenue | 619-224-4623 | $

Hodad's is just good, old, fun and cheap eating. This hamburger place is famous for its food and devil-may-care attitude. Hodad's is a true original taste of San Diego.

ORIGINAL PANCAKE HOUSE
3906 Convoy Street | 858-565-1740 | www.originalpancakehouse.com | $

The Original Pancake House serves good American food—and plenty of it. Try the apple pancakes when you visit this family-owned eatery.

CHIVE
558 Fourth Avenue | 619-232-4483 | www.chiverestaurant.com | $$

Chive is a hip bistro that serves a variety of food. Your experience here will be modern, crisp, and still fun. Visit Chive when you want to add a hint of sophistication to your diet.

DICK'S LAST RESORT RESTAURANT
345 Fourth Avenue | 619-231-9100 | $$–$$$

Sometimes it's fun to be treated badly while you eat good food. The waitstaff of Dick's is, well, one of a kind. I promise you will have an experience you won't soon forget. This place can be a bit over the top for some. It is not for the faint of heart and can be a bit risqué.

Hotels

HOTEL OCCIDENTAL
410 Elm Street | 619-232-1336 | www.hoteloccidental-sandiego.com | Economy/Moderate

The rooms aren't big and the frills aren't much, but that's what they call

European. However, this place is amazing for the price. Most of us won't spend too much time at the hotel anyway, and you can't beat the Occidental for value and location.

THE BRISTOL

1055 First Avenue | 619-232-6141 | www.thebristolsandiego.com | Moderate

The Bristol is a neat boutique hotel within walking distance of some of the best shopping and entertainment in San Diego. The guest rooms have been recently upgraded, and their sleek, yet casual, design makes it a pleasure to call the hotel your home away from home. When you stay at the Bristol, you are just steps away from the Gaslamp Quarter and San Diego's trolley. If you are thinking about a get-together, consider the Starlight Ballroom. The ceiling actually opens up to reveal the balmy starlit nights (or sunny days if you prefer)! The Transit Authority is less than a block away, so you have ready access to the city buses.

THE SOFIA HOTEL

150 West Broadway | 800-826-0009 | www.thesofiahotel.com | Moderate

The Sofia is a modern hotel in a historic building. It is also a remarkable value. It's hard to find this level of luxury and service at a better price in San Diego.

PACIFIC TERRACE HOTEL

610 Diamond Street | 858-217-5469 | pacificterrace.reachlocal.net | Luxury

The Pacific Terrace is a great place to stay—if you can afford it. The hotel has a great view of the ocean, and I have rarely encountered a better service staff.

SAN FRANCISCO, CALIFORNIA

San Francisco Visitor and Convention Center
Visitor Information Center
900 Market Street
San Francisco, CA 94102
415-391-2000
www.onlyinsanfrancisco.com

"The coldest winter I ever spent was a summer in San Francisco." It has been said that Mark Twain made this statement. However, reliable sources dispute that. All I know is that when I was in San Francisco in July, I wore a heavier sweater there than I had much of the winter in Arkansas. Well, maybe that is an exaggeration but take a light jacket, no matter what time of year it may be. Honestly, the City by the Bay is one of those rare places you can comfortably visit any time of the year. The Pacific Ocean keeps things nice and mild. San Francisco is truly a unique place. I know you hear the "something for everyone" line a lot, but this city is more than that. I must caution you, San Francisco can indeed steal your heart, and you, too, will be singing that unforgettable song "I left my heart . . ."

Getting There

San Francisco's perch on the West Coast of the United States makes it more than a hop, skip, and jump for most of us. As usual, the airlines will give you the most options. Amtrak serves the area with the California Zephyr from Chicago, and if you dare to drive in California, a car will get you there too.

SAN FRANCISCO INTERNATIONAL AIRPORT (SFO)
San Francisco International is a well-run ultramodern airport. It ranks among the busiest in the world but still maintains a San Francisco feel. The AirTrain system can ease some of the strain from moving around such a large facility. There are public art displays and other distractions throughout the airport.

AirTrain. The AirTrain connects the terminals and links them to short-term parking garages, BART, and the rental car center. Note that the Red

Line runs in a loop to each terminal, while the Blue Line branches out to the rental car center in addition to running the loop.

Taxi. Taxi stands are located outside terminals 1 and 3 on level 1 and the international terminal on level 2. The fare to downtown will cost $35.00–$45.00, including a $2.00 airport origination fee. I recommend using the BART system to get into town. If you don't feel like walking to your hotel, you can always catch a cab at a downtown stop. This will be a lot cheaper than a cab ride all of the way from the airport.

Shuttle. You have several shuttle options, but the best bet is to go with a door-to-door service. That way you'll know it will get you where you want to go. The rates aren't bad either and should run you about half the cost of a taxi for one person. Some shuttle companies, such as www.bayshuttle.com, offer discount coupons on their Web sites. So check them out and save a little money!

Limo/sedan. There are plenty of options when it comes to limo service at SFO. It is advisable to make arrangements in advance; however, courtesy phones in the terminal connect directly to several companies. *Do not* take a ride from anyone who comes up to you offering limo service. These people are not authorized, and you could end up getting ripped off.

Rental car. All of the big guys have on-site rental desks at SFO, but the desks are located in the detached rental car center. To get there, take the free Blue Line AirTrain.

BART. BART, the regional rail system, has a station in the airport and stops at several places in San Francisco. Call ahead to your hotel, and find out the closest stop and its distance from the hotel. BART is clean and safe; it can also save you money. However, do not buy a multiple-day BART pass unless you plan on traveling outside San Francisco proper. You will use MUNI to travel within the city.

OAKLAND INTERNATIONAL AIRPORT (OAK)
www.flyoakland.com

Oakland International Airport is the San Francisco area's discount port of entry. It does not have the appeal or services of SFO and is farther from the city center. Nevertheless, you can sometimes save a good chunk of money on your airline ticket by flying here. It *will* cost you more to travel to town, so take that into consideration when making your flight plans.

Taxi. Taxis are available outside the departures area. A trip into San Francisco costs at least $50.00 each way.

Shuttle. The scheduled van services are not as extensive as your options at SFO. Plan on spending about half of what you would on a taxi. Be sure to check the airport's Web site for the latest information.

Rental car. OAK has a detached rental car center housing a desk for all of the majors. The shuttle stops are marked outside the terminals, and it runs every ten minutes during most of the day.

BART. To hop the BART from Oakland International, you have to take the AirBART shuttle to the closest BART stop. There is no on-site BART station at the airport. The shuttle runs regularly and costs about $2.00. The shuttle doesn't start until 5:00 AM, so that can be a problem with early morning flights on your way home. The station itself isn't in the best part of town, but taking BART will save you some money.

AMTRAK

The Amtrak station for San Francisco is actually closer to Oakland. If you come in by train, you will more than likely use BART or take a cab to get into town. San Francisco is the terminus for the California Zephyr, which originates in Chicago. You can also hop a train to San Fran from Seattle, Southern California, Sacramento, and points in between.

Getting Around

Unlike many other California cities, San Francisco has a public transportation system worth mentioning. It combines environmentally friendly buses, electric streetcars, and a subway. San Franciscans call their transit system MUNI. It is easier to use, cleaner, and feels safer than the systems in other large cities. If you feel comfortable reading a map or asking for directions, you can use the MUNI system to get to many places you want to go. Convenient day passes give you unlimited rides on any MUNI vehicles. They even have a handy trip planner at www.transit.511.org/tripplanner/index.asp, which tells you the routes to take.

Hippies, grand masters, notorious convicts, and eccentric millionaires have left their marks on San Francisco. There are too many great sights to fit in this book. I urge you to take some time, explore the city, and find some jewels of your own.

While making your plans to visit San Francisco, check out the San Francisco City Pass (www.citypass.com). The City Pass includes six attraction admissions plus a seven-day MUNI Cable Car Passport. It is one of the most effective ways to combine sightseeing and saving a little money. You can purchase your City Pass either online or when you reach San Francisco.

ALCATRAZ

Pier 33, Hornblower Alcatraz Landing | 415-981-ROCK | www.alcatrazcruises.com | Tour dates and times vary | Cost: $20.00–$30.00

I must insist that you make time for Alcatraz. It is not a place you'll want to visit every time you go to San Francisco, but it deserves your attention at least once. I doubt I need to explain the island's history to anyone, but just in case I'll let you know that it is the site of what was once the country's most notorious prison. In the middle of the bay, surrounded by cold water and brisk currents, the prison was said to have been inescapable. As a result the federal government chose to house such luminaries as Al Capone there. The audio tour of the decaying structures is very well produced and provides fascinating stories about life on the island. Purchase your tickets in advance because these tours often sell out. Ranger tours, given by the U.S. Park Service, are fascinating and free. My sister Red Hatters and I agree that one of our favorites is the "Children of Alcatraz" tour. Guards' families lived with them on Alcatraz, and the children were ferried to San Francisco each day for school. To learn more, visit Alcatraz. When you are on the island, take as much time as you need; just make sure you are on the last ferry out. There is a night tour during the summer that can be as eerie as it is interesting.

FISHERMAN'S WHARF

On the water | 415-391-2000 | www.fishermanswharf.org

You haven't been to San Francisco until you have been to Fisherman's Wharf. The Wharf is a collection of restaurants, attractions, oddities, and buskers assembled on piers and the land around them. Pier 39 is the top attraction with retail shops and gimmicky food stops galore. Follow your nose to K Dock where a motley crew of wild sea lions hang out. The Aquarium of the Bay and world-famous San Francisco Carousel are also housed on Pier 39. Step off the pier and back onto dry land, and you'll find some of the freshest and tastiest seafood in the country. You will also run into any number of street performers, from innocuous silver mimes to scary walking bushes. Many good places to eat, from nice to dive, are around here. Don't get pulled in by the Pier 39 restaurants. Walk around some and find something you really like.

BLUE & GOLD FLEET BAY CRUISE

Pier 39 west of the marina at Beach Street and the Embarcadero, 2 blocks east of Fisherman's Wharf | 415-773-1188 | www.blueandgoldfleet.com | Cost: $18.00 for adult; $14.00 for 62+

I am a big fan of harbor cruises. The view from the water when you turn to see the city is mystifying. The one-hour harbor cruise will give you a broad overview of the sites around the bay, including Alcatraz and the Golden Gate Bridge. It will certainly whet your appetite and give you a little history of the area and things to do. It can be chilly out on the water, so take along a jacket.

CALIFORNIA PALACE OF THE LEGION OF HONOR

Thirty-fourth Avenue and Clement Street | 800-777-9996 | www.thinker.org/legion | Hours: Tuesday–Sunday, 9:30 AM to 5:15 PM | Cost: $10.00

In a city full of wonderful museums this one is my favorite. The building is a beautiful replica of its Paris original, and the view cannot be outdone. Your journey through four thousand years of art, with a European focus, begins with the massive *Thinker* sculpture by Rodin. Many of his other works grace the galleries. The museum is somewhat out of the way and requires a bus ride or taxi to reach it. However, its location in the middle of Lincoln Park is one of the most remarkable things about it. The Palace is well worth the journey, and you'll want to give yourself at least a couple of hours to enjoy the extensive collection.

CABLE CARS
Various stops | Hours: vary | Cost: $5.00

The Golden Gate Bridge and the cable cars seem to be in an epic struggle for prime icon of San Francisco. It is hard to imagine the city without either one. The cable car system doesn't really serve a practical purpose. It has been superseded by modern transportation, but that hasn't hurt its popularity with visitors and residents. The wait can be an hour or two, especially at the Fisherman's Wharf stop, but many will tell you the experience is worth the wait.

GOLDEN GATE BRIDGE
www.goldengatebridge.org | Cost: free to walk

I wanted to throw this in here because I only found out about it the last time I visited the city. Not the bridge—I knew about that. I found out that you can walk across the bridge. It's a good distance but a flat walk, and the views from the bridge are spectacular. If you don't think you can make it all the way across and back, just go halfway. And FYI: the bridge is *not* in Golden Gate Park.

SAN FRANCISCO MUSEUM OF MODERN ART
151 Third Street | 415-357-4000 | www.sfmoma.org | Hours: vary; closed Wednesday | Cost: $12.50; $8.00 for seniors

If your visit to the Palace of the Legion of Honor has you thirsty for more art but from a different era, then take a trip to the San Francisco Museum of Modern Art. SFMOMA is one of the premier facilities of its kind in the world. Casual art observers will find plenty of pieces here to keep themselves interested while art lovers could spend hours poring over the collection. The building itself is an icon that many visitors will recognize. SFMOMA has really grown into its space over the last decade and is truly a fascinating destination.

MUIR WOODS NATIONAL MONUMENT
San Francisco, CA | www.visitmuirwoods.com | Cost: $3.00

Home of the giant redwoods, Muir Woods is just 12 miles north of San Francisco. It is an unexpected oasis just a few miles away from San Francisco. One-thousand-year-old trees towering over 260 feet high create a fairyland feeling as you stroll along the paths and trails. Walking trails and hiking paths vary in length and difficulty. There is something for everyone, including a cafe and gift shop!

Shopping

Millions of people come to shop in San Francisco every year, and very few leave disappointed. The bargain hunters flock to Chinatown where you can get a cheap (knockoff) version of just about anything. Chinatown is also a great place to pick up little gifts for your friends back home. For super-chic shopping, stroll around Fillmore Street at California where you'll find trendy boutiques galore. On top of these shopper-centric centers you will find interesting stores around most tourist areas.

Entertainment

SAN FRANCISCO GIANTS
sanfrancisco.giants.mlb.com

The San Francisco Giants play in one of baseball's nicest stadiums, AT&T Park. The classic design is set on the water's edge and includes an eighty-foot Coca-Cola bottle. Tickets range from $20.00 to a whole lot more. Of course, there is nothing quite like a baseball game.

SAN FRANCISCO 49ERS

www.sf49ers.com

The 49ers currently play at Monster Park, but that might change soon. The team is looking for a new home and isn't even 100 percent certain that it will stay in San Francisco. Catch the team while you can during the football season. Tickets start around $50.00.

AMERICAN CONSERVATORY THEATRE

415 Geary Street | 415-749-2ACT | act-sf.org/index.cfm | Show times and dates vary

San Francisco's American Conservatory Theatre, or A.C.T., is a force on the national theater scene. It is considered one of the best houses outside New York. A.C.T. performs a well-rounded schedule of many styles and eras of theater.

SHN-BROADWAY REFRAMED

1182 Market Street | 415-551-2075 | www.shnsf.com | Show times and dates vary

SHN owns three historic touring houses in San Francisco: the Curran, the Golden Gate, and the majestic Orpheum. SHN uses these theaters to bring in the hottest shows just off Broadway. Thanks to this multiple-theater arrangement, they are able to ensure that something great is playing in town almost every night.

SAN FRANCISCO OPERA

301 Van Ness Avenue | 415-861-4008 | www.sfopera.com | Show times and dates vary

San Francisco Opera is considered to be a premier opera company in North America (just behind the Met). Here productions are done on a grand scale with exceptional talent. San Francisco Opera has a reputation for discovering rising stars in the opera world, a recent find being the renowned countertenor Gerald Thompson.

TEATRO ZINZANNI
Pier 29 | 415-438-2668 | www.love.zinzanni.org | Cost: $120.00–$140.00

What do you get when you combine acrobats, gourmet food, jugglers, singers, dancers, and some crazy? You get Teatro ZinZanni! This one-of-a-kind (not counting its Seattle sister) production is not to be missed. The price is steep, but you get what you pay for.

Eateries

DELESSIO MARKET AND BAKERY
1695 Market Street | 415-552-5559 | www.delessiomarket.com | Dessert | $

DeLessio is without a doubt the sweetest place in San Francisco. Its variety of chocolate concoctions is to die for and its choice of cakes scrumptious. Open for breakfast, lunch, and early dinner, this bakery can satisfy your sweet tooth almost any time of day.

IT'S TOPS COFFEE SHOP
1801 Market Street | 415-431-6395 | $

It's Tops is a 1950s-style diner, but not in a cheesy 1990s chrome re-creation way. It's a 1950s-style diner because it hasn't changed since the 1950s (and it's low on the chrome). The down-home-style food is hard to find elsewhere in San Francisco, and they aren't lying about having the best hotcakes in town.

L'OSTERIA DEL FORNO
519 Columbus Avenue | 415-982-1124 | $$–$$$

Every major city has at least one great authentic Italian restaurant. L'Osteria del Forno answers that call for San Francisco. Here you will get incredible food that tastes as though you have been transported to Italy.

THE STINKING ROSE
325 Columbus Avenue | 415-781-7673 | www.thestinkingrose.com | $$–$$$

It has been said that the easiest way to find the Stinking Rose is to follow your nose. This San Francisco institution features dishes with garlic. From appetizer to dessert, garlic is king. This place is also good fun. Breath mints are highly recommended.

A. SABELLA'S
2766 Taylor Street (Fisherman's Wharf) | 415-771-6775 | www.asabellas.com | $$$–$$$$

A. Sabella's is the top spot for sit-down seafood in town. This fancy restaurant has been serving up the best crab in the Bay Area since 1920. So gussie up a little and make a reservation. You'll enjoy treating yourself at A. Sabella's.

Hotels

HOTEL REX
562 Sutter Street | 415-433-4434 | www.thehotelrex.com | Moderate

The Hotel Rex is a hip joint modeled after San Francisco drawing rooms of the 1920s. The Union Square location is convenient to shopping and public transportation to various hot spots. Hotel Rex really gives you the "San Francisco" vibe.

ARGONAUT HOTEL
495 Jefferson Street at Hyde | 415-563-0800 | www.argonauthotel.com | Luxury

The Argonaut Hotel is the best place to sleep at Fisherman's Wharf. The rooms offer spectacular views, and the hotel is a cute, quirky boutique. The location also puts you in walking distance of several major destinations.

PARC 55 HOTEL
55 Cyril Magnin Street | 415-392-8000 | www.parc55hotel.com | Luxury

Formerly connected to a large chain, the Parc 55 recently shed its corporate labels and reclaimed its independent status. This four-star hotel is well known throughout San Francisco for its luxury and frequent celebrity guests.

SEATTLE, WASHINGTON

Seattle's Convention and Visitors Bureau
701 Pike Street, Suite 800
Seattle, WA 98101
206-461-5800
www.visitseattle.org

Seattle is one of my favorite places to visit when traveling with my Red Hat sisters. People from the Emerald City are nice, the history is fascinating, and the food is great. Forget the Seattle stereotype of gray clouds and rainy days. Think more of sipping a double tall latte while gazing at the snowy peaks of the Olympic Mountains. Take a trip in the summer and you'll have plenty of clear skies and mild temperatures. On the far side of Puget Sound, ferry boats come and go across Elliott Bay. Seattle boasts one-of-a-kind attractions, world-class performances, and priceless views. Seattle also offers the most relaxing atmosphere on the West Coast. Its open and inviting atmosphere welcomes everyone, no matter who you are or how different you are.

Getting There

Seattle is served by every major form of transportation available. You can get there by car, train, airplane, and boat. However, because of its location in the extreme northwestern part of our country, most of us will be most efficiently served by the airlines.

SEATTLE-TACOMA INTERNATIONAL AIRPORT (SEA)

Seattle-Tacoma International Airport, or Sea-Tac, is nestled in its own township between, uh, Seattle and Tacoma. Sea-Tac is a pleasant airport and currently has a light rail connection under construction, but getting from the airport to the Seattle city core can be a bit confusing. Heck, getting from the terminal to the taxi stand can be a little confusing.

Taxi. Most airports locate their taxi stands in the departures pickup area. Counterculture Seattle, on the other hand, keeps the stands in the parking garage. After you get off your plane, take an escalator down a floor, and pick up your bags, you will need to go up two floors, across a catwalk, down one floor, and *then* look for the taxi line. The good news is, there are usually taxis. Taxi fare to downtown will set you back around $35.00. Considering what I am about to say about the shuttles, it's a pretty good deal. For taxi information call 206-246-9999.

Shuttle. I have never been anywhere with a more confusing airport shuttle scheme. The problem arises because Sea-Tac serves such a geographically vast area. Each shuttle serves different areas, and if you get the wrong one, you could go *way* wrong. Gray Line has a downtown shuttle that stops at several hotels. If your hotel isn't on the list, you'll want to double-check beforehand to see if it stops nearby. Gray Line does have a connector service that goes to other hotels. All I know is that the last time I landed in Seattle and tried to work it all out, I eventually gave up and took a cab. It is best to call your hotel and ask about the shuttle route it is on before you arrive. Gray Line can be reached at 800-426-7532. It will cost $10.00–$20.00, depending on connections.

Limo/sedan. Seattle is a good place to splurge a little and get a limo or Town Car to pick you up. You'll enjoy the extra comfort while taking in the amazing views. Using an on-call limo service to downtown will cost only $5.00–$10.00 more than a cab. To arrange a limo or Town Car, call 206-431-5904.

Rental car. All of the majors have desks in the airport, but only Alamo, Avis, Budget, Hertz, and National have cars on-site. You'll be hopping a shuttle for the rest.

AMTRAK

Amtrak can be an adventure if you like trains and live on the line. Seattle is served by routes down the West Coast and the Empire Builder route out of Chicago. You can visit www.amtrak.com for a full list of stops and schedules.

BOAT

I did mention boat as a way to Seattle. Many major and smaller cruise companies use Seattle as a port of call. It can be an easy add-on to the end or beginning of an Alaskan cruise.

Getting Around

Seattle's Metro buses can provide an inexpensive way to see Seattle and King County. With a visitor pass you can ride all day for only $5.00. The service makes a rental car optional. The visitor pass is not sold on board the buses, however, so you will have to visit a customer service office at 1301 Fifth Avenue or 201 South Jackson Street or purchase the tickets online. Call 206-461-5840 or go to www.seeseattle.org for more information.

Attractions

History, art, architecture, nature, and interesting people—Seattle has it all. A unique blend of attractions keeps this city interesting even after a dozen visits. There is even more to see outside downtown. However, you'll need to rent a car to see any of that.

SEATTLE ART MUSEUM
1300 Union Street | 206-654-3180 | www.seattleartmuseum.org |
Hours: Tuesday– Saturday, 10:00 AM to 5:00 PM; Thursday–Friday, 10:00 AM
to 9:00 PM; closed Monday | Cost: $13.00 for adult; $10.00 for 62+; $7.00 for student

The Seattle Art Museum (SAM) has just reopened in a spectacular new facility. This modern, state-of-the-art building provides the perfect space for presentation of great art. And there is plenty of great art. Opened in 1933, SAM's collection originally focused on Asian art. However, the museum seems to have expanded into most styles out there, and you will see ancient Grecian urns and giant undulating ice packs. No matter what era of art excites you, you will find something you love. The museum displays countless masterpieces and maybe even a few pieces of questionable artistic merit. SAM is a definite must-see on the list of Seattle to-dos.

BILL SPEIDEL'S UNDERGROUND TOUR

608 First Avenue | 206-682-4646 | www.undergroundtour.com | Tour dates and times vary | Cost: $14.00 for adult; $12.00 for 60+ or student

Let me get this out of the way: If you have trouble standing for a long time or using stairs, this attraction is not for you. Unfortunately the historic and derelict nature of the site makes it impossible to accommodate persons who are disabled. Usually that would be a reason to leave it out of the book, but the Seattle Underground Tour is just too cool. You see, many years ago, after a big fire, Seattle's town fathers decided to raise Seattle a couple of dozen feet above sea level. That meant the first stories of any buildings already built would be buried. So instead of destroying and rebuilding all of those buildings, they just raised the streets! After years of declining use, the whole thing was sealed off with walkways, storefronts, and bank teller cages intact. Over the decades the Underground was practically forgotten and fell into ruin. It wasn't until the 1970s that columnist Bill Speidel revived interest in the Underground and saved the Pioneer Square neighborhood from the wrecking ball. Thanks to Bill, you can now take a trip back in time to Seattle's Underground. The knowledgeable tour guides love to share interesting and historic facts about Seattle. You'll be amazed at what you'll learn about the city's seamstresses.

SEATTLE CENTER

www.seattlecenter.com

A short monorail ride from downtown, Seattle Center is home of several of the city's most famous attractions. The parklike area features several fountains, some of which are interactive. There are also several theaters and other entertainment venues in the Seattle Center area.

THE MONORAIL

www.seattlemonorail.com | Cost: $4.00 round-trip

Seattle's two-stop monorail is the first commercial monorail system in the world. It runs between downtown and Seattle Center. A round-trip is only $4.00, which is a whole lot cheaper than taking a cab from downtown.

SPACE NEEDLE
www.spaceneedle.com | Cost: $16.00

Built for the 1962 World's Fair, the Space Needle is Seattle's most recognized landmark. Take a trip to the top and see matchless views of Mount Rainier and Elliott Bay. The Space Needle costs $16.00 to visit, and that includes the trip up *and* down. There is an extensive gift shop at the base of the attraction.

EXPERIENCE MUSIC PROJECT
www.emplive.com | Cost: $15.00; $12.00 for seniors

Unless you just love pop music, Jimi Hendrix, or Frank Gehry, there is not much reason to go to EMP. It is usually full of school groups and other kids. Admission to EMP also gets you into the adjacent Science Fiction Museum and Hall of Fame.

SCIENCE FICTION MUSEUM AND HALL OF FAME
Seattle Center | 325 5th Avenue North | Seattle, WA 98109 | 877-367-7361 | www.empsfm.org | $15.00; $12.00 for seniors

It shares a building with EMP, but the experience couldn't be more different. Set up like a traditional museum, the Science Fiction Museum allows you to view and learn about thousands of items, including science fiction props, ephemera, and robots. Admission to the Science Fiction Museum also gets you into the Experience Music Project.

PIKE PLACE MARKET
85 Pike Street | 206-625-7453 | www.pikeplacemarket.org | Hours: vary | Cost: *free*!

It is hard to think of Seattle without thinking of Pike Place, the oldest continuously operating farmers' market in the country. Here you can meet local artists, pick up trinkets, grab a bushel of veggies, and watch the fishmongers toss fish bigger than your golden retriever. There are antique shops, family restaurants, and even the original Starbucks. You won't find many supergood deals, but the prices are fair and the selection eclectic.

ARGOSY CRUISES

1101 Alaskan Way | 206-623-1445 | www.argosycruises.com

Argosy Cruises offers several ways to go into the harbor and see Seattle. The most popular tour is the Harbor Cruise. It is a one-hour trip around Seattle's harbor and includes an interesting narration about the city's history. Argosy offers renowned lunch and dinner cruises around the bay and the sound. The dinner cruise often includes live music, and patrons are encouraged to dance. Group rates and private tours are available.

Shopping

A wide variety of shopping awaits you in Seattle. As you're walking around the city, keep your eyes open for neat little shops. If you're not careful, you'll walk right past some interesting ones. Westlake Center, one of the monorail stops, has a good selection of national mall chains and some local flavor. Downtown Seattle still has a few big department stores left and upscale shopping areas. The Seattle Premier Outlets is located away from the city center. If you have time and really love outlet shopping, you can rent a car and be there in twenty or thirty minutes. While you're there you can walk over to the Tulalip Casino. It's not Las Vegas, but it passes the time.

Entertainment

Always happy to be hip, Seattle offers plenty for a Red Hat to do after the sun sets.

ACT THEATRE

700 Union Street | 206-292-7676 | www.acttheatre.org | Show times, dates, and prices vary

ACT, Seattle's premier regional theater, boasts a national reputation. The schedule tends to lean toward modern productions, but the company presents a wide variety of plays. As with any company, it all depends on the show. Check the Web site or call to see what is playing. If it sounds interesting, go. If it's at ACT, you will not regret the cost of the ticket.

THE 5TH AVENUE THEATRE

1308 Fifth Avenue | 206-625-1900 | www.5thavenue.org | Show times, dates, and prices vary

The 5th Avenue Theatre is one of the top producing musical theater companies outside New York City. In fact, several of its shows have transferred to Broadway. The building itself is a masterpiece and should delight anyone who is a fan of historic structures. Check what is playing and when. Who knows? You might see something that months later will be on the Broadway stage.

READINGS AT THE ELLIOTT BAY BOOK COMPANY

101 South Main Street | 206-624-6600 | www.elliottbaybook.com | Hours: reading times vary | Cost: most readings are free but some require advance tickets

Seattle has been called the most literate city in America. Well, the center of all that literacy is Elliott Bay Book Company. The new and used bookstore features more than 150,000 titles, but the key attraction is the dozens of author readings held each month. From relative unknowns to multiple best sellers every author worth his or her salt has presented here. Check out the Web site or stop by the store to see who's in town.

TEATRO ZINZANNI

2301 Sixth Avenue | 206-802-0015 | dreams.zinzanni.org | Hours: shows Wednesday–Saturday | Box office is opened: Monday through Saturday 11:00 AM–6:00 PM | Show times: 6:30 PM Wednesday through Saturday and 5:30 PM on Sundays. The lobby opens for drinks 1 hour before showtime. | Cost: $104.00–$125.00 per person

Teatro ZinZanni bills itself as "dinner and dreams," and that is exactly what it is. Experience a dinner like no other as you eat a gourmet meal and watch acrobats fly. The food is great, and the entertainment is in the high art, if sometimes zany, circus style. The price is high, but if your budget can handle it, your evening at Teatro ZinZanni is one you won't soon forget.

GELATIAMO
1400 Third Avenue | 206-467-9563 | Dessert | $$

Gelatiamo is *the* place in Seattle to eat something sweet. The gourmet ice cream, pastries, and drinks are the best in town. The menu here is varied with classics and some innovations mixed together. Your sweet tooth will go into shock as you enter the establishment. The sights, sounds, and smells would be overwhelming, were they not so sweet. When you go, be sure to pick up something for me.

CJ'S EATERY
2619 First Avenue | 206-728-1648 | $

We stumbled upon this place during our last Red Hat trip to Seattle. The locals eat at CJ's, a diner-style restaurant on a nondescript corner of First Avenue. The food is great, the service is friendly and speedy, and the atmosphere is relaxed. Since the CJ's secret is so well kept, you almost never have to wait for a table. It is open for breakfast and lunch.

T. S. MCHUGH'S IRISH PUB & RESTAURANT
21 Mercer Street | 206-282-1910 | www.tsmchughs.com | $$–$$$

After you leave an evening event at Seattle Center, do yourself a favor, and grab a bite at T. S. McHugh's. The menu might be pub fare, but it's no slop. The chef has taken traditional Irish dishes to a new level, and your taste buds will thank him. McHugh's can be crowded after big events, but feel free to call ahead and make reservations. It is also a place you can let your hair down a bit and not worry about disturbing the other diners (as if we would worry!). It is open for lunch and dinner.

UNION SQUARE GRILL
621 Union Street | 206-224-4321 | www.unionsquaregrill.com | $$$

Recently transformed from a classic steakhouse, Union Square Grill prides itself on delivering the most innovative cuisine in Seattle. Don't let that scare you. *Innovative* doesn't mean crazy or weird, but it does mean delicious. The restaurant hasn't lost all of its steakhouse past; it still has some of the best steaks in town. Right across the street from ACT Theatre, the Grill is a perfect place for a preshow dinner. It is also open for lunch.

SHUCKERS
411 University Drive | 206-621-1984 | $$$–$$$$

It wouldn't be Seattle if I didn't include seafood! Shuckers provides a fun, friendly atmosphere combined with some of the best seafood you can find. Oysters are specialties, so if that's your game, don't miss this place. Shuckers is located inside the Fairmont-Seattle and offers outside seating when the weather is good. This isn't the only great seafood house in town, but if you find yourself in the neighborhood, you should stop and have a bite. It is open for lunch and dinner.

Hotels

From ultramodern to turn-of-the-century throwback, Seattle offers myriad styles of hotels.

MARQUEEN HOTEL
600 Queen Anne Avenue North | 888-445-3075 | www.marqueen.com | Moderate/Luxury

The MarQueen is a gem of a hotel. The building was constructed in 1918 as an apartment building and still retains much of its original charm. Since the rooms were once residences, they include a full-sized refrigerator, stove, and plenty of room. There is one drawback to this small, three-story hotel: it has no elevator. But if you can manage the stairs, just have one of the strapping bellboys carry your bags for you. Those of us who don't like climbing stairs can request a ground-floor room when making reservations. The MarQueen is just a block away from Seattle Center and its attractions.

THE EDGEWATER HOTEL

2411 Alaskan Way, Pier 67 | 800-624-0670 | www.edgewaterhotel.com | Luxury

They call it the Edgewater because it is the only place that is, well, on the edge of the water. The Edgewater is built on a pier in Seattle's harbor. The harbor side rooms hang over the water. We had one the last time we stayed there, and I fed seagulls out of my hand from our third-story room. The rooms are large, with excellent bathrooms and gas fireplaces. The Edgewater staff is also top-notch. From janitor to manager they are nice and eager to help. The Edgewater was built in the 1960s but has been recently renovated and feels brand new. Even if it's only one night, it's worth it to stay in a harbor view room.

HOTEL MAX

620 Stewart Street | 866-833-6299 | www.hotelmaxseattle.com | Luxury

The Hotel Max isn't for everyone, but if the sight of a modernist nude painting in the lobby doesn't bother you, you'll do fine. The Max provides an ultramodern, superhip place to stay in the middle of downtown Seattle. All of the rooms feature originals from local artists commissioned by the hotel. Other artworks are distributed throughout the building, and guests are encouraged to walk the various floors to view them. Each room has a unique photograph laminated on the door, so if you forget your room number, you just have to remember what the door looks like. Hotel Max is close to shopping, movies, and other downtown attractions.

AIRPORT AREA HOTELS

The Sea-Tac Airport is a good distance from downtown, and if you encounter a lot of traffic, it can be a very long drive. I usually recommend that people spend their last night in an airport area hotel that offers a free shuttle. Some of the nice airport hotels are a bit cheaper than their counterparts in the city. Search online or ask the hotel about specials. Last time I was there one of the hotels had a dinner and a movie package that got me a room, a pizza, drinks, and a movie—all cheaper than any other room on the trip!

WASHINGTON, D.C.

Washington, D.C., Convention and Visitors Association
901 Seventh Street NW, 4th floor
Washington, D.C., 20001
800-422-8644
www.washington.org

Washington, D.C., is a great vacation spot for all ages. However, there is so much to do in Washington, D.C., proper and the surrounding areas, you don't have the concentration of the crowds all at one place at one time as you do with Disneyland. Getting into a Capitol tour may be difficult, but with a little planning D.C. during cherry blossom time is certainly doable and something you should have on your list. If I had to pick a favorite thing about D.C., it would be difficult, but I can tell you that almost all of my favorite things about D.C. have something in common: many of them are *free!*

Request the *Washington, D.C., Official Visitors Guide* by calling 800-422-8644. It does a wonderful job of providing information about hotels, maps, attractions and tours, the arts, and almost anything else of interest. It is updated twice a year so it covers any new planned events or upcoming special events.

Getting There

Washington, D.C., is within thirty minutes of three major airports. Trains, taxis, SuperShuttle, and the Metro serve the airports, making them easily accessible for travelers. When shopping for your tickets, remember that prices may vary depending on the airport.

RONALD REAGAN WASHINGTON NATIONAL AIRPORT (DCA)

Metrorail, shuttles, taxis, and rental cars serve Ronald Reagan Washington National Airport. The Metrorail has a stop dedicated to Reagan National that serves the immediate Washington, D.C., Maryland, and Virginia regions.

Taxi. Cab stands are located near the arrivals area of each terminal (near baggage claim). Dispatchers on duty at each stand help you determine which taxi will best serve your destination. No advance reservations are required. Taxi fare to downtown is approximately $15.00.

Shuttle. SuperShuttle provides unscheduled, door-to-door, shared ride service. Follow the signs toward ground transportation to the Super-Shuttle boarding area, which is located curbside at each terminal. You can easily spot a SuperShuttle guest coordinator. The guest coordinators are on duty between 6:30 AM and 11:30 PM. If your arrival is other than that, call 800-258-3826 and press 1 for dispatch or 2 for reservations. Fares to and from Washington, D.C., are approximately $12.00 for the first passenger and $8.00 for each additional passenger in the same party, up to five.

Limo/car service. Prearranged car or limousine service pickup is at the second curb outside terminals B and C.

Metrorail. The Washington, D.C., Metrorail system station is located on the concourse levels of terminals B and C. Two enclosed pedestrian bridges just off each concourse will connect you to the station. If you are in terminal A, exit the terminal and board any airport shuttle. Go to parking garage B (bus shelter #3) or C (bus shelter #5), and an enclosed bridge will connect you to the Metrorail station.

When departing the airport, you will be accessing the Yellow or Blue Metrorail lines. Consult the Metrorail station map to determine which line will take you to your destination. Purchase Metrorail fare cards at machines located at all entrances to the airport Metrorail station.

Rental car. Rental car counters are located on the first floor in parking garage A. The parking/rental car shuttle stops at each terminal just outside the baggage claim area. You can also walk to the rental car area, about ten minutes away from terminals A and B. If you are a member of a rental car club, you can proceed directly to that rental agency located on the third or fourth floor of garage A.

WASHINGTON DULLES INTERNATIONAL AIRPORT (IAD)
1 Saarinen Circle | Dulles, VA 20166-7506

Washington Dulles is located twenty-six miles west of Washington, D.C.

Taxi. Washington Flyer Taxicabs serve Dulles exclusively and provide service twenty-four hours a day. Taxis accept American Express, Diners Club, MasterCard, Discover Card, and Visa. Taxi fare to downtown is approximately $55.00 to $60.00. No reservation is necessary when leaving the airport. The taxi passengers area is located on the lower level of the main terminal. Wheelchair accessible minibuses are available.

For service to the airport, call 703-661-6655. I recommend making your return reservation in advance.

Metro connection. Washington Flyer Coach Service provides very economical service to the Metro's West Falls Church Station for just $9.00 each way. You can purchase your ticket just inside Door 4 on the arrivals/baggage claim level. The trip takes twenty to twenty-five minutes, depending on traffic. For more information, call 888-WASHFLY. Once you are on the Metro, trains bound for New Carrollton will take you toward downtown Washington, D.C. Know where you want to disembark and how far it is from your accommodations before deciding this is the best way to start your D.C. adventure. Being economical is always good, but consider the stress and hassle of juggling three pieces of luggage while navigating multiple modes of transportation.

Shuttle. SuperShuttle provides door-to-door shared ride van service to and from Union Station and other locations in Washington, D.C. The shuttles operate on an on-demand basis. Go to the baggage claim area, and follow the signs toward ground transportation/shared ride vans. The SuperShuttle ticket counters are on the lower level just before the exit. After you purchase your ticket or check in for your reservation, wait until you hear your ticket number called, then proceed outside to the uniformed guest service representative. The ticket counter is open from 6:00 AM until 10:30 PM. The guest service representatives are on duty until 12:00 AM. Fares from Dulles to Washington, D.C., are $25.00 for the first passenger and $8.00 for each additional passenger in the same party, up to five. For more information on the SuperShuttle, go to www.supershuttle.com or call 800-BLUEVAN.

Rental car. Rental cars at Dulles are listed as on-airport. You shouldn't have to go anywhere to pick up your car. All the majors have desks.

BALTIMORE–THURGOOD MARSHALL AIRPORT, MARYLAND (BWI)

I'm not going into detail for BWI, but lots of people use it as an alternative to Reagan National and Dulles. However, getting from BWI to downtown D.C. can easily negate any savings you realized from flying there in the first place.

THE SUBWAY (METRO)

For those of you who have never been on the subway before, the Washington, D.C., Metro is the perfect one to learn on. It is clean, convenient, and extremely easy to use. Fares run from $1.35 to $3.90, and day passes are available for $6.50. The Metrofare kiosk takes cash, Visa, and MasterCard (no AmEx). It is easy to use and very forgiving, so take your time and follow the steps. It's really kind of fun. Also, the person in the booth does not sell tickets, so go ahead and brave the kiosk. Almost any hotel will have Metro maps available; they are also available at each station. If you want to see one in advance, you can get it online at www.wmata.com.

The rail map will help you familiarize yourself with where you want to go and which lines you will be riding. At www.wmata.com you can use a trip planner: Input an address or landmark and it will tell you which station is closest, which direction to go, and where to exit. It is very handy, especially if you enjoy the planning side of things. The good part about the Metro is that it is so rider friendly, you will do just fine if you don't plan far ahead. However, learn how to read the Metro map. I tend to ask directions if I am the least bit unsure, but more than once the lady in the booth had me going in the wrong direction. If I had not consulted my handy pocket guide, I would have lost a lot of time.

Accessibility

Washington, D.C., claims to be one of the most accessible cities in the world. There are several options for people with mobility challenges. I haven't actually used them, but the Washington, D.C., Convention and Tourism Corporation lists them on its Web site.

CITY SCOOTER TOURS
888-441-7575 | www.cityscootertours.com

They have wheelchair and scooter rentals and will give you a free estimate when you call. DisabilityGuide.org (also known as Access Information,

Good to Know

Most buildings in the Washington, D.C., area require you to go through security before entering, so be prepared to have your purse, backpack, shopping bags, and camera case opened and checked by security people. In some places you will have to place your electronic items, cameras, and bags in plastic bins very similar to those at an airport; however, the security is not nearly as intensive. You do not have to remove your shoes or watch. In other places, you will have to open only your purse or backpack for the guard to look through; it really is quick and painless.

When visiting Washington, D.C., take a good pair of walking shoes. If you can walk a few miles a day before your trip, you will enjoy it that much more. If you are not a walker, Washington, D.C., is not outside your reach either.

Inc) provides detailed accessibility information for D.C. attractions including restaurants and bars. 301-528-8664

Attractions

There is a lot to do in D.C., and almost all of it is related to our federal government, from the working Congress to massive monuments. The architecture of the city is grand and like nothing else on this side of the world.

TOURING THE WHITE HOUSE
www.whitehouse.gov

To experience certain aspects of Washington, D.C., you must do some pre-planning. Touring the White House now requires you to request the visit via your congressman or senator three to six months in advance. The White House offers tours Tuesday through Saturday in the morning.

When you submit your request to your congressman's or senator's office, be prepared to give the following security information: social security number, birth date, and full name as it appears on a government-issued picture ID for all members of your party. Typically you will find out whether the tour has been approved three to four weeks before the scheduled date of your tour. I checked several senators' Web sites to get the scoop on how to request these tours, and most provided the same information. Some stated that you had to have a group of ten; however, not all listed that as a requirement. Once you decide you are headed to D.C., call your U.S. senator's or congressman's office and find out the recommended procedures. Also, if you have never called your representative's office, just do it for the experience. I found the employees to be very helpful and a bit uplifting!

TOURING THE PENTAGON

The Pentagon, headquarters of the Department of Defense, is a city in itself with a workforce of approximately 23,000 military and civilian employees. Pentagon tours originated in May 1976 to support the nation's Bicentennial celebration and have continued since then. The general public must contact a representative to request a Pentagon tour. Tour requests must be made at least two weeks in advance.

TOURING THE CAPITOL

Touring the Capitol is free, but tickets are required. The Capitol is open 9:00 AM to 4:30 PM, Monday through Saturday. There are no tours on Sunday. It is also open all federal holidays except Thanksgiving Day, Christmas Day, and New Year's Day. The tickets are given out on a first-come, first-served basis beginning at 9:00 AM, and they usually run out. Once they are gone, no more for that day. Currently the tickets are available at the Capitol Guide Service kiosk. It is located near First Street SW and Independence Avenue. I say near because it isn't really at the intersection but a bit off to the left on a curving sidewalk. Be aware that the tickets are given out one at a time to one person at a time, so unless you call and make special arrangements, don't count on one member of your group getting up early to obtain tickets for the whole group. The maximum tour size is forty at one time.

If you happen to be in D.C. when the House and the Senate are in session, you can go to your respective representative's office to request passes to the Gallery. You will not be able to tour the Capitol building with these passes, but if you have ever wanted to see what happens while our public servants are in session, it can be interesting. You can tell that the House and Senate are in session when the U.S. flags are flying over their buildings. For more information go to the U.S. Capitol Guide Service at www.house.gov/house/tour_services.shtml.

THE SMITHSONIAN MUSEUMS
SI Building, Room 153, MRC 010 | 202-275-2000 | www.gosmithsonian.com

The Smithsonian Museums number seventeen in Washington, D.C., alone. Ten of them are within one mile of each other on the National Mall. The Smithsonian Information Center is housed in the easily identifiable red building often referred to as the Castle. The Castle is a great place to start your journey through the museums. Cafes and grills are scattered among the museums, and the gift shops have unique, interesting treasures that are almost as hard to resist as dessert!

The Smithsonian Museums are truly amazing. My brief descriptions in no way give any of them the honor that they deserve. If by some chance, your time in D.C. does not allow you to visit each museum, I have listed what I think are the four must-sees first.

Air and Space Museum. The National Air and Space Museum opened in 1976, and it is touted as the most-visited museum in the world. The museum tells the story of flight before the days of Kitty Hawk and beyond. Also, not to be missed are the Lockheed Martin IMAX Theater and the Albert Einstein Planetarium. They add a great touch to the adventure and an opportunity to sit down for a while and rest those weary tootsies.

American History Museum. The National Museum of American History collects artifacts of all kinds. From Lincoln's top hat to Dorothy's ruby slippers to Kermit the Frog, this museum will touch each of you with something from your past.

Portrait Gallery. The National Portrait Gallery (NPG), housed in the Donald W. Reynolds Center, is my all-time favorite. The portraits, anecdotes, and videos tell the stories of the great Americans who made our nation what it is today. Not so many years ago, our presidents were known to many of us only by the pictures and few occasional sightings on television. Through the very portraits hanging in this museum, people were able to put a face with the name. I hate to admit it, but visiting this museum taught me more about the previous presidents than I ever learned in school.

Natural History Museum. The Natural History Museum's wonders of the natural world await you beneath the dome of this classical building, which has recently undergone extensive renovation. This museum complex holds more than 126 million specimens, some of which are brand new and some of which were collected almost two hundred years ago during early voyages and explorations of the world. The vast exhibition halls focus on the earth and its evolution into the world in which we live today, with wondrous displays of animals, plants, fossils, rocks, minerals, and cultural artifacts.

National Zoo. The National Zoo is one of only four in the nation that is home to a giant panda. Book signings and lectures are often held at the National Zoo. You can check out www.nationalzoo.si.edu for schedules.

Postal Museum. The Postal Museum is not on the National Mall but on Capitol Hill at the corner of First Street and Massachusetts Avenue NE, just west of Union Station. The building was originally the Washington City post office from 1914 to 1986. If you were ever a stamp collector, even if it was only long enough to earn your Girl Scout badge, you will want to visit the Postal Museum.

Smithsonian Institution Building, the Castle. The Castle is the Smithsonian Institution's original home. Now the Smithsonian Information Center, it is by far the easiest building to locate on the National Mall.

UNITED STATES HOLOCAUST MEMORIAL MUSEUM
100 Raoul Wallenberg Place SW | www.ushmm.org | Hours: Daily 10:00 AM to 5:30 PM including weekends; closed Yom Kippur and Christmas Day

The United States Holocaust Memorial Museum is a history lesson that you should not miss. It presents a comprehensive narrative history through multiple modes of media, including photographs, films, eyewitness testimonies, and artifacts. The permanent exhibit is designed for audiences ages eleven and up. The exhibit *Remember the Children: Daniel's Story* is recommended for visitors eight years and up. Although entrance to the museum is free, you must have an entrance pass to go through the permanent exhibit. (To get tickets in advance, go to www.tickets.com, or call 800-400-9373 or

202-488-0400.) The passes are timed and allow a controlled flow to ensure that everyone is able to view the exhibits and videos without excessive crowding. The passes are given out for fifteen-minute intervals beginning at 10:00 AM and ending at 3:45 PM. During the busy spring and summer seasons, there may be a line at the entrance of people waiting to obtain passes. I recommend lining up to get your pass as soon as you arrive. There may be a wait between the time you get your pass and the time you are allowed to enter the permanent exhibit. Take the opportunity to browse through the exhibits that do not require an entrance pass.

THE NATIONAL MALL

The National Mall (or just "the Mall") is the centerpiece of Washington, D.C. It stretches nearly two miles connecting the Capitol building and the Lincoln Memorial. The Mall is home to some of the most impressive and famous memorials in the world. These include the following:

Washington Monument. This prominent obelisk is open daily from 9:00 AM to 4:45 PM. You'll need to pick up a free ticket in advance at the monument kiosk or online at www.reservation.gov.

Lincoln Memorial. Its image on the back of a penny makes the Lincoln Memorial one of the most recognized buildings in the world. You can visit it for no cost twenty-four hours a day. Park rangers are around to answer questions between 9:30 AM and 11:30 PM.

World War II Memorial. The impressive WWII Memorial is the latest addition to the Mall. It is open twenty-four hours a day with rangers available between 9:30 AM and 11:30 PM.

Franklin Delano Roosevelt Memorial. A newer but still important part of the Mall, the FDR Memorial captures the president as very few have seen him—in his wheelchair. The memorial is open twenty-four hours a day with rangers on-site between 9:30 AM and 11:30 PM.

Korean War Veterans Memorial. This memorial honors the sacrifice of American soldiers during the Korean War. It is open twenty-four hours every day.

Vietnam Veterans Memorial. This stark reminder of the cost of war can be viewed twenty-four hours a day. Few of us will be unable to find a friend, brother, cousin, or neighbor among the 58,256 names (eight of them were women).

Shopping

D.C. isn't the shopping mecca that you might think it would be, but it has several places that will help you part with your money. Union Station houses trains and a shopping mall. There are no stand-out stores, but the atmosphere is second to none. The Fashion Centre at Pentagon City is a short Metro ride from downtown. Here you will find Nordstrom, Benetton, Armani Exchange, J. Jill, Talbot, Cache, and more. (There is an indoor mall located in the heart of the city.)

Entertainment

Washington, D.C., is more than just stones and statues. It also has plenty of live action.

THE CHERRY BLOSSOM FESTIVAL
www.nationalcherryblossomfestival.org

The Cherry Blossom Festival has become an annual event in Washington, D.C. It officially runs for a two-week period around the first two weeks in April. You can check the above-mentioned Web site or the National Park Service Web site (www.nps.gov) for the exact days that the festival is in full swing. It truly is a sight to behold. The Washington, D.C., cherry trees were gifts from Japan in 1912. Since that time, they have come to symbolize the coming of spring to our nation's great capital city.

SHAKESPEARE THEATRE COMPANY
450 Seventh Street NW | 202-547-1122 | www.shakespearedc.org | Show times and prices vary

Shakespeare Theatre Company is one of the top presenters of the Bard's work in the world. If Shakespeare isn't your cup of tea, the company performs other works. The company moved into wonderful new digs, which should further enhance the world-class productions.

FORD'S THEATRE

511 Tenth Street NW | 202-347-4833 | www.fordstheatre.org | Show times and prices vary

This theater is best known for its role as the site of the assassination of President Abraham Lincoln. However, you can still catch a modern stage production. The Presidential Box is decorated as it was that fateful night. You can't help feeling one with history when you watch a show here. The productions consist of musicals and straight plays that are family friendly. Check for daily tour information.

Eateries

MARKET INN

200 East Street SW | 202-554-2100 | www.freshcrabcakes.com | $$–$$$

The Market Inn is the place in Washington for fresh seafood. Market Inn has been serving up crustacean and other sea life since 1959. The steak isn't bad either.

OLD EBBITT GRILL

675 Fifteenth Street | 202-347-4800 | www.ebbitt.com | $$–$$$

The Old Ebbitt Grill has been a Washington, D.C., landmark since 1856. It is close to the White House and several other attractions. It is a great place to stop for lunch or after a long day of sightseeing adventures.

ROSA MEXICANO

Various | www.rosamexicano.com | $$$–$$$$

Rosa Mexicano is a small chain of upscale Mexican restaurants. The chefs take traditional Mexican cooking to levels previously unknown.

TTHE QUINCY

1823 L Street NW | 202-223-4320 | www.quincysuites.com | Moderate

The Quincy is a hip, little all-suites boutique hotel in downtown D.C. It is close to the Metro and some attractions. If you would like a quirky, non-corporate place to stay, the Quincy is it.

RESIDENCE INN–CAPITOL

333 East Street SW | 202-484-8280 | www.marriott.com | Moderate

This hotel has good-sized rooms and is within walking distance of many D.C. attractions. And a Metro stop is just around the corner when you want to go farther away. If you stay here, you'll be able to get just about anywhere in town quickly and easily.

HE HAY-ADAMS

Sixteenth Street and H Street NW | 202-638-6600 | www.hayadams.com | Luxury

The Hay-Adams is the city's top hotel. It sits across the street from the White House and is close to several other attractions. This place is pricey, but it has no rival for class and personalized service.

Special Thanks

Jerry Glidewell
Cole Wakefield
Emily and James Glidewell
Eldon and Betty Pence
Joel Farthing

Travel Partners

Cory Allen
Kathy Glidewell
Sarah Sawyer
Michelle Harris
Jason Hunt
Debby and Dennis Hunt
Zack Wakefield

Helpful People on the Road

American Eagle, Fort Smith, Arkansas: You all are the best! Thank you, thank you, and thank you again for the many times that you have made leaving home just a little bit easier.

Chris Bebo: Hotel Max, Seattle, Washington. The hotel was great. The introduction to your mother, Liz, and her inspirational story . . . priceless!

Gayla D. Schaftlein: Greater Louisville Convention & Visitors Bureau

Rachelle Wilson

Lynn Winter

Carol MacMasters

Debby Gilliatt

Jennifer Schak: Bloomington Convention & Visitors Bureau

Christine DeCuir: New Orleans Metropolitan Visitors and Convention Center

Simone Rathle

Matt Wakefield: Seattle Convention and Visitors Center

Contributors

Packing Tip Contributers

Marilyn Puett | Red Hat Rovers | Huntsville, AL
Sharon Simpson | Ladies of the Lake | Abbeville, AL
Marlene Aylor | Lady Marlene | Tea Birds | Harrison, AR
Judy Kessler | Madam Shaddow Catterly | Happy Hatters of Jane | Bella Vista, AR
Coolleen Arwine | Ruby Red Hots | Cypress, CA
Carol Betush | Rebellious Elegant Dames | Redding, CA
Sue Ellen Cooper | Fabulous Founders | Fullerton, CA
Peggy Diller | Red Hatters for Heart Matters | Covina, CA
Cathy Fagan | Wild Women of Wildwood | Penn Valley, CA
Lorraine Fauntleroy | River City Classy Sassy Divas | Sacramento, CA
Virginia Hosford | Santa Teresa Red Hots | San Jose, CA
Lynn Hunter | Corona Cuties | Corona, CA
Linda Lohman | The Dessert Queen | Anything Goes SuppHose to Chapeaux |
    Sacramento, CA
Chris Maston | Gold Country Mad Hatters | Rescue, CA
Buffy Oster | Red Hat Classy Lassies of Palm Desert | Palm Desert, CA
Elizabeth Weaver | HatCourters | Buena Park, CA
Barbara Whitener | Ding Dong Belles | Palm Desert, CA
Patsy McElroy | Red Hot Boa Babes | Castle Rock, CO
Sharron Newman | Arsenic & Lace | Grand Junction, CO
Joan Croce | Scarlet O'Hatters | Cheshire, CT
Wendy Barr/Holmes | Red Magnolia Ladies of Encore | Ormond Beach, FL
Jo Derby | Scarlet O'Hatters of Trinity | Trinity, FL
Patricia Gillen | Red Hot Cruisers | Fort Myers, FL
Linda Murphy | Fabulous Founders | Tarpon Springs, FL
Gail Safarikas | Scarlet O'Hatters of Trinity | Trinity, FL
Sharleen Whitman | Red Hat Treasures | Panama City Beach, FL
Jacqueline Signori | Scarlet O'Hattas | Fairfield, IA
Nancy Thorsen | Crimson Cronies | Idaho Falls, ID

Katherine Bibber | Twisted Sisters of Cyberspace | Batavia, IL
Carol Hall | Deco City Divas | Napier, IL
Janet Taylor | Graceful Gals | Georgetown, IL
Leah Durr | Bright Red Hats | Lawrenceburg, IN
Mary Dye | Boogie Woogie Redhatters of Evansville | Evansville, IN
Rosalie Hunt | Hoosier Honeys | Fortville, IN
Mary K. Page | SASS (South's Awesome Sassy Sisters) | Lawrence, KS
Susan Buchanan | Red Hat Hons of the Millennium | Bel Air, MD
Judy Slaughter | The Swing'n Red Hat'rs | Linden, MI
Barbara Domke | Mod Hatters | Blaine, MN
Karen Aitken | Red Hot Fillies | Smithville, MO
Beryl Ferranto | Lady Queenbee | Swinging Mississippi Belles | Picayune, MS
Phyllis Grant | Red Hats Go 4 Fun | Statesville, NC
Jackie Tarpinian | Jewels of the Prairie | Jamestown, ND
Elizabeth Ketner | Ramblin' Rosies | Stella, NE
Barbara Noakes Aldrich | Tootee Flutee Red Hats | Omaha, NE
Sharon Smith | Ruby Rebels with Purple Passion! | Palmyra, NE
Maria Clapp | Hats 'R Us | Franklin Township, NJ
Judith A. Yannarelli | Dizzy Dames of Unknown Fame | Clifton, NJ
Anita Tucci | Red Hat Tamales | Las Vegas, NV
Carole Barris | Ruby-Hatted Rascals | Bellmore, NY
Mindy Nadworny | Vinni's Vixens | Fresh Meadows, NY
Mickey Pilson | Yadda Yadda Sisterhood | Ridley Park, PA
Carol Downton | Mad Red Hatters | Nashville, TN
Virginia Duke | Gaudy Gals | Manchester, TN
Gloria Kirkland | Juliet Red Hatters | Mount Juliet, TN
Linda Roberts | Nonpareils | Knoxville, TN
DeeDee Clark | Victorian Ladies | Gainesville, TX
Janie Russell | Big D Re-Gal | Garland, TX
Elna Swofford | Duchesses of Bedford | Oakton, VA
Carol Slaughter | Vashon Island Red Tides | Vashon Island, WA
Georgean Kruger | Red Zippity Do Dahs | Shell Lake, WI
Maryanne Niesen | Red Hot Cheesy Chicks | Whitefish Bay, WI
Lisa Vesnaver | The Queentessential Adelaide Red Hats | Adelaide, Australia
Dorothy Vallillee | Yarmouth Seaside Red Hatters | Yarmouth, Nova Scotia, Canada
Betty Gamperl | Scarlett Shady Ladies | Kingsville, Ontario, Canada

Donna Hreceniuk | Dpyenne Dunlaith of Eire | Rose City Dollies | Windsor, Ontario, Canada

Safety Contributors

Sharon Simpson | Ladies of the Lake | Abbeville, AL
Lorraine Fauntleroy | River City Classy Sassy Divas | Sacramento, CA
Linda Lohman | Anything Goes SuppHose to Chapeaux | Sacramento, CA
Elizabeth Weaver | HatCourters | Buena Park, CA
June Tragesser | Royal Red Hat Sisters of the Road | Newark, DE
Jo Derby | Scarlet O'Hatters of Trinity | Trinity, FL
Jackie Tarpinian | Jewels of the Prairie | Jamestown, ND
Elizabeth Ketner | Ramblin' Rosies | Stella, NE
Barbara Noakes Aldrich | Tootee Flutee Red Hats | Omaha, NE
Carole Barris | Ruby-Hatted Rascals | Bellmore, NY
Cory Allen | Royal Red Hat Sisters of the Road | Tulsa, OK
Gloria Kirkland | Juliet Red Hatters | Mount Juliet, TN
Janie Russell | Big D Re-Gal | Garland, TX
Elna Swofford | Duchesses of Bedford | Oakton, VA
Donna Hreceniuk | Rose City Dollies | Windsor, Ontario, Canada

Discount Contributors

Sharon Simpson | Ladies of the Lake | Abbeville, AL
Marlene Aylor | Tea Birds | Harrison, AR
Maude Jeter Rogers | Royal Red Hat Sisters of the Road | Fort Smith, AR
JoAnn Trapp | Flaming Fedoras of Phoenix | Phoenix, AZ
Carol Betush | Rebellious Elegant Dames | Redding, CA
Sue Ellen Cooper | Fabulous Founders | Fullerton, CA
Peggy Diller | Red Hatters for Heart Matters | Covina, CA
Lorraine Fauntleroy | River City Classy Sassy Divas | Sacramento, CA
Virginia Hosford | Santa Teresa Red Hots | San Jose, CA
Lynn Hunter | Corona Cuties | Corona, CA
Linda Lohman | Anything Goes SuppHose to Chapeaux | Sacramento, CA
Chris Maston | Gold Country Mad Hatters | Rescue, CA
Buffy Oster | Red Hat Classy Lassies of Palm Desert | Palm Desert, CA
Barbara Whitener | Ding Dong Belles | Palm Desert, CA

Patsy McElroy | Red Hot Boa Babes | Castle Rock, CO
Sharron Newman | Arsenic & Lace | Grand Junction, CO
June Tragesser | Royal Red Hat Sisters of the Road | Newark, DE
Wendy Barr/Holmes | Red Magnolia Ladies of Encore | Ormond Beach, FL
Jo Derby | Scarlet O'Hatters of Trinity | Trinity, FL
Patricia Gillen | Red Hot Cruisers | Fort Myers, FL
Linda Murphy | Fabulous Founders | Tarpon Springs, FL
Gail Safarikas | Scarlet O'Hatters of Trinity | Trinity, FL
Sharleen Whitman | Red Hat Treasures | Panama City Beach, FL
Jacqueline Signori | Scarlet O'Hattas | Fairfield, IA
Nancy Thorsen | Crimson Cronies | Idaho Falls, ID
Katherine Bibber | Twisted Sisters of Cyberspace | Batavia, IL
Rosalie Hunt | Hoosier Honeys | Fortville, IN
Susan Buchanan | Red Hat Hons of the Millennium | Bel Air, MD
Barbara Domke | Mod Hatters | Blaine, MN
Karen Aitken | Red Hot Fillies | Smithville, MO
Beryl Ferranto | Swinging Mississippi Belles | Picayune, MS
Barbara Noakes Aldrich | Tootee Flutee Red Hats | Omaha, NE
Elizabeth Ketner | Ramblin' Rosies | Stella, NE
Sharon Smith | Ruby Rebels with Purple Passion! | Palmyra, NE
Phyllis Grant | Red HATS GO 4 FUN | Statesville, NC
Jackie Tarpinian | Jewels of the Prairie | Jamestown, ND
Maria Clapp | Hats 'R Us | Franklin Township, NJ
Judith A. Yannarelli | Dizzy Dames of Unknown Fame | Clifton, NJ
Anita Tucci | Red Hat Tamales | Las Vegas, NV
Carole Barris | Ruby-Hatted Rascals | Bellmore, NY
Mickey Pilson | Yadda Yadda Sisterhood | Ridley Park, PA
Carol Downton | Mad Red Hatters | Nashville, TN
Gloria Kirkland | Juliet Red Hatters | Mount Juliet, TN
DeeDee Clark | Victorian Ladies | Gainesville, TX
Carol Slaughter | Vashon Island Red Tides | Vashon Island, WA
Georgean Kruger | Red Zippity Do Dahs | Shell Lake, WI
Maryanne Niesen | Red Hot Cheesy Chicks | Whitefish Bay, WI
Lisa Vesnaver | The Queentessential Adelaide Red Hats | Fulham Gardens SA |
   Australia
Dorothy Vallillee | Yarmouth Seaside Red Hatters | Yarmouth, Nova Scotia,
   Canada

Betty Gamperl | Scarlett Shady Ladies | Kingsville, Ontario, Canada
Carol Hall | Deco City Divas | Napier, New Zealand

Train Travel Tip Contributors

Lynn Hunter | Corona Cuties | Corona, CA
Elizabeth Weaver | HatCourters | Buena Park, CA
Jacqueline Signori | Scarlet O'Hattas | Fairfield, IA
Judith A. Yannarelli | Dizzy Dames of Unknown Fame | Clifton, NJ
Maryanne Niesen | Red Hot Cheesy Chicks | Whitefish Bay, WI
Lisa Vesnaver | The Queentessential Adelaide Red Hats | Adelaide, Australia

Car Travel Tip Contributors

Marlene Aylor | Tea Birds | Harrison, AR
Chris Maston | Gold Country Mad Hatters | Rescue, CA
Barbara Whitener | Ding Dong Belles | Palm Desert, CA
Julie Cole | Royal Red Hat Sisters of the Road | Ferriday, LA
Susan Buchanan | Red Hat Hons of the Millennium | Bel Air, MD
Judy Slaughter | The Swing'n Hed Hat'rs | Linden, MI

Dining Contributors

Marilyn Puett | Red Hat Rovers | Huntsville, AL
Sharon Simpson | Ladies of the Lake | Abbeville, AL
Marlene Aylor | Tea Birds | Harrison, AR
Michelle Harris | Royal Red Hat Sisters of the Road | Fort Smith, AR
JoAnn Trapp | Flaming Fedoras of Phoenix | Phoenix, AZ
Carol Betush | Rebellious Elegant Dames | Redding, CA
Sue Ellen Cooper | Fabulous Founders | Fullerton, CA
Peggy Diller | Red Hatters for Heart Matters | Covina, CA
Cathy Fagan | Wild Women of Wildwood | Penn Valley, CA
Lorraine Fauntleroy | River City Classy Sassy Divas | Sacramento, CA
Virginia Hosford | Santa Teresa Red Hots | San Jose, CA
Lynn Hunter | Lady Lawless, Questionable Queen | Corona Cuties | Corona, CA
Cathy Kiley | 007REDHATS | Folsom, CA
Linda Lohman | Anything Goes SuppHose to Chapeaux | Sacramento, CA

Chris Maston | Gold Country Mad Hatters | Rescue, CA
Reba J. Moorman | Kindred Sisters | Fremont, CA
Elizabeth Weaver | HatCourters | Buena Park, CA
Barbara Whitener | Ding Dong Belles | Palm Desert, CA
Patsy McElroy | Red Hot Boa Babes | Castle Rock, CO
Sharron Newman | Arsenic & Lace | Grand Junction, CO
Joan Croce | Queen Joan | Scarlet O'Hatters | Cheshire, CT
Wendy Barr/Holmes | Red Magnolia Ladies of Encore | Ormond Beach, FL
Jo Derby | Scarlet O'Hatters of Trinity | Trinity, FL
Patricia Gillen | Red Hot Cruisers | Fort Myers, FL
Linda Murphy | Fabulous Founders | Tarpon Springs, FL
Gail Safarikas | Scarlet O'Hatters of Trinity | Trinity, FL
Sharleen Whitman | Red Hat Treasures | Panama City Beach, FL
Jacqueline Signori | Scarlet Hattas | Fairfield, IA
Nancy Thorsen | Crimson Cronies | Idaho Falls, ID
Katherine Bibber | Twisted Sisters of Cyberspace | Batavia, IL
Mary Dye | Boogie Woogie Redhatters of Evansville | Evansville, IN
Rosalie Hunt | Hoosier Honeys | Fortville, IN
Susan Buchanan | Red Hat Hots of the Millennium | Bel Air, MD
Barbara Domke | Mod Hatters | Blaine, MN
Karen Aitken | Red Hot Fillies | Smithville, MO
Phyllis Grant | Red Hats Go 4 Fun | Statesville, NC
Jackie Tarpinian | Jewels of the Prairie | Jamestown, ND
Noakes Aldrich | Tootee Flutee Red Hats | Omaha, NE
Elizabeth Ketner | Ramblin' Rosies | Stella, NE
Sharon Smith | Ruby Rebels with Purple Passion | Palmyra, NE
Beryl Ferranto | Swinging Mississippi Belles | Picayune, MS
Maria Clapp | Hats 'R Us | Franklin Township, NJ
Judith Yannarelli | Dizzy Dames of Unknown Fame | Clifton, NJ
Anita Tucci | Red Hat Tamales | Las Vegas, NV
Carole Barris | Kween Carole | Ruby-Hatted Rascals | Bellmore, NY
Mindy Nadworny | Vinni's Vixens | Fresh Meadows, NY
Jacqueline Pickering | Queen City Crimson Belles | Cincinnati, OH
Carol Downton | Mad Red Hatters | Nashville, TN
Gloria Kirkland | Juliet Red Hatters | Mount Juliet, TN
Linda Roberts | Nonpareils | Knoxville, TN
Sue Stein | Hen-der-hatters | Hendersonville, TN

Janie Russell | Big D Re-Gal | Garland, TX
Eina Swofford | Duchessess of Bedford | Oakton, VA
Carol Slaughter | Vashon Island Red Tides | Vashon Island, WA
Marilyn Huset | Mazo Railroadin' Reds | Mazomanie, WI
Maryanne Niesen | Red Hot Cheesy Chicks | Whitefish Bay, WI